CREATING PLACES OF
POWER

"The archaic lore that traditional builders in Europe once used to bring structures into creative harmony with their physical and spiritual environments has become all but inaccessible to students of the mysteries in today's world. *Creating Places of Power* remedies that, placing a wealth of once-secret lore in the reader's hands. Encyclopedic in its scope and detail, this is the definitive work on a crucial dimension of old earth magic."

JOHN MICHAEL GREER, AUTHOR OF
THE SECRET OF THE TEMPLE AND
THE TWILIGHT OF PLUTO

"In *Creating Places of Power,* Nigel Pennick, an established authority on folklore, folk magic, and ancient beliefs with more than 60 books to his name, hones his work on the European ancestral heritage of geomancy, sharing fascinating facts and practices that are accessible and also of value today. Crammed with a generous sharing of wisdom, this illustrated book is highly recommended."

JUNE KENT, PUBLISHER AND EDITOR OF
INDIE SHAMAN MAGAZINE

The geomantic layout of the city of Karlsruhe, Baden, Germany.
(Nigel Pennick)

CREATING PLACES OF
POWER

Geomancy, Builders' Rites, and Electional Astrology in the Hermetic Tradition

NIGEL PENNICK

Inner Traditions
Rochester, Vermont

ACKNOWLEDGMENT

I would like to thank Patrick McFadzean
for his help with astrological texts.

Inner Traditions
One Park Street
Rochester, Vermont 05767
www.InnerTraditions.com

Text stock is SFI certified

Cataloging-in-Publication Data for this title is available from the Library of Congress

ISBN 978-1-64411-584-8 (print)
ISBN 978-1-64411-585-5 (ebook)

Printed and bound in the United States by Lake Book Manufacturing, Inc.
The text stock is SFI certified. The Sustainable Forestry Initiative® program
promotes sustainable forest management.

10 9 8 7 6 5 4 3 2 1

Text design and layout by Debbie Glogover
This book was typeset in Garamond Premier Pro with Gill Sans MT Pro,
Grand Cru, Kapra Neue Pro and Nexa used as display typefaces

To send correspondence to the author of this book, mail a first-class letter to the
author c/o Inner Traditions • Bear & Company, One Park Street, Rochester, VT
05767, and we will forward the communication.

Contents

Preface to
the New Edition

Since I wrote this book a quarter century ago, the inexorable process of human dislocation from Nature has continued apace. Global destruction of the natural world, ecological degradation, and the proliferation and use of weapons of war has expanded and accelerated. This vanishing world is in need of rescue, but the powerful glamour of technologies that produce an illusion of mastery are accelerating its destruction. Gleefully, exponents of virtual, digital illusions assert that place, time, and space have ceased to have any real meaning. But virtual reality is only an illusion. It has not replaced the realities of existence, the nature of the planet we live on, or the stark fact of the human condition. Whether or not we choose to comprehend it, we are in the real world. We are subject to the same forces, the same conditions, as our ancestors. They developed cultures that worked with Nature, conducting life in harmony with the cycles of the cosmos. They understood that we are part of Nature and when we deny this, we demolish the foundations supporting life on Earth. But the ancient skills and wisdom that sustained our ancestors have been banished to the borderlands and in some places, utterly extinguished. Traditional cultures the world over are based upon the archetypal realities of the physical world, and a spiritual understanding of our place within a system far greater than ourselves. In the vast span of time that humans have lived on this planet, this present phase is clearly an aberration. The current effects of unbridled human activity on the environment are obvious to all except those who wear virtual-reality headsets.

I offer this new edition as a record and a teaching of the eternal principles that exist at a far more fundamental level than the conflicting political and religious theories and ideologies that currently have hegemony over most of the peoples of the world.

NIGEL PENNICK
OLD ENGLAND HOUSE
ST. WINNAL'S DAY—MARCH 3, 2022

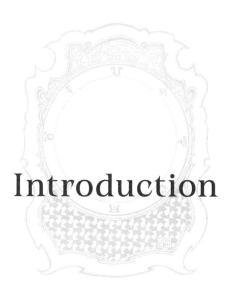

Introduction

And do not ask me by chance who is my master or which deity protects me. I am not bound to revere the word of any master.

HORACE, *NULLIUS IN VERBA: EPISTLES*

Nothing in existence exists separately—everything that is present in the cosmos is continuous with its surroundings and is the product of its own unique historical circumstances. Wherever we choose to look, there is nothing that exists now, or that has existed in the past, that has not come into being because of a multiplicity of events and processes. Everything can be traced back to the time when the world came into being aeons ago, and even before that. When humans make things, there is a precise moment when the artifact comes into being as a separate entity. Although it has not been created out of nothing, it has a precise time of birth. Because each time has its own quality, it affects whatever comes into being at that instant. There is a right time to do something, and a wrong time. We have the power to decide this moment.

All physical artifacts occupy space. Buildings especially define space by enclosing and articulating it. When space is used with understanding, a tangible reality is created. This is presence. There is no presence without time, and it is in time that all things exist. All material things have physical and temporal dimensions. Just as their presence is defined

1

Figure I.1. European traditional building techniques date back over 7,000 years. This is a modern reconstruction of a Celtic lake village (original before 500 BCE) at the Pfahlbaumuseum at Unteruhldingen, Lake Constance, Germany. (Nigel Pennick)

by where they begin and end in space, so they are also defined by where they begin and end in time. Because there are both favorable and unfavorable times to begin a venture, or to finish an artifact, it is desirable to have the ability to distinguish them. If we ignore the possibility of knowing, then we increase the likelihood of doing something at the wrong time and failing in whatever we do. So, throughout history, people have employed various techniques to determine the qualities of particular moments. Divination, chronomancy, and astrology came into being to inform us of the nature of these time qualities, and to predict them.

This book is about recognizing and dealing with earthly time and space, especially in the spheres of sacred and secular building. In this book, I reassemble the European ancestral heritage of geomantic practice. Its principles have existed in Europe in some form or other for over 7,000 years. In this book, I give instances of this tradition that come from various parts of Europe and beyond. Such principles have been present throughout history and are found within both Pagan and monotheistic religions for they recognize an archetypal perception of human existence on Earth. Because they are eternal, they are meaningful today and of value to everyone who uses them.

NIGEL PENNICK
BAR HILL
JULY 26, 1998 CE

CHAPTER 1

Patterns of Existence

Consciousness, the Gods, and the Stars

The octave teaches the saints to be holy.
Latin inscription on a medieval capital
at the Abbey Church of Cluny, France

PATTERNS

Since ancient times, people have recognized that nothing in the world occurs by mindless, random chance, but has a meaning related to the structure of existence. Every time that we recognize a pattern, this reality is reasserted. The form of patterns is almost infinitely diverse. Since the earliest times, people have seen human faces in rocks, humanoid forms in trees, animal shapes in the clouds, and other seemingly non-random patterns. These they have taken as evidence for the creative, communicative action of a conscious cosmos that sometimes they personified as divine beings. By scrutinizing natural or generated patterns, diviners learnt to extract information from the given natural world. Through study and experience, the skilled diviner can have an intimate knowledge of the common pattern that he or she can see, comparing it with an inner conceptual image. When the outer patterns of the world concur with the diviner's inner patterns, then meaning is recognized, and the status of the patterns can be evaluated. When they do not concur, then by close comparison the differences can be determined and evaluated, too.

The patterns that we experience in Nature recur infinitely at different scales of time and space. The spiral forms of distant galaxies are identical to the spiraling water going down the plughole. Dendritic formations of tree branches echo the shape of river deltas; cloud patterns look like sand dunes, snowdrifts, and the coloring on the side of a fish. These common patterns were recognized by our remote ancestors. Our language recalls this. The feather patterns on the birds called starlings reflect the night sky studded with stars. A "mackerel sky" resembles the fish patterning, and kidney stone looks like the bodily organ. All these patterns are the result of the underlying physical laws of the universe. If these laws were slightly different, then physical matter as we know it would not exist, and life would be impossible. Our very existence is dependent on these laws of the behavior of matter. They are the underlying causes of life. Those who can understand them can gain useful information about the present state of existence and its immediate future.

Patterns appearing in physical structure are the visible results of the unseen energy within the natural order. The dynamic relationships between matter and energy naturally take certain forms, which humans express through mathematical formulae and geometrical illustrations. Patterns produced by Nature are the same regardless of material and are scarcely affected by scale. They range from the galactic to the molecular, in inorganic systems and in life itself. Dynamic, self-organizing systems are the driving force of physical and cultural evolution. Their patterns work best when they approximate as nearly as they can to the natural patterns inherent in the universal order. When we live according to them, we are truly at one with all existence.

It is through our own physical, psychological, and spiritual existence that we recognize the patterns of existence. We can only experience the world through our own being as physical human bodies that have awareness and consciousness. So we describe the world according to our own bodily being. This was recognized in antiquity in archaic creation myths. It has been restated continually by priests and philosophers, poets and visionaries ever since. It was put most elegantly by the German mystic, Jakob Böhme (1575–1624). In his *Vom übersinnlichen Leben* (Dialogues on the Supersensual Life; 1624), Böhme expressed the traditional European spiritual understanding that the human body

> is the visible World; an Image and Quintessence, or Compound of all that the World is; and the visible World is a manifestation of the inward spiritual World, come out of the Eternal Light, and out of the Eternal Darkness, out of the spiritual compaction or connection; and also an Image or Figure of Eternity, whereby Eternity hath made itself visible; where Self-Will and resigned Will, viz., Evil and Good, work one with the other.

AUGURY AND ASTROLOGY

Ancient symbolic ways of understanding existence were based upon the principle expressed much later by Jacob Boehme. The ancient, pre-monotheistic European spiritual tradition recognized that patterns are the outward manifestation of transcendental powers. These were viewed anthropomorphically as gods and goddesses, giants and spirits. Viewing these patterns as signs, systems of interpretation evolved with schools of experts who specialized in various aspects. By seeking and examining these signs, the experts hoped to determine the will of the gods.

Divine approval or disapproval of human acts could be detected through these signs, which included the appearance of lightning, clouds, running water, the flight and song of birds, and, inside the human mind, dreams. According to this worldview, a right relationship existed between the world of humans and the divine powers, so long as divine laws remained unbroken. In Latin, this is called the *Pax Deorum* (Peace of the Gods). To maintain the *Pax Deorum*, ritual purity was called for at certain places and times. Before entering a shrine, or crossing a river, one had to wash so as not to disturb the sanctity of the place. It was also necessary to perform particular rites and ceremonies at certain places at certain times. The *Pax Deorum* was affirmed and enhanced by art in the form of fine buildings, beautiful artifacts, and harmonious performances. Divine guidance that some imbalance had occurred came as the result of omens (called *ostenta*). These could come either spontaneously from the gods, or alternatively after humans had made formal requests through prayer and offerings.

Like illness, omens, portents, and auspices can only be recognized when one knows what is normal, so a formal understanding of normality and omens was preserved by colleges of specialists. In ancient Rome, sacred rites were conducted by the high priest called the Rex Sacrorum, who was accompanied originally by three Augurs. It was they who observed the auspices and from them interpreted the will of the gods. They also knew the appropriate remedies and procedures for instances when the gods were displeased. Some, if not all, of the rites and ceremonies of the Roman Augurs were a continuation and development of the earlier Etruscan practices known collectively as the Etruscan Discipline. In turn, some Etruscan practices probably originated in Babylonian divination techniques.

Originally comprising three members, the Roman College of Augurs was later expanded to six, then nine and fifteen. Finally, a sixteenth was added by Julius Caesar. The senior Augur blessed growing crops and military actions, authorized magistrates, and "inaugurated" the Rex Sacrorum and the priests of Jupiter, Mars, and Quirinus. Sacred buildings and lands were also inaugurated by the Augurs. Their main work as state officials was the maintenance of the *Pax deorum* through the performances of rites and the interpretation of *auspicia* (omens).

After a magistrate had invoked the appropriate tutelary deity over the matter in hand, he asked for an appropriate sign. The Augur sat blindfold at the *templum,* the place of observation, while the magistrates watched the sky for omens. The Augur then interpreted any sign that subsequently appeared. When the order of nature was seen to be disrupted by human action, then it was the task of the Augurs to rectify it by appropriate measures.

At the same period when Roman Augury was developing, in Babylon and Assyria there existed an extensive literature on omens both terrestrial and celestial. Many exist from the reign of the Assyrian king Ashurbanipal (668–626 BCE). Their comprehensive complexity shows that they are part of a much more ancient tradition going back to the middle of the third millennium BCE. These texts appear to be the basis of Western astrology. The Greeks and Romans had calendars that defined auspicious and inauspicious days, but astrology took this further. Astrology enabled experts to determine favorable and unfavorable times independently of calendar days. Just as spontaneous omens were the outward manifestation of transcendental powers, so were the more predictable movements of celestial bodies. Sophisticated astrology allowed the prediction of possible public catastrophes, and hopefully the means to avert them.

In the years following the conquests of the Macedonian king Alexander the Great, Mesopotamian astrology reached the Mediterranean region. The Egyptian city of Alexandria became the center of astrological research and teaching. Astrology was transmitted to Rome by way of the Chaldeans. Lucretius called astrology the "Babylonian doctrine of the Chaldeans." In Rome, the astrologers were separate from the Augurs, and their practices seem not to have concurred. In 139 BCE, for example, Chaldeans were expelled from Rome along with the Jews as undesirable astrologers. But the stellar art proved too useful, and the Chaldeans came back. By the second century CE, court astrologers were members of the court of the Roman emperors. In later years, the practices of the astrologers were used to find the best times for performing important actions, and their traditions were merged with those of the Augurs. The coming together of various strands of divination and inauguration laid the foundations of later European spatial traditions that include builders' rites and ceremonies, weather forecasting, and navigation on land and at sea.

In Europe, techniques of observation, divination, and ceremony were not separated until the 1700s. In a medieval account of a pilgrimage to Jerusalem by Frater Felix Faber (Fabri), the Christian monk tells of the many related skills possessed by those who navigated the vessel. Faber recounts how, on board ship, besides the pilot,

> there were other learned men, astrologers and watchers of omens (auspices) who considered the signs of the stars and sky, judged the

winds, and gave directions to the pilot himself. And, all of them were expert in judging from the sky whether the weather would be stormy or tranquil, taking into account besides such signs as the colour of the sea, the movements of dolphins and fish, the smoke from the fire, and the scintillation when the oars dipped into the water. At night, they knew the time by an inspection of the stars.

Such a level of sophisticated knowledge today is rare indeed, but it is a level of conscious awareness to which we can all aspire.

RIGHT ORDERLINESS IN THE BUILT ENVIRONMENT

Mens sana in corpore sana *may also include the body of the house and the house itself.*

PROFESSOR PETER SCHMID,
*STRUCTURAL COMPLETION FOR AN INTEGRAL,
BIOLOGICAL ARCHITECTURE* (1975)

The Roman *Pax Deorum* was a state of ritual purity, in which human beings behaved according to divine principles and were rewarded accordingly. Such traditions do not exist for nothing, nor in a social and spiritual vacuum. They are the distilled essence of millennia of human skills and wisdom, practiced in harmony with natural principles, developed and perfected through practical application in the real world. To this day, elements of the *Pax Deorum* continue. One instance is European traditional building. Traditional buildings are made through the application of certain well-understood skills, techniques, and principles, all of which are founded in Nature. When things are not done according to natural principles, as they generally were in former times, then various forms of disruption will be felt. This is not a theoretical, intellectual, or occult concept, but something at the very heart of real existence. "Do not make a custom, and do not break a custom," advises the old Irish proverb.

But during the twentieth century, certain theorists published manifestos that declared the coming of a new world whose main ethos was based upon admiration for the inhumanity of the machine. The concept of the *Pax Deorum,* either in its older Pagan form, or its later Christian one, was anathema to them. These men preached the deliberate destruction of everything old—except militarism and patriarchy—without regard to values. The year when this destructive faction emerged was 1908. In that year, an Austrian architect, Adolf Loos (1870–1933) published an essay that proved highly influential. Titled "Ornament und Verbrechen" (Ornament and Crime), Loos's essay equated ornament in architecture with criminality and disorder. "The evolution of culture," wrote Loos, "is synonymous with the removal of ornament from articles of everyday utility . . . not only is ornament produced by criminals* but it also commits a crime itself by causing grave injury to human health, to the natural economy, and hence to cultural development."

In the next year, one of the main theorists of the Futurist art movement, Filippo Marinetti (1876–1944), wrote *The Founding Manifesto of Futurism* (1909). In it he proclaimed "We will glorify war—the world's only hygiene—militarism, patriotism, the destructive gesture of the anarchist, beautiful ideas worth dying for, and scorn for women." This was a defining text for militant modernity, and many copied it. In 1911, the *Manifesto of Futurist Dramatists* asserted, "Every day, we must spit on the altar of Art." The Futurist artist Umberto Boccioni (1882–1916) wrote "Necessity = Speed" (and nothing else!), while in the *Manifesto of Futurist Architecture* (1914), Antonio Sant'Elia (1888–1916) wrote: "We are the men of the great hotels, the railway stations, the immense streets . . . luminous arcades, straight roads, and beneficial demolitions." Sant'Elia wrote that in his ideal world, the house would be "remarkably ugly in its mechanical simplicity." Thus modernism, the movement that projected itself as founded on rational principles, in fact was the result of the obsessions and fanaticism of a few men who nevertheless were good self-publicists. And so the future envisaged by these brutal men came to be.

Rather than continuing the development of human conscious-

---

*Loos is alluding here to tattoos on the body.

ness and technique that had been going on for thousands of years up to then, many architects chose to operate as though there were no historical and cultural background to their work. The idea that buildings should be in harmony with the earth and the heavens was abandoned. Falsely, they equated progress with the willful destruction of all tradition, art, beauty, and symbolism. Because many modern architects have ignored common-sense principles, preferring theories based ultimately upon Futurist political doctrines, both "right" and "left" or other make-believe, the detrimental effect of buildings constructed without right orderliness is known to all. As the Danish architect Paul Hennigsen noted, "Building houses is playing with human lives," and Heinrich Zille wrote, "One can kill a man with a house just as well as with an axe."

In the early Roman imperial period, Vitruvius wrote of the integrated skills that an architect should have. His *Ten Books on Architecture* (written between 33 and 14 BCE) encapsulate the main concerns of the European tradition. His description of the skills and knowledge needed by an architect are telling:

He should be both spiritually gifted as well as eager for knowledge. Because giftedness without knowledge or knowledge without giftedness can never produce a complete artist. He must possess knowledge of language; handle a competent drawing pen; be well versed in geometry; have knowledge of light; be experienced in arithmetic; be acquainted with many historical facts; have been attentive in listening to the philosophers; know music theory; be not ignorant of the studies of health; be knowledgeable on the pronouncements of judges and lawyers; and possess knowledge of astrology and the ratios of the heavens. . . . Philosophy perfects the architect to be a broad-minded man, so he will not be arrogant. Rather [he] will be willing, and what is more important, just, honest, and free of greed. Since, indeed, no work shall prosper without honesty and unselfishness. Moreover, philosophy furnishes us with an explanation of the essence of Nature, in Greek called psychology which he must have studied with more than usual industry as this includes many and divergent problems in the area of nature.

THE ATTEMPT TO ABOLISH
TIME AND PLACE

By him first men also, and by his suggestion taught,
Ransack'd the center, and with impious hands
Rifled the bowels of their Mother Earth
For treasures better hid. Soon had his crew
Open'd into the hill a spacious wound,
And diggéd out ribs of gold. Let none admire
That riches grow in Hell; that soil may best
Deserve the precious bane.

JOHN MILTON (1608–1675), *PARADISE LOST* (1667).
(ON MAMMON, WHO, ACCORDING TO
MILTON'S COSMOLOGY, WAS CAST OUT OF
HEAVEN ALONG WITH SATAN)

Since it came into existence in the early years of the twentieth century, militant modernity has progressively attempted to dispense with traditional human culture. Among the first cultural activities to be attacked were the rites and ceremonies of human existence. This may be because they possess deep psychological and social meaning that was perceived to support a way of life contrary to the ruling ideology of modern industrial society. Throughout the twentieth century, there were those who, using military terminology and styling themselves "avant-garde," adopted a minimalist, ostensibly emotionless, colorless mode of existence. Describing this soulless state by emotive words like "cool rationality," they projected the inertness of idealized geometry and the unfeeling machine as their images of perfection. Individuality and character were discouraged in this worldview, which emphasized uniformity, conformity, and the paramount status of economics.

The militant moderns attempted to replace the spirited, pluralistic, cyclic world of Nature with the obsessive concerns of "tidiness" and "order." All that they succeeded in doing was to destroy much that was humane in society. To replace humaneness, they proposed an emphatic void that existed almost without past or future, day or night, seasonal cycles, omens or auspices. Although associated mainly with the twentieth century, this tendency was already recognized in the middle of the nineteenth by spiritual people. In his *The Key to the Masonic Parables* (1894), the French occultist Eliphas Levi (1810–1875), wrote: "There are three rebels: the rebel against Nature; the rebel against knowledge; the rebel against truth. They were symbolized in the hell of the ancients by the three heads of Cerberus." Militant modernity embodies all three.

Wishing to deny their own finite natures, fearing change and death, the militant moderns attempted to be timeless through making things they believed to be timeless and changeless. Rather than through dynamic participation in the ceremonies of the endless cycle of time, the militant moderns attempted to erase continuity with the past so that their vision of existence would not be "tainted" by the remains of former ages. In the pursuit of novelty, they made repeated but futile attempts to separate human activities from the universal order. So the ancient skills and wisdom of traditional Philosophy were ignored. States of ritual purity, rites of foundation, and ceremonies of passage were discarded as unfit for the streamlined modern machine-made world.

Architecture was to be the means by which the shape of things to come would be made concrete. As a beginning, they chose to negate most of the intellectual and ethical virtues recommended by Vitruvius. Inside the "machines for living" that would replace homes, the Futuristic new order of modernity would triumph, once the old was destroyed, so they told us. Among the most characteristic artifacts of this militant modernity are the buildings dubbed "glass stumps" by Prince Charles that tower above almost every city in the world. These are the geometrical modern ferroconcrete glazed buildings that lack all transcendent symbolic meaning. There can be no human dimension in such buildings, for they are designed heartlessly. These enormous structures portray no more than the power and material wealth of those who ordered them to be built. Sheer size is used as a means to impress people by the degree to which they are dwarfed. The competition to build the tallest or biggest structure on earth still continues, as though size brings contentment.

Enormousness for its own sake was a theme beloved of totalitarian systems, whether they were ruled by Napoleon, the British

Empire, Italian and Spanish Fascists, the Nazis, Soviet and Chinese Communists, or contemporary Capitalists. The "reign of quantity," as the French philosopher René Guénon (1886–1951) called this mass delusion, is none other than John Milton's Mammon, appearing in his modern guise. Mammon is a state in which quantities of objects mask the inner spiritual emptiness of materialism.

The external vastness of the works of militant modernity signifies and only serves to emphasize the enormous empty space inside. This is epitomized in Britain by a typical example of Futurist grandeur, the so-called "Millennium Dome" built with mountains of taxpayers' money on the banks of the Thames in East London. This folly was made for no purpose other than to "celebrate" the year twenty hundred, the last year of the twentieth century, which the organizers mistakenly believed to be the beginning of the twenty-first century.

THE FLIGHT FROM REALITY

The final result of militant modernity has been to revere the medium to the detriment of the message. The technology that most distinguishes the present era from the past is the use of electronic media for communication and entertainment. When used uncritically, the electronic media devalue reality, because they allow any unsubstantiated idea, illusion, speculation, misunderstanding, delusion, and outright lie to be propagated throughout the world as the equal of truth without the checks required to determine veracity. In the world of the electronic media, presentations, rooted neither in place or space, are separated from our physical existence, which does exist in space, place, and time. On the screen, places are often presented as abstract objects, existing in the absence of human presence and activities. Frequently, holy places are depicted without the human rites and ceremonies that are their very reason for existence. They are reduced to an inert spectacle.

As presented by those who make their living from the electronic media, life consists of a constant and rapid succession of edited and distorted images and fantasies, which may or may not be rooted in physical reality. The balanced cosmos of the *Pax Deorum* is utterly obliterated.

Generally, these images are presented outside any context that allows us to distinguish fact from fiction, fallacy, fantasy, and lie. There are many vested interests, both individual and collective, that want to keep it that way. Militant modernity has evolved its own superstitions that sustain its socioeconomic success. All of this flight from reality has a detrimental effect upon the way that we perceive place and time. The sense of place and time is easily destroyed by the Futurist illusion. The boundaries of our personal space are blurred by electronic illusions and those who benefit from presenting them as more important than physical existence itself. If we fall into the trap of relying upon this electronic collective make-believe, then immediately we disempower our individual humanity.

The electronic media also have the effect of removing the ceremonial from life. Because the mass media collectively are a 24-hour-a-day business, their main concern is to ensure an unbroken supply of images. Images from the past and the present, fact, fiction, and fantasy, appear in a never-ending cavalcade, one after the other. Because the producers of this material are in competition with one another, they must seek continually to excite their audience, tending always to take excess to

Figure 1.1. Traditional European building techniques are maintained by the craft guilds of central Europe. Here, a new timber-frame building was under construction near Hohenzollern in south Germany, summer 1998. (Nigel Pennick)

even further excess. There is little place for calm, step-by-step, reflective ceremony in such a highly pressurized environment. Ceremonies are broadcast as part of fiction at times when they are inappropriate. Their place within time is blurred. When actual ceremonies are broadcast as they happen, which is uncommon, they are generally disempowered by commentators who confuse individuals with roles. In the mass media, individual identity is everything, and ceremonial roles, especially anonymous ones, do not fit. The value of rites is confused further when the trappings of ceremony are used to introduce popular shows or in advertising. Related rites in the real world are thereby reduced in value even to many of those who experience them directly. In this virtual world, even the awesome *ostenta*—omens and portents that came from the gods—are repackaged as Fortean entertainment.

TRADITIONAL
RITES AND CEREMONIES

The solemn rites are well begun,
And, though but lighted by the moon,
They show as rich as if the sun
Had made his night his noon.
But may none wonder that they are so bright,
The moon now borrows from a greater light.
Then, princely Oberon,
Go on.
This is not every night.

BEN JONSON (CA. 1572–CA. 1637),
THE MASQUE OF OBERON (1611)

Traditional rites and ceremonies exist on a different level. They are not primarily spectacles of entertainment, but a means for people to identify directly with their own immediate environment, in both the physical and spiritual realms. They affirm and maintain the *Pax Deorum*, maintaining right orderliness in the world. The rites and ceremonies celebrated in this book are of two kinds, the official and the vernacular. Official rites and ceremonies are conducted by priesthoods and organizations, while the vernacular are performed as an everyday thing by ordinary people. Official rites have a precise structure—a script— through which they are conducted in a more or less standard way. They include foundation rituals, consecration and blessings by priests, the rites of Freemasonry, and the ceremonies of trade and craft guilds. These merge imperceptibly with vernacular usages, in which ordinary people conduct ceremonies whose nature is somewhere between the official and the personal. The most effective ceremonies are constructed according to principles that reflect and reinforce the meaning of what is being done. Rites and ceremonies mark and empower the beginning and end of significant parts of any human work or enterprise. They are witness to the constructive effort, both on the collective, human level and in the realm of spirit.

Unlike much of modernity, the sacred architecture of the West is not empty, but enspirited. Western sacred architecture is the result of several thousand years of continuity and development, based upon the principle of balance embodied in the *Pax Deorum*. Traditional temples and cathedrals portray images or iconic representations of divine beings and sacred history. They are transcendent visions of Nature on all levels. They are not separated from the world, nor from the otherworld, for they are places where sanctity is re-created continuously by human activity. Regardless of religion, sacred buildings and artifacts are re-empowered periodically by sacred rites and ceremonies. It is universal practice to bless or reconsecrate sacred things on holy days.

Also, at times when they are not the object of religious ceremonies, when passersby recognize that an object or sign is holy, they experience pious thoughts and feelings. The sacred thing is thereby re-empowered. There is an identical effect in all belief systems. An image of a Hindu deity in India, or an effigy of a saint in a Roman Catholic country have the same effect. A devout person will acknowledge its holiness with a short prayer, or an offering, which re-charges the object with spiritual power. If consecration creates a special psychical state inside and around an object, then it will also be reinforced by devotions. Buildings protected by spiritual objects are held to bring harmony where there was discord, health where once was illness, and plenty in place of shortage. To all but the committed militant modern ideologue, the health and harmony, peace and plenty of the *Pax Deorum* is better to live in than "the Futurist reconstruction of the Universe" as they put it.

Figure 1.2. Traditional building according to spiritual principles has resulted in the great masterpieces of European architecture. King's College Chapel, Cambridge, England. (Nigel Pennick)

CHAPTER 2

Ceremonial Beginnings

Finding and Marking the Place

*We want to crystallize the infinity of the cosmos and give
expression to it in form.*

HENDRICUS THEODORUS WIJDEVELD (1885–1987),
"NATUUR, BOUWKUNST EN TECHNIEK"
(NATURE, ARCHITECTURE, AND TECHNOLOGY; 1923)

CREATION

Beginning anything is an act of creation. It is a small reenactment
of the primal act of coming-into-being of all things that is described
symbolically in human-made myths of creation. In their own ways, all
myths tell of how once chaos was the only state of being. Then, at a
precise moment, a change came about, bringing existence into being.
According to myth, existence was brought about either by the action
of a divine being or by a spontaneous change in the state of the cosmos. The symbolism of how we view our own beginnings depends upon
the symbolism of the tradition in which we work. The Judeo-Christian
myth tells how the supreme being acts sequentially to bring the various orders of existence into being, culminating in the human being,
who is in the creator's image. The northern European myths tell of the
interplay of cosmic forces and principles. The opposites of fire and ice

19

Figure 2.1. Traditional symbolic representations of dragon slaying,
such as St. George shown here, denote the fixation of the moment
of foundation, when the dragon is pierced by the first stake
driven into the ground. (Nigel Pennick)

come together to initiate a series of events that culminates in the emergence of the world and life. The elemental components of creation—fire, water, ice, salt, venom, and blood—play certain roles in this cosmic drama of coming-into-being. Whichever mythos we use, our rites of commencement refer to these and other elements. They reappear in the "subsequent performance" of creation that is each beginning.

Beginning with a proper state of mind, augmented by proper rites and ceremonies, is essential for any enterprise. The most developed ceremonies of beginning are in European building traditions. One of the best explanations of this is by the Italian Renaissance architect, Leon Battista Alberti, in his influential book, *De re aedificatoria* (On the Art of Building; 1452). Alberti wrote:

> It is undoubtedly proper . . . to set about our work with a holy and religious preparation. . . . We ought therefore to begin our undertaking with a clean heart, and with devout oblations, and with prayers to almighty God to implore his assistance and blessing upon the beginnings of our labour, that it may have a happy and prosperous ending, with strength and happiness to it and its inhabitants, with content of mind, increase of fortune, success of industry, acquisition of glory, and a succession and continuance of all good things.

Every beginning must be marked in some way that distinguishes the time after from the time before. The fundamental recognition of time and process, and one's own place in that continuity, takes place when one conducts a beginning consciously. As with other beginnings, in founding a building, there are a number of points that can be taken as the beginning—choosing the site, clearing the place, digging the first hole, and laying the first stone.

SOME TRADITIONS OF SITE LOCATION

The Etruscan Discipline and its Roman development were formal, official systems of taking omens to decide on the suitability of places for building. In their full form, they were used for the foundation of cities, temples, and civic buildings. In his *Ten Books on Architecture,* the Roman architectural writer Vitruvius wrote:

> When about to build a town or a military camp, our ancestors sacrificed cattle that grazed at the place and examined their livers. If the first victims' livers were dark colored or abnormal, they sacrificed

others. If they continued to find abnormalities, they concluded that the food and water supply at such a place would be equally unhealthy for people, so they went away to another locality, their main objective being healthiness.

It is clear that there have always been similar less official, local techniques with the same function, both in Italy and across the rest of Europe. They have been practiced since time immemorial and exist to this day in folk traditions all over Europe, and they are by no means out of use. The objective of the locator is to determine the true ambience of the land. According to widespread European folk tradition, place-spirits sometimes object to humans building on their land, and so they must be consulted before a decision to build is made. In the early medieval Norse *Kormákssaga* (Saga of Kormak), the place-spirits are asked through a ritual of measurement. The Norse builders measure the building-place three times. If the measurements come out the same thrice, then the place is a good location to build, but if the measurements are different, this is an omen that the place should not be built upon. A later northern technique employs the magnetic compass to determine the suitability of a building plot. In the Faroe Islands, a compass is laid upon the site. If it does not show true North, then the *huldrafolk* ("hidden folk") there have rejected the proposed building, and another site must be sought.

A south Slav site-testing tradition rolls a wheel-shaped loaf of bread around the area where a building is to be erected. If the bread falls upper-side-up, then the *anima loci* permits building there. But if it is inverted, then the place-spirit has rejected the humans' wishes, and the building should not be started. An Estonian custom involves laying stones all over the proposed site. If, after three days, there are worms beneath them all, then the place is all right to build on. If not, then not. White settlers in the Ohio Valley in North America sited their farmhouses "right with the earth"—in a proper and appropriate place with regard to terrain, watercourses, and orientation for sun and winds—until the nineteenth century. In India, construction is abandoned if anything untoward is found when digging the hole for the main post. If bones, a skull, hair, ash, chaff, timber-work, or red earth is found, then work must be abandoned. Brick or stone is auspicious.

There are many instances in Celtic literature that tell how priests and monks of the Celtic Church used animal augury to discover appropriate places for monasteries, chapels, and churches. They are mostly legends, as far as can be ascertained, yet they record genuine traditions of place-divination. Traditions dating from the sixth century onward speak of place-omens being given by insects, birds, swine, cattle, and deer. The priests of the Celtic Church were inheritors of a syncretic tradition that incorporated elements of Jewish, Egyptian, Greek, Roman, and pre-Christian Celtic practices. The Celtic Church saw foundation of new settlements in terms of sowing or planting, and many foundation legends display sowing symbolism.

St. Dyfrig, the priest legendarily said to have crowned King Arthur, walked around his lands at Inis Ebrdil in south Wales, looking for a suitable place to build his monastery. In a meander of the River Wye, on land covered by thorn bushes, Dyfrig discovered a wild white sow with her piglets. This was the omen he sought, and there he built the monastery called Mochros, the "swine moor." In Celtic symbolism, the wild pig denotes fruitfulness, because in autumn it tramples the seeds into the earth. The sow herself is the epitome of motherhood, for she gives birth to many young. Like the earth, the sow also devours her own young. The Celtic monks who followed the ascetic practices taught by St. Anthony of Egypt were enthusiastic pig-keepers and in Celtic monastic legend, the tradition easily merged with the earlier Pagan swine-cultus of the corn goddesses, Ceres and Cerridwen.

A legend of St. Carannog from Carhampton in Somersetshire, England, tells how he borrowed a spade from a peasant, and began to dig the foundations of his new church. During rests from digging, Carannog whittled a pastoral staff cut from the local wood. While he was whittling, a wood pigeon flew out of a tree, picked up some of the wood shavings, and carried them off. The monk followed the bird, and discovered that it had dropped all of the wood chips at a certain place preparatory to nest-building. He took this as an omen and built his church there instead of at the original place he had chosen.

According to another Welsh legend, St. Patrick's disciple, the Welsh saint Ieuan Gwas Padrig was told by an angel not to found his church on his own land at Llwyn in Ceinmeirch, but to walk southward until he saw a roebuck, and to build there. At Cerrig y Drudion, he came across the roebuck, and the church was built. Sometimes, an unusual incident during a hunt revealed a holy place, which then was honored. A Breton legend tells how Conmor, the Count of Poher, was hunting near Carhaix. Without warning, the stag he was pursuing stopped at a special place, and the hounds refused to kill it. The count examined the place and found the forgotten grave of St. Hernin. A church was built there to commemorate the miracle. The city of Bern in Switzerland was also founded after a strange hunting incident, when a knight beheld a miraculous apparition of a bear. It was taken as an omen to found a new city, which was named after the bear. Bears have been kept at Bern ever since, as the "luck" of the city.

Figure 2.2. Locational practices in European geomancy often take into account observed solar phenomena. This nineteenth-century engraving (1859) of Elm, near the Segnes Pass in Switzerland, shows the illumination of the church of St. Martin by a sunbeam passing through a mountain cave also named after the saint. (Nideck)

Testing the site was important in Renaissance building. Following the ancients, in *De re aedificatoria,* Alberti wrote a chapter titled "Of some more hidden conveniences and inconveniences of the region which a wise man ought to inquire into." In it, he states:

> We ought further to enquire carefully, whether the region is used to be molested with any more hidden inconveniency. Plato believed that in some places the influence of spirits often reigned, and was sometimes mischievous, and at others propitious to the Inhabitants. It is certain there are some places where men are very subject to run mad, others where they are easily disposed to do themselves a mischief, and where they put an end to their own lives by halters or precipices, steel or poison. It is therefore very necessary to examine the most occult traces of nature, everything that can be attended with such effects. It was an ancient custom, brought down even from Demetrius's time, not only in laying the foundations of cities, but also in marking out camps for the armies, to inspect the entrails of the beast that grazed upon the place, and to observe both their condition and color. In which if they chanced to find any defect, they avoided that place as unhealthy. Varro informs us of his own knowledge, that in some places the air was full of minute animalcules as small as atoms, which being received together with the breath into the lungs . . . caused dreadful raging diseases, and at length plagues and death.

This intelligent, conscious approach to the ambience of the land was defined perfectly by the French landscape architect Antoine-Joseph Dezallier D'Argenville (1680–1765):

> To make a complete Disposition and Distribution of a general Plan, Respect must be had to the Situation of the Ground: For the greatest Skill in the right ordering of a Garden is, thoroughly to understand, and consider the natural Advantages and defects of the Place; to make use of the one, and to redress the other: Situations differing in every Garden. . . . 'Tis, therefore, the great Business of an

Architect, or Designer of Gardens, when he contrives a handsome Plan, with his utmost art and good Economy to improve the natural Advantages, and to redress the Imperfections, Shelvings, and Inequalities of the Ground. With these Precautions he should guide and restrain the Impetuosity of his genius, never swerving from Reason, but constantly submitting, and conforming himself to that which suits best with the natural Situation of the Place.

This principle was expressed more poetically by Alexander Pope (1688–1744) in his *Epistle to Richard Boyle, Earl of Burlington* (1732):

> *Consult the genius of the place in all;*
> *That tells the waters or to rise or fall,*
> *Or helps th'ambitious Hill the heav'n to scale,*
> *Or scoops in circling theatres the vale.*

SWEEPING OUT

In beginning things on the earth, we first must clear the place of whatever exists there before we start. This can involve cutting down trees, rooting out shrubs, and removing debris. Sweeping is a very visible act of cleansing, removing dirt and bringing order to a place. A site should be swept ritually before the commencement of any other activities. The Roman bard Ovid (43 BCE–17 CE), in his *Fasti,* tells how in his time, shepherds ritually purified their sheep at twilight on ground first sprinkled with water and swept with a broom.

Sweeping is an act of transformation, conducted ceremonially by a person dressed in ritual disguise that emphasizes the role being performed and not the individual. In European culture, the broom is both revered and feared as a magical tool. The traditional English besom is made from three woods. The stick itself is made from ash wood. Tied to it by osiers are birch twigs. Birch symbolizes purification, the driving out of uncleanness, both physical and spiritual, from the place. Like all ceremonial tools, besoms are made ceremonially. In East Anglia, the birch twigs are cut at Michaelmas. Once they are attached to the besom,

Figure 2.3. Ritual sweeping plays an important part in the preparation of the ground for beginning buildings or conducting ceremonies. The Mepal broom dancers, dressed in East Anglian ceremonial costume, perform the Cambridgeshire Broom Dance at Whittlesey in Cambridgeshire, England. (Nigel Pennick)

they should never be cut. In England, East Anglian Broom Squires sometimes make the brush end of besoms from ling (heather), trimmed at the end. The ling is tied by split bramble thongs. During ceremonial use, the besom is bedecked with red and green ribbons that denote the performance of a special event. The stick can be painted with a sunwise spiral of blue, red, green, and yellow to distinguish it from mundane broomsticks.

Ceremonially new brooms should be made each year. In Westphalia and Mecklenburg, Germany, the new broom is made at the beginning of the new year, on Twelfth Night. It is made in springtime in Switzerland, when snow still lies on the ground. Children are left in the house, while the adults leave it to fetch the new broom, singing the ritual song "Der Zug in's Besenreis" in a circle. In old Bohemia, it was traditional to renew the broom at Easter, and in Austria, on

St. George's Day (April 23). It is inauspicious in England to make a new broom of birch twigs or green broom during the Twelve Days of Christmas or the merry month of May.

In the British Isles, custom demands that dust should always be swept inward. If the sweeper should sweep the dust outward, then she will sweep away the luck of the house. When the outsweeper is a bride who is sweeping her house for the first time, then disaster will follow. As a customary rite, it is necessary to sweep on a certain day of the year. The date of ritual sweeping is a fundamentally important aspect of the ceremony to re-empower a place. At Eyam in Derbyshire, central England, there is the tradition that unless one sweeps one's doorstep on the first of March, then the house will be infested with fleas for the rest of the year. At Laneshaw Bridge, near Colne in Lancashire, it is customary to sweep the old year out and the new year in. The rite involves ceremonial sweepers in ritual disguise—men, women, and children with faces blackened or masked. They go from house to house on New Year's Eve between ten o'clock and midnight, having the customary right to enter any house whose door is unlocked. Without a word or a song, the sweepers enter the house and dust the living room and the hearth. In Handsworth, Sheffield, the mummers' performer, Little Devil Doubt, sweeps out the houses.

When someone dies in Saxony, it is customary not to sweep the house all the time that the body remains there. Once the coffin is taken to the cemetery, a besom is used to sweep out the place where the coffin was, the threshold and any place where pieces of wreath may have fallen. After the funeral, the house is cleansed with salt and swept thrice. Then the besom is abandoned, never to be used again. It is left lying on a beam in a barn or outhouse, or alternatively taken to the churchyard or a field and left there.

Any place must be ceremonially cleansed before being used. This is a basic ritual principle. Before mechanization, it was traditional in Ireland to sweep the threshing-floor ceremonially with a heather broom before the threshers began their work in the goafstead. Scottish guising sides have a broom-man who first sweeps a circle in which the action then takes place. In the Plough Monday traditions of the

Cambridgeshire Fens, it is also customary to have a man with a broom of some kind. It serves to sweep away mud, snow, ice, and bad luck from the dancing-ground where Molly Dancing or the Broom Dance is to be performed. It is the "badge of office" of the bearer, who also carries the box to collect money from the spectators. In traditional street parades, the officials and participants are preceded by a ceremonial sweeper. In the City of London, it is the custom that two wine-porters, clad in new aprons and carrying new brooms, should sweep the street in front of the officials of the Vintners' Company processing to the church of St James Garlickhythe for their annual service. In central Europe, the Fasching (Shrovetide) parades in the Steiermark, Eifel, and Tyrol regions have a man with a broom who sweeps the way. The path is thereby cleansed both physically and spiritually for the passage of the procession.

MAKING A MARK

After the area is cleansed ritually, the next steps can be taken. The act of changing the earth's surface most usually involves digging into the surface, making a mark that was not there before, but which remains as a memory of what was done there. By digging, we make a change at a specific place at a specific time. The earth cannot return to its former condition now. After this event, the place is changed. Foundation ceremonies involve making a mark in the ground, digging the first spadeful "turning the first sod," or creating a boundary around our special place. When the first sod is turned, this is the moment of "birth" of the new place. Then, further digging takes place, as much as is needed for the construction.

For at least 3,000 years, European tradition has recognized that foundation has an ideal form that reflects the perceived pattern of the cosmos. In the early years of the first millennium BCE, the Etruscan augurs marked the central point of their sacred sites by sinking a shaft into the ground. In cities, ideally this lay beneath the future crossroads from which the rest of the area was to be laid out. This shaft, called the Mundus, received sacrifices and offerings of the first fruits and all things deemed good and necessary. Then it was ceremonially consecrated and finally sealed with the *Lapis Manalis*. This may mean "ghost stone." In its shape it was a wheel or disc of stone resembling a millstone. The Roman writer Varro tells us that this Mundus formed the gateway to the Gods of the Nether Regions. Festus asserts that this stone "was reckoned to be the gate of Hades, through which the souls of people in the underworld, who are called ghosts, pass to the people above." Once the Mundus was dug, consecrated, and sealed, a stone or other upright marker was set up over the shaft. Then the rite of foundation was deemed complete.

Digging the first ditch around a place was the next act of foundation in ancient times. According to the Roman foundation legend, after following bird omens, Romulus founded the city of Rome and delimited its boundary by ploughing around the area, turning the clods of earth inward. This made a ditch with a bank on the inside, a defensive earthwork. According to Ovid, this was said to have taken place at the festival of Pales, the Parilia:

> A trench was dug down to the solid rock, the earth's fruits were cast into the bottom of it, and along with them earth brought from the region nearby. The trench was filled up with humus, and on it was set up an altar and a fire duly lighted on a new hearth. Then, leaning on the plough-handle, he drew a furrow to delineate the line of the walls; yoked were a white cow and a snow-white bull.

In his *De re aedificatoria,* Alberti asserted:

> The ancients used to found the walls of their cities with the greatest religion, dedicating them to some god who was to be their guardian . . . they fabled that Saturn, out of his care of human affairs, appointed semi-gods and heroes to be guardians over cities and to protect them by their wisdom.

According to ancient Egyptian tradition, Menes, legendary founder of the kingdom of Egypt, delineated the boundary of the holy city of Memphis, which he surrounded with a white wall. White is the sacred

Figure 2.4. In London in 1722–1723 architect Nicholas Hawksmoor designed and built this pyramidal tower of the church of St George, Bloomsbury, London, recreating the design of the Mausoleum at Halicarnassos, one of the "Seven Wonders of the World." A statue of King George I in ancient robes stands on top like a guardian god of the city. He is accompanied by guardian beasts, a lion and a unicorn. (drawing by Nigel Pennick)

color of the mother-goddess Nekhbet, protectress of Upper Egypt. When each new pharaoh came to Memphis to be inaugurated, he performed a ritual circuit of the White Wall around the holy place. Only after the ritual reenactment of the foundation was he recognized as king of Egypt.

Historically, Rome was delineated by a ditch around the area that later became the Comitium. The first fruits of the fields and handfuls of soil from the settlers' home localities were thrown into the ditch. Like the Etruscan pit, the Roman ditch was called Mundus, meaning "the world," or "sky," according to Plutarch, "the same as that of the universe." This original boundary was a ritual line called the Pomerium. In republican times the Pomerium was delineated by a line of stones. It marked the boundary between the city and the country.

Ovid mentions dividing up the land with earthen baulks known as *limites* by a "careful measurer." According to Varro in his *Antiquities* (47 BCE), these baulks originated in the Etruscan Discipline. Plautus, in the prologue to *Poenulus,* puts these words in the actor's mouth: "I shall now delimit its areas, *limites,* and boundaries; I have been appointed its Finitor" (a Finitor was a "definer" rather than a "diviner"). New Roman foundations in the Empire were divined and defined by a three-man committee called the *Tresviri Coloniae Deducendae* (Three for Founding [literally *leading out*] a Colony). Defining the boundary is an act that penetrates the earth, either by making a furrow with a plough, or by driving posts into the ground. The boundary is marked with a sacrifice. Roman custom required the fruits of the earth. In Russia, it is traditional to mark out the boundary with barleycorns, while in Bohemia, the custom used linden-wood charcoal, grain, and chalk.

The first hole is acknowledged by some offering put into it before the post is driven or the stone is laid. Breton custom requires eggs and oil, wine and spirits, to be put into the ground to acknowledge the genius of the place and to mark the beginning. Once this rite is finished, then further artifacts may be added to the place. In the Scandinavian cultural sphere, holy and sacred places were defined by a fence composed of *tjösnur* (sg. *tjasna*). These are phallic-shaped hazel posts made of hazelwood and set up around a holy area called the *vé*. Linked by ropes or ribbons, they form the sacred fence known as the *vébönd*. Four *tjösnur* were used to pin down the animal hide on which the combatants fought in the single combat known as *hólmganga*. They are the forerunner of the four posts that support the ropes in the contemporary boxing ring. Once such a boundary fence is set up, then the area is separated from the normal, profane world, and timeless ceremonies can be performed there.

CHAPTER 3

Foundation

Offerings, Sacrifices, and Relics

There is no sure foundation set on blood,
No certain life achieved by others' death.
WILLIAM SHAKESPEARE, *KING JOHN* (1595)

HUMAN FOUNDATION
SACRIFICES AND RELICS

Foundation sacrifices or deposits have been customary in the west since time immemorial. It is likely that at least some of them have been the remains of sacrifices made to test the site as told by Vitruvius above. Archaeological excavations of several prehistoric earthworks in Britain have revealed traces of human inhumation at the time that the ramparts were constructed. Places where they have been found include South Cadbury in Somerset, where the remains of a young adult male were recovered, and at Reculver in Kent, where children's skeletons were unearthed. Excavations of similar defensive works in the Holy Land, dating from the first millennium before the Common Era, have also revealed the remains of many sacrificed children in the foundations. This practice is referred to in the Bible. There, we are told, Hiel the Bethelite built a gatehouse and "laid the foundation thereof with the loss of Abiram his first-born." When Seleuceus Nicator founded the city

Figure 3.1. The central pillar of the Chapel of the cross at Mont-Sainte-Odile in Alsace, France, has the bound hands of victims carved in stone at the four lower corners, recalling the grim practice of sacrificing human beings in church foundations. (Nigel Pennick)

of Antioch on the Orontes in 300 BCE, his high priest sacrificed a virgin at the moment chosen as most auspicious by the astrologers. She formed the foundation of the city.

In the time of the Irish holy man St. Columba (521–597 CE), it is recorded that a Celtic Christian monk named Oran was buried alive as a monastic foundation sacrifice on the holy island of Iona. The Irish monastery of Clonmacnois is also reputed to have been consecrated by the living burial of a hapless leper who was foolhardy enough to follow St. Patrick. Perhaps these burials were in imitation of ancient Jewish practice, or as a continuation of a pre-Christian Celtic sacrificial tradition. Much later British churches have been found to contain similar sacrifices or deposits. When the church at Holsworthy in Devon was rebuilt in 1885, a skeleton was found embedded in the southwest angle of the wall. According to England Howlett in his *Sacrificial Foundations* (1899), there was "every indication that the victim had been buried alive." In 1895, reconstruction after a gale of the church tower at Darrington in Yorkshire revealed the remains of a man under the west side. He lay in "a sort of bed in the solid rock," with "the west wall actually resting upon his skull."

The body in the rock is a classic foundation-sacrifice position, when, killed and buried at an auspicious moment, the victim becomes the literal foundation of the building. The victim's bones are the link between the rocky "bones of the earth" below and the stone fabric of the building above. The building is thus a tomb, a principle overtly expressed in Roman Catholic rites of church consecration. Other possible foundation sacrifices are the two human skeletons found beneath the church at Brownsover, near Rugby, in 1876. These skeletons, laid out oriented north–south, in the Pagan polar direction, were each covered by oaken boards that appeared to be carpenters' benches. It was speculated at the time by the workmen who found them that secret craft rites had been performed in founding the church.

Although sacrificial foundations of churches are a historic reality, the custom was obviously at variance with orthodox Christian teaching, and harmful to human society. In addition to adults, children are also known to have been buried in the foundations of churches in the Oldenburg region of Germany at Blexen, Ganderkesee, and Sandel. However, it was not only in churches that the practice took place. According to a Danish folktale, when the ramparts of Copenhagen were being built, they subsided. So twelve stonemasons took a little girl and built an arch over her, walling her in. The walls then stood firm. When demolished in the nineteenth century, we are told, the Bridge Gate of Bremen revealed the skeleton of a child in its foundation. There are also numerous similar child-foundation legends told at places in Austria, Silesia (Poland), and Greece.

Legend asserts that the Master Mason who designed Cologne Cathedral, unable to make the tower stable, volunteered to be buried beneath it to ensure success. Another legend tells that when a broken dam on the River Nogat near the city of Danzig (Gdansk, Poland) was repaired in 1463, the peasants engaged on the reconstruction were approached by a supernatural river monster that advised them to sacrifice a living man. So they accosted a passing vagabond, made him drunk, and cast him alive into the foundations. This tradition was still strong in 1843, when a new bridge was under construction at Halle, Germany, and "the common people got an idea that a child was wanted to wall up in the foundations." Similarly, the famous medieval bridge at Mostar in Herzegovina, destroyed in the Bosnian war of the early 1990s, was said to have a Romani woman buried in its foundations.

RELICS AS FOUNDATION DEPOSITS

Apart from the interment of whole human beings beneath or within the fabric of a building, there are many instances of fragments of human beings being used. Of course, in the mainstream Christian tradition, it is considered essential that some "relic" should be buried in the fabric or held in the church so that its spiritual power will protect and sanctify the building. Human bones play an important part in Christian practice if not in written doctrine. For doctrinaire reasons, this strong element of ancestor worship in the Christian religion is given another name.

Relics such as bones of saints, or artifacts deemed to have association with Jesus and his immediate entourage, were and are placed in foundation stones, altars, and on top of spires. The center of Western Christendom, St. Peter's in Rome, was founded on an ancient cemetery, the Vatican, an oracle-place of the Great Mother Goddess Cybele. It was designed to incorporate the reputed tomb of St. Peter at a key point in its sacred geometry. As early as the year 150 CE, the Church at Smyrna referred to the remains of the martyr Polycarp as "more precious than the most exquisite jewels," depositing them where the faithful might gather round them "to celebrate the anniversary of his martyrdom."

Later, certain prominent teachers in the Church tried to stop the worship of bones, for by then they were being dug up and traded. St. Augustine condemned the monks who traded in Christians' bones, "retailing the limbs of martyrs, if martyrs they are." In the year 386 CE, an edict was issued that said, "Let no one remove a buried body; let no one carry away or sell a martyr." As late as the year 538 CE, the Church had no bone-related rituals for dedicating churches, but attempts to prevent the faithful from practicing the cult of bones finally failed and relics became essential. Since the late sixth century, Christians have carried bones around and buried them in churches to provide on-lays as part of their consecration rites. Because Christian writers do not see their religion anthropologically, they cannot recognize their ancestral cult of bones for what it is. Perhaps the first people to comment on this were the indigenous Pagans of Madagascar, who refused to become Christians because, as they told the missionaries, Jesus was clearly the ancestor of the "white man," and they already prayed to their own ancestors.

When the present basilica of St. Peter's replaced the original mother church in Rome, Ippolito Aldobrandini (Pope Clement VIII, 1592–1605) incorporated several reputed relics into the cross upon the lantern of the dome. The topping-out ceremony involved depositing ritually two leaden caskets in the cross at the summit. These caskets contained reputed pieces of the True Cross as well as pieces of St. Andrew, St. James the Great, and the early Popes Clement, Callixtus, and Sixtus. As well as these relics, the caskets contained seven Agnus Dei, ritual "Lamb of God" medallions cast from the wax of Easter candles that had been mixed with the dust of martyrs' bones. The apical cross of St. Peter's is thus a powerful repository of ancestral fragments, providing powerful magical protection for the basilica and the city.

Figure 3.2. Baroque high altar in the Muenster Unserer Lieben Frau
(Minster of Our Lady) Cathedral in Konstanz, Germany, containing the
skull of a martyr or saint. Counter-Reformation Catholic churches
displayed skulls, bones, and even complete skeletons behind glass
as objects of veneration. (Nigel Pennick)

Many Roman Catholic churches contain pieces of dead human
beings actually on public view. They are considered to empower the
sanctity of the place, being physical witnesses to the cult of the ancestral
dead that is one of the key features of Catholic Christianity. Detached
arms, legs, and heads are popular. Drogheda in Ireland has the grisly
mummified head of the Catholic martyr Oliver Plunkett, in a glass case.
In Germany, the splendid eighteenth-century baroque altar of Konstanz
(Constance) cathedral contains mummified heads with jewels in their
eye sockets, looking out on the congregation through portholes. The
cathedral of Arles, in Provence, France, has a whole chapel full of wonderful golden and bejeweled reliquaries that display the bones, blood,
and clothes of saints.

In London, Westminster Cathedral has the reassembled relics of a saint who was hanged, drawn, and quartered by Protestants. Many churches in Italy have whole bodies, often of local notables considered to be "martyrs" and "saints." For instance, the "martyr" Maria Goretti, murdered in 1902, lies in state at Nettuno. One of the most famous visible body-relics is that of the Jesuit missionary St. Francis Xavier, preserved in the church of Bom Jesu in Goa, India. He is not intact, as his right arm was taken away to Rome, and later exhibited in America. The Catholic tradition of having mummified bodies on view has been taken up in the twentieth century by political movements. At some time or other, the corpses of Vladimir Lenin, Joseph Stalin, Eva Perón, and Ferdinand Marcos have been displayed to the faithful.

BLOOD FOUNDATIONS

Blood symbolizes the life of the human being, and sometimes it has been an important ingredient in buildings. In religious terms, it is a significant element in both the northern European creation myth and the mysteries of Jesus Christ's death. The twelfth-century writer Geoffrey of Monmouth tells how blood was a necessary component in difficult building situations. In the legend of the discovery of Merlin, the foundations of a new castle at Mount Erith refused to stand. King Vortigern's magicians recommended the sacrifice of an illegitimate boy "so that the mortar and stones could be sprinkled with the boy's blood," after which they would stand. The boy they found was Merlin, who avoided being sacrificed by telling the king's wizards that dragons were the cause of the castle's instability. There are many recorded instances of blood being used in European foundation and building ceremonies. In the eighteenth century, the walls of Portsmouth Dockyard were built using mortar into which the blood of bulls had been poured. It has been common in many lands to mix blood with mortar, serving both magically and physically to bind the walls together strongly. In Swabia, there is the related custom of mixing wine or milk with mortar. In Christian symbolism, wine is the blood of Jesus Christ. Scottish builders' ceremonies once included smearing the foundation stone with human blood, or killing a chicken and allowing its blood to run over the stone.

There are several explanations for these sacrifices. The spirit theory explains that the earth (or the spirits of the place) must receive a gift before they will allow the building to stand there. If they did not get an offering, they would throw the building down, or psychically persecute the inhabitants with hauntings and bad luck. The Christian theory appears to be that the saints' bodies or body parts contain a spiritual force that drives away the powers of the demonic empire, simultaneously protecting the devout and reinforcing their faith. Another idea is that the spirit of the sacrificed one will remain in the building to protect it against supernatural attack. Many legends are a synthesis of these three beliefs.

An important origin motif in the Indo-European tradition is the foundation of buildings or other structures upon a slain human form. In the northern European creation myth, the androgynous giant Ymir was killed by the gods, and a great river of blood gushed forth, drowning "all the race of rime-giants." Ymir's body was then ripped apart by the gods in a ritual frenzy of destruction/creation, for as the giant was torn apart, elements of his-her physical substance became the world. On the giant's death, the world was built.

Fragments of the giant's body formed various aspects of the world: Ymir's bones became the rocks; his-her blood filled the earth's hollows to become the seas, and the cranium formed the dome of the heavens. The moment of the death of the anthropocosmic giant was thus also the moment of the creation of the world. In the Hindu tradition, Mahapurusha, the Cosmic Man, who displays all existence in his body, serves a similar function.

These beings are related to the Jewish mystical concept of Adam Kadmon and the classical European idea known now as "Vitruvian Man." There, humans' subtle body geometry defines the proportions and structure of architecture, and is used in the traditional European martial arts. This link with the cosmos is expressed in the Hermetic maxim "As above, so below." In Christian architecture, the body of the crucified Jesus Christ symbolically underlies the body of the church, and the bones of his followers literally do. Although the geometric plan of churches is ostensibly the body of the crucified Jesus Christ, actual representations of him in foundations are extremely rare. It seems that crucifixes were only used at places where the on-lay needed to be most

Figure 3.3. Man the Microcosm.
(Nigel Pennick)

powerful. One example was the Christian monastery built on the site of
the Pagan holy oak tree at Romowe (Romuva) in East Prussia. There, a
golden crucifix and a triangular "ring" inscribed with Christian sacred
texts was buried in the foundations.

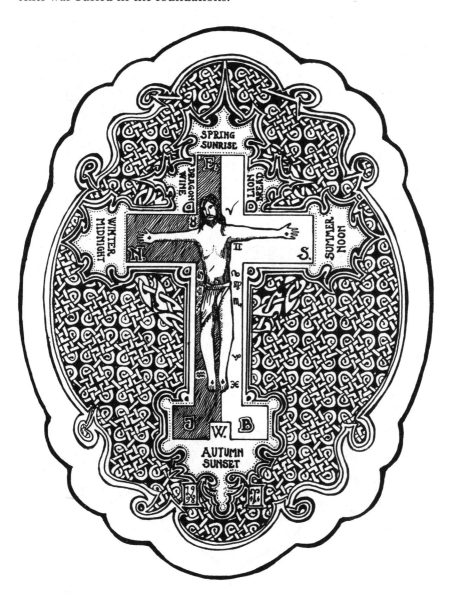

Figure 3.4. Traditionally, Christian churches are laid out according to the
image of the crucified Christ, paralleling the slain giants of Northern
Tradition and Hindu cosmology. (Nigel Pennick)

A most remarkable symbolic artifact relating to the human body as foundation is preserved in the National Museum in Dublin. Found on an artificial island known as a *crannog* at Ballinderry, near Moate, County Westmeath in Ireland in October 1932, it is an early medieval wooden gameboard. It is square with a protruding carved human head at one end, and a handle at the other. The playing part is only about nine-and-a-half inches (24 cm) square, making it readily portable, like a modern traveling chess set. Forty-nine holes arranged in a square are drilled in the board, for playing the game called *Brandubh*. The central hole, in which the main king-piece, the Brenin, which began the game,

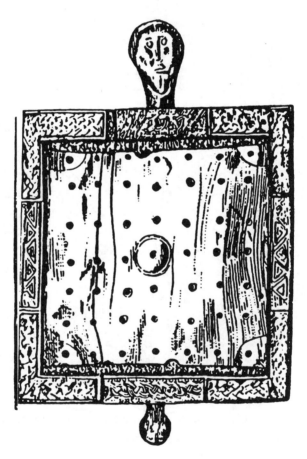

Figure 3.5. The navel of the Earth related to the human body:
Ancient Celtic Gameboard from Ballinderry, Ireland.
(Nigel Pennick)

has circles around it, marking it as the navel of the board, which it is in relation to the head. The Ballinderry gameboard thus symbolizes the slain giant that underlies the world, countries, and buildings in Indo-European cosmology. The use of real human victims in remote antiquity may be the origin of this legendary being.

ANIMALS IN FOUNDATIONS

The horse was a holy animal in Pagan northern Europe. The Celts revered a goddess of the horses, Epona. Before they were destroyed by Christian missionaries in the twelfth century, certain religious places of the Germani, Angles, and Wends included fenced sacred enclosures in which sacred horses were kept. No one was allowed to ride them, and they were sacrificed on occasion in honor of the gods. Then, a holy meal of horseflesh was taken, and the sacrificed animal's skull was set on a post as a witness and memory of the sacrificial rite. Often the post was draped with the horse's skin and hung over a holy well or sacred pool. In later years, once eating it had been banned by Christian edicts, horseflesh was considered to be the diet of giants and witches, and the Norwegian trolls were said to play their otherworldly melodies on flutes made from horses' leg-bones. But despite the Christian dietary law, horses have been used continuously until the present day in non-Christian rites and ceremonies. Horse skulls continued to protect buildings, appear in ritual performances, and be buried as the foundation of buildings.

Just as in life, horses are the faithful companions of humans, so they are connected with human burials. In many parts of Europe, horsemen and women were buried with their animals, which were probably killed to accompany them to the grave. This Pagan tradition was not halted by the introduction of the Christian religion. There are numerous recorded examples of horse sacrifice in medieval and later times. Horses were sacrificed at the funerals of King John of England in 1216 and the Holy Roman Emperor Karl IV in 1378. In 1389, the knight Bertrand Du Guesclin was buried at Saint-Denis in France. At his funeral, several horses were sacrificed after being blessed by the Bishop of Auxerre. In

1499, the *Landsknechte* (men-at-arms) sacrificed a horse to mark the end of the Swabian Wars. In 1791 at Trier in the Rhineland, the horse of General Friedrich Kasimir was killed and buried with him in his grave. The horse belonging to Queen Victoria's leading huntsman was shot at his funeral at Sunninghill church in Berkshire, England, in 1866. Its ears were put in the huntsman's coffin and buried with him.

Horses were also used in building foundations and fabric. In 1318, a horse was sacrificed at the foundation of Königsfelden monastery in Germany. St Botolph's church at Boston, Lincolnshire, had horse bones embedded in the floor. Forty horse skulls were found laid in ranks under the floor of a seventeenth-century house at Bungay in Suffolk. The Folk Museum in Cambridge has several horse relics recovered from old buildings. Half a horse's jawbone, dating from the seventeenth century, was found between two courses of brickwork in the chimney of a house at Histon in Cambridgeshire. Another horse relic from Histon is a horse leg bone found in the brickwork of a chimney arch. The Folk Museum itself, formerly the White Horse Inn, has on show a horse leg bone once part of the stables of the inn itself. A horse's head was buried in 1897 as a foundation-offering beneath the Primitive Methodist Chapel at Black Horse Drove in an isolated part of the Cambridgeshire Fens in eastern England. The builder poured a libation of beer over it as "an old heathen custom to drive evil and witchcraft away."

Eight horse skulls were embedded in the pulpit of the Bristol Street Meeting House in Edinburgh. At Llandaff Cathedral in Cardiff, Wales, horse skulls were concealed in the choir stalls. It seems that here the skulls have an acoustic function. Traditions from as far apart as Ireland and the northern German regions of Dithmarschen and Holstein tell how horse skulls were laid beneath threshing floors in barns. This is because a good threshing floor should "bend to meet the flail," and then the flails will "sing." Also, horse skulls laid under the flagstones of a house improve the sound when the occupants dance over them.

To this day, horse skulls are used in traditional performances. The skull is mounted at the end of a pole, and a person carries it. Both pole and person are covered with a horse skin or blanket, and the performer impersonates the horse in a dance or play. Traditional British performances using the horse skull include the midwinter outings of Welsh mummers disguised as Mari Lwyd and various "horse-plays" in the English mumming tradition. There are Old Ball of Lancashire, the "Poor Old Horse" play of Derbyshire and South Yorkshire, the boundary-claiming ritual of Huntingdon, and the Hoodening Horse of Kent. In some instances, the horse skull is buried in the earth between performances. The appearance of the horse-guisers at one's house is considered to be a luck-bringing event.

It was not only horses and their parts that were buried as traditional foundation offerings. A former German foundation custom was to bury a living blind dog beneath the threshold of a stable so that cattle would be prevented from straying. Lithuanian folk tradition asserts that to have peace and harmony within a house, a dog should be buried as a foundation-offering. The tradition was reasserted in England in 1984. Then, a mummified whippet dog was discovered under the tackroom floor of the former stables of the 1898 public house The Carlton in Leigh-on-Sea, Essex, which was undergoing reconstruction. It was reburied ceremonially in a wooden box lined with red velvet. With it were a sprig of yew and a piece of thyme, and a message for the dog that read: "We apologise for disturbing you and hope you will continue to act as guardian to the Carlton and the shops. . . . A sprig of yew and the herb thyme, two plants associated with mortality and protection, have been put with your carcass to help you in the role."

Cats are far more common as foundation and other building offerings. During the 1980s, the present author collected over one hundred instances of them in England alone. Many cats are found in the roof spaces of old houses, where they were placed ceremonially as apotropaic offerings against fire and infestation of vermin. Others were buried in the thresholds, hearths, and chimneys of houses. Sometimes, animal foundation offerings were considered to be "witchcraft." In 1703, an elder of the church at Oyne in Aberdeenshire, Scotland, was charged with "witchcraft and charming" because he buried a cat beneath the hearth of his house to keep witchcraft and bad luck away. Like cats, chickens have also suffered burial in walls. Examples have been recorded in England, France, Denmark, Germany, Poland, Austria, and Greece.

Figure 3.6. East Anglian foundation and building deposits.
Top row (left to right): Mummified cats from the city of
Cambridge and Sudbury, Suffolk.
Middle row: A jawbone from Billericay, Essex,
and mummified rat from Cambridge.
Lower row: A Cambridgeshire witch bottle from
Willingham in Cambridgeshire and a mummified Whippet dog
from Leigh-on-Sea, Essex. (Nigel Pennick)

Animal offerings beneath buildings have included many domestic and wild species. In the eleventh century CE, wolf skulls were buried in the foundation of a tower at Bury St Edmund's Abbey in Suffolk, England. In Bulgaria, lambs or cocks were sacrificed in the foundations of houses. Churches in Denmark had the remains of sacrificed lambs buried beneath their altars. Russian house-building customs include the husband and wife together beheading a chicken and burying the body and head beneath a front corner of the house. Russian water-mill

Figure 3.7. A mummified cat preserved in Dirty Dick's public house, Bishopsgate, London. (Nigel Pennick)

builders propitiated the water-spirits called *Wodjanoi* with offerings of cows, sheep, horses, or pigs. Excavated foundations of mills in Silesia, Poland, have yielded jars containing bones of lambs and chickens.

Wild birds are occasionally discovered in foundations when buildings are renovated. A swallow and a dove were sacrificed in the church foundations in Knottingen, Germany, at Luib, on the Isle of Skye, Scotland, a pied wagtail was immured in the bridge. The egg, symbol of creation and the omphalos, has been used in many lands as a foundation deposit. An origin legend of the city of Naples in Italy tells how it was "founded on an egg." In Germany, eggs in the foundation are said to protect a house against lightning strikes. They are known from many places, including Highgate in London, and Berlin, Deilmissen, and Trempen in Germany.

Figure 3.8. The Etruscans marked omphalos sites with carved stones such as this one preserved at Fiesole, near Florence, Italy. (Nigel Pennick)

WITCH BOTTLES

The eastern counties of England possess a tradition of foundation deposition that has a recorded magical function and theory—the Witch Bottle. The use of them was recorded by Joseph Glanvil in 1681 in his *Sadducismus Triumphatus, or, Full and Plain Evidence Concerning Witches and Apparitions* (published 1689). Glanvil tells how William Brearly, a priest educated at and a Fellow of Christ's College, Cambridge, took lodgings in a Suffolk village. He soon found out that his landlady was unwell, having been haunted by "a thing in the shape of a bird." He reported the phenomenon to an old man "that travelled up and down the country." He recommended that the woman's husband should "take a bottle, and put his wife's urine into it, together with pins and needles

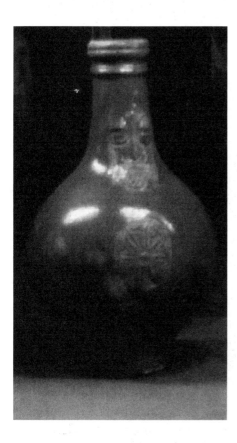

Figure 3.9. 'Bellarmine' witch-bottle Bury St Edmunds, Suffolk, England. (Nigel Pennick)

and nails, and cork them up, and set the bottle to the fire, but be sure the cork be fast in it, that it will not fly out."

The husband followed the old man's instructions, but the cork blew out, and the remedy failed. But at the second attempt, "The man did accordingly, and his wife began to mend sensibly, and in competent time was well recovered. But there came a woman from a town some miles off to their house with a lamentable outcry, that they had killed her husband . . . at last they understood that her husband was a wizard and had bewitched this man's wife, and that this counter-practice prescribed by the Old Man, which saved the wife from languishment, was the death of that wizard that had bewitched her."

Glanvil recounts the traditional magical remedy of the Witch Bottle, which was prepared in this way and then buried beneath the threshold or in the chimney-breasts of houses to ward off bad luck and ill-wishing. The most common Witch Bottle in eastern England is the Bellarmine or Greybeard. This is a squat, roundbellied stoneware bottle with a handle. Bellarmines are saltglazed with a rich brown or gray finish, and imprinted on the neck with a bearded face, with either a coat of arms or an eight-branched sigil beneath it. The name "Bellarmine" comes from the supposed resemblance to the Roman Catholic inquisitor Cardinal Bellarmine (1542–1621), who persecuted the Protestants in the Low Countries during the wars between the two Christian sects. First produced in the German Rhineland around 1500, their manufacture spread through the Low Countries to England. Production finally ceased around 1700. They were installed in buildings well into the nineteenth century: the famous wizard Cunning Murrell of Hadleigh was practicing the craft until his death in 1860. Many museums in eastern England have Witch Bottles on display. The contents of many have been analyzed, and found to concur with Glanvil's account.

Less common than Bellarmines are the Cambridgeshire Witch Bottles. These are glass, and much smaller than Bellarmines, which measure between 5–9 inches (13–23 cm) in length. Cambridgeshire Witch Bottles are made of greenish or bluish glass. They are long and narrow, and contain strands of thread of various colors, with red predominant. They are deposited in apertures in walls and windowsills. Like the Bellarmines, their function is to ward of bad luck and ill-wishing. Human hair has been found in a similar bottle at Hof Füllberg at Ahrenfeld in Germany.

PLANT OFFERINGS AND BUILDERS' TOKENS

Polish housebuilding customs include laying green herbs or consecrated garlands under the four cornerstones of new houses. A Flemish tradition from Denderleeuw and elsewhere in Belgium deposits consecrated palms or flowers beneath the foundation stone. These are lustrated with holy water. Religious medallions are also used in Catholic parts of the Low Countries. On the holy island of Rügen in the Baltic, branches of Juniper are laid in foundations "to keep out the Devil and evil spirits." Wendish builders buried a hymn book beneath each of the four supports of their windmills (*Bockmühlen*).

During construction, contemporary builders often embed objects and messages in walls or beneath door and window frames during construction. Some objects are traditional, representing a continuity that certainly goes back for several centuries, and perhaps longer. Welsh plasterers kill flies and embed them in the middle of each wall they are plastering. In the English midlands, plasterers embed coins at the bottom corner of walls they are covering with plaster. Contemporary workmen finding old coins during repair work will replace them, and add a new one, if possible dated "this year." A few years ago, a workman in Wellingborough, Northamptonshire, told me that in 1990 he found four old coins together, the earliest dating from the eighteenth century, and the newest from the beginning of the twentieth. He added a fifth coin, dated 1990, to the pile when he reburied them.

In his *Builders' Rites and Ceremonies* (1894), G. W. Speth speculated that coin burial was a substitute for "a living human sacrifice" that "our forefathers" had buried in the foundations. "Their sons substituted an animal," Speth continued, "their sons again a mere effigy or other symbol; and we, their children, still immure a substitute." These are coins bearing the effigy "of the one person to whom we are most loyal, and whom we all most love, our Gracious Queen." By embedding the coin in the structure, Speth asserts, we symbolically "provide a soul for the structure."

Documents concealed by workmen often include the names of the people working there, the date, and some other information. Sometimes this information is deposited beneath foundation stones, and the two practices are clearly contiguous with one another. Speth comments that if one asked a bystander the reason why these deposits were made, "He would probably answer that if at any time the stone was removed, evidence might be forthcoming of the circumstances attending the function; that, in fact, these objects were placed there for a future witness and reference." Although this is a seemingly reasonable supposition, Speth continues, "it is obviously an absurd one, for surely the hope of all concerned in the ceremony is that the foundation stone will never be removed, and that the witness will forever remain dumb."

The twentieth-century practice of burying so-called time capsules under buildings is a development both of the formal records laid in foot-stones, and of the vernacular practice of workmen's messages. A famous time capsule was buried at the site of the New York World's Fair at noon on September 23, 1938. It contained objects that were supposed to last for 5,000 years and show people in the year 6938 how New Yorkers lived in 1938. They included a Silver Dollar, a Mickey Mouse plastic cup, comic strips, and the Lord's Prayer printed in 300 languages. "May the time capsule sleep well," said A. W. Robertson, chairman of the Westinghouse Electric and Manufacturing Company, lowering the capsule into the ground, "When it is awakened five thousand years from now, may its contents be found a suitable gift to our far-off descendants."

The practice of burying time capsules continues. In 1996, on October 3, one was buried by the Minister of Transport beneath the floor of a new tramcar maintenance facility at Southbank in Melbourne, Australia. It contained tramway memorabilia, company staff registers, model trams, and a list of people who attended the ceremony. Unlike the New Yorkers, the Australians were less ambitious about the length of time it will last, for the Melbourne capsule "will remain sealed for at least fifty years."

CHAPTER 4

Consecration, Evocatio, and Blessings

The Sacred and the Profane

Know what you have to do, and do it.
WILLIAM MULREADY,
QUOTED BY JOHN RUSKIN (1819–1900)
IN *THE SEVEN LAMPS OF ARCHITECTURE* (1849)

Once a new thing is begun, after the rites of construction have been completed, ceremonies should be performed that state the spiritual nature of the entity that has been brought into being. Consecratory or dedicatory rites activate the inherent qualities of the new venture, displaying them to all in the public domain. They are a statement to the community that all is well and in proper order. Dedication commemorates the arrival of the new thing in the sphere of human society. It is the parallel of the customary baptisms and naming ceremonies for infants, marking the moment at which they take their place as distinct individuals in the world.

Ceremonial dedication of holy places and things has been performed for the greater part of recorded history. Plutarch, in his *Life of Theseus,* tells how on his voyage back from Crete, the hero came ashore at Delos. There, he consecrated an image of Aphrodite in a temple. Then, he danced with his male followers

a dance which they tell is still performed by the Delians, in imitation of the circling pathways of the labyrinth, composed of certain
rhythmic involutions and evolutions. Dicaerchus tells us that the
Delians call this sort of dance the *Crane.* Theseus danced it around
the altar called *Keraton,* built of horns taken only from the left side
of the head.

This Greek *geranos* crane dance is performed today as a winding
line-dance that spirals in and out in the manner of a labyrinth, though
it is no longer a ceremonial dance of dedication, having long since lost
its sacred function. Rites like this are the mainstream way of celebrating
and dedicating new things. Only militant modernity has attempted to
dispense with them, to the psychological and spiritual detriment of all
of us.

The forms of sacred rites and ceremonies are skilled performances
in their own right. The religion to which they belong gives them their
color, but not their structure and function. In Europe, rites of dedication and consecration exist in their fullest form in the various sects
of the Christian church. They are clearly in continuation of ancient
Egyptian, Babylonian, Greek, Etruscan, Roman, and Jewish ritual
forms, modified and refined to express the particular doctrines of the
religion and the sect within it. They emphasize proper order within
everything that is done, for that which is done on the physical level
is reflected in the spiritual. The details of the rites vary according to
the type of thing to be consecrated. They are very precise and understanding of their context. In the Church of England, for instance,
there are separate rites for consecrating churches and burial grounds.
The latter includes powerful invocations such as: "From lightning
and tempest; from plague, pestilence, and famine; from battle and
murder, and from sudden death, Good Lord, deliver us." There are
numerous other different rites with appropriate actions and words for
dedicating fonts, windows, church bells, and schools, and the opening
of hospitals. The Anglican, Roman Catholic, and Orthodox churches
have further rites for blessing secular buildings, wells, fields, roads,
animals, and vehicles.

CATHOLIC TRADITIONS OF CHURCH CONSECRATION

The earliest record of Roman Catholic church consecration is in a letter from Pope Vigilius to Profuturus of Braga in the year 538 CE. At that time, a church was deemed to be dedicated by simply celebrating the Mass in it. The church was not cleansed first with holy water. When relics were available, they had to be deposited in the church before the first Mass was said. Around sixty years later, Pope Gregory's letters deal extensively with church consecration. By his time, centralization of power with the pope meant that no church could be consecrated without papal authorization.

Early church rites of consecration recreate a foundation-burial ritual by bringing the holy relics (the foundation deposit, usually the bones of a saint) to the completed church and then sealing them in the altar. Rites recorded in the *Gelasian Sacramentary* tell how church consecration begins at an already consecrated place. The litany is said there, and relics are placed on a paten on which a white linen cloth is laid, and then covered with a silk veil. Then, the bishop and his clergy set out in ceremonial procession to the new church, carrying the relics. During the procession, a psalm is chanted, and when the new church is in sight, the litany is begun. The bishop hands the relics to a priest and then, accompanied by two or three other clergymen, he enters the church. He takes some water, exorcises it, mixes it with some drops of holy oil, and mixes it with the mortar that will be used to seal the altar-stone. Then he takes a sponge previously dipped in the exorcised water and washes the altar with it once. After this, the clergy leaves the church, and concludes the litany with a prayer.

Then the bishop sprinkles the remains of the exorcised water over members of the public assembled there. He then carries the relics into the church and takes them to the altar. The altar has a cavity prepared for the reception of the bones. Then, after anointing the four corners of the cavity with holy oil, he seals in the relics, using the sacred mortar. The altar thus becomes the grave of the fragmental saint, and the church his tomb. After further prayers, the rite is ended.

The ancient Gallican rites were recorded at the end of the ninth century in the Episcopal School at Rheims in France and in the *Sacramentary of Angouleme*. They follow the Roman ceremonial structure, with a bishop bringing relics from another place, after an all-night vigil has been observed with them. The church to be consecrated is empty, save for a single clergyman. Twelve candles are burned all night, arranged around the inside of the walls. When the bishop arrives, he touches the lintel of the door with his pastoral staff, and then is admitted by the priest inside. The bishop and clergy enter, and all prostrate themselves on the church floor.

Next, the bishop proceeds to the northeastern corner and walks diagonally across the church to the southwest, making the letters of the alphabet with his pastoral staff. From the southwest, he goes to the southeastern corner, and does the same to the northwestern corner. returning from the northwest to the altar, the bishop blesses first water and then salt. The salt is then mixed with ashes, and the mixture sprinkled on the holy water in the sign of the cross in three separate passes. The bishop then pours in wine and dips his finger into the "lustral water" thus made. He traces the sign of the cross at each of the four corners of the altar, and then makes a sevenfold sunwise circuit of it while sprinkling holy water on it with a bunch of the Hyssop plant (*Hyssopus officinalis*). Then, with the Hyssop, the bishop makes a threefold circuit of the inside of the church, sprinkling the walls with holy water. At the same time, clergymen sprinkle the outer walls. Once this is done, the bishop sprinkles the pavement along the centerline of the church from altar to west door, then at right angles to this across the center of the church.

After further prayers, the altar is anointed with the remains of the holy water. Then the altar is censed with incense and anointed in the center and at the four corners with the sign of the cross. This is done three times, twice with ordinary blessed oil, and lastly with the holy chrism. Next, the bishop anoints the church walls with the holy chrism. Back at the altar again, he makes a cross out of grains of incense, and lights them. As they burn, he recites a consecrational prayer. Once this is done, the subdeacons bring linen and sacred vessels for the bishop to bless. The paten and chalice are anointed with holy chrism.

Next, the bishop and clergy leave the church and go to the place where the relics are being guarded by the people. They are collected and brought in procession to the church. Then the lay people are allowed to enter it for the first time. When the bishop enters the sanctuary, a curtain is dropped so that the lay people cannot see the final rite of enshrinement of the relics. As in the Roman rite, the bishop seals the relics into the altar. Then, the church lights are lit, and the bishop celebrates the Mass.

CHURCH OF ENGLAND CONSECRATION RITES

Church consecration in England traditionally follows the following procedure. There are no relics, and no altar in Protestantism, but the symbolic rites are as well thought out as those of any other religion. Before the consecration, all legal documents concerning the church are shown to the bishop. These include the deeds to the ground on which the church stands, the nomination of the minister who is to preside there, and any other relevant documentation. If this is all in order, the bishop issues an Act or *Sentence of Consecration* for the church. Eight days before the consecration, a notice is fixed to the church door giving the day and hour when the church will be consecrated. Before the day of consecration, the church must be fully finished, including all of its furnishings. A chair for the bishop is set in the sanctuary, and sufficient seats provided for his chaplains and other attendants. Seats outside the sanctuary, and a table with pen, ink, and blotting paper, are provided for the chancellor, registrar, and apparitor.

At the day and hour appointed, the congregation being already inside the church and waiting, the bishop and his entourage arrive at the entrance where they are received by the church's clergy. A petition, signed by the incumbent minister and the churchwardens is handed ceremonially to the bishop, requesting him to consecrate the church. The request is also spoken, and the bishop agrees. Then a procession begins. It makes a complete circuit of the outside of the church, sunwise, while Psalm 24 is sung. It begins: "The earth is the Lord's, and all that therein is: the compass of the world, and they that dwell within. . . ."

Once the ritual circuit is finished, the procession halts at the west door. The bishop knocks upon it three times with his pastoral staff, saying, "Open me the gates of righteousness: that I may go into them, and give thanks unto the Lord. Lift up your heads, O ye gates, and be ye lift up, ye everlasting doors: and the King of Glory shall come in." He is answered from within with "Who is the King of Glory?" and the bishop replies, "Even the Lord of Hosts: He is the King of Glory." At this, the door is opened, and the keys of the church are given to him.

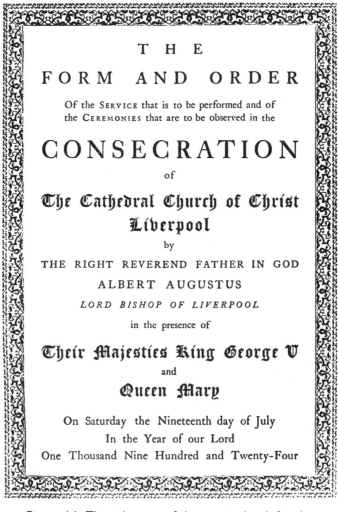

THE
FORM AND ORDER

Of the SERVICE that is to be performed and of the CEREMONIES that are to be observed in the

CONSECRATION

of

The Cathedral Church of Christ Liverpool

by

THE RIGHT REVEREND FATHER IN GOD

ALBERT AUGUSTUS

LORD BISHOP OF LIVERPOOL

in the presence of

Their Majesties King George V

and

Queen Mary

On Saturday the Nineteenth day of July
In the Year of our Lord
One Thousand Nine Hundred and Twenty-Four

Figure 4.1. The title page of the service book for the consecration of Liverpool Anglican Cathedral, 1924. (Nideck)

The bishop then pronounces peace upon the house, enters the church, and says a prayer of invocation: "Enter, O Lord, we beseech thee, this house which is built to thy glory, that it may be hallowed by thine abiding presence, and within the hearts of thy faithful people establish for thyself an everlasting habitation." After another saying from the Bible, the procession moves through the church from west to east, singing Psalm 122, which tells of the house of the Lord in Jerusalem. When the psalm has ended, the officiants are at the east end, and the bishop lays the church keys upon the Holy Table (as the Protestant altar is called).

Next comes the dedication. After a prayer about the Key of King David, the bishop asks the congregation to kneel and pray in silence for the church and those who shall worship there. This is followed by the hymn "Veni, Creator Spiritus," which invokes the Holy Ghost. While it is being sung, the bishop makes the sign of the cross together with the Greek characters *alpha* and *omega* upon the pavement with his pastoral staff. A more complex, and older, form of this rite involves the bishop writing all of the letters of the Roman and Greek alphabets with his pastoral staff in a cross made of ashes on the pavement of the new church. Although this rite represents the symbolic sigils of Christ, who is described as α (*alpha*) and ω (*omega*), the beginning and the end. Both characters have the meanings of riches and abundance in Greek alphabet lore. This rite is a continuation of the ceremony conducted by the ancient Pagan augurs and agrimensors when laying out a sacred site for a temple. In the church, it is a rite of on-lay that signifies taking possession of the ground upon which the church stands in the name of Jesus Christ.

Next, the bishop requests God to accept his service and see and hear all that will take place in the church. This is followed by a request for God to accept, sanctify, and bless the church to be a sanctuary of the Most High, and to send down his spiritual benediction and grace, "that it may be the House of God to him, and to us the gate of heaven." After this, the procession forms up once more, led by the cross-bearer, and visits the font and "other places here appointed." The bishop blesses the font, then the chancel step, the lectern, and the pulpit. If there are any secondary chapels, they are blessed next, with the Holy Tables within them. The bishop traces the sign of the cross at the four corners and in the center of each Holy Table, with a prayer.

Once this is finished, the bishop's entourage re-enter the chancel and take their places once more. Then comes the consecration proper. Facing east, the bishop invokes the divine power to "descend upon this place in the fullness of sevenfold grace . . . that whensoever thy holy name is invoked within these walls, the prayers of those who call on thee may be heard by thee, O Lord, merciful and gracious." At the Holy Table (altar), the bishop calls upon God "to bless, hallow, and sanctify this Holy Table, and to bless, hallow, and consecrate this whole building with the everlasting fullness of thy sanctifying power." At the moment he says "Holy Table," the bishop traces the sign of the cross at its four corners and center.

Psalm 84 is then sung and, during it, the Holy Table is vested with "frontal, frontlet, and fair linen cloth," and the "ornaments and vessels" are presented to the bishop, who puts them on the altar. After the psalm, the bishop lays his hands on each ornament and vessel and says a prayer of dedication. Next comes a hymn, during which the ornaments are placed in position, the vessels taken away to the Credence, and candles are lit. The Holy Tables in any other chapels are also vested. Once this is done, the bishop sits, and the Chancellor of the Diocese reads out the *Sentence of Consecration*. The bishop then signs the document and "gives instructions for its safe custody." Once this is done, the bishop stands, and, holding his pastoral staff in his hand, faces the congregation and states: "Good people, by virtue of our sacred office in the Church of God, we do now declare to be consecrate, and for ever set apart from profane, common, and ordinary uses this House of God, under the dedication of [name of saint or other holy name]." This is followed by the Lord's Prayer, and then the bishop blesses the people. The service ends with further prayers, a sermon, and blessings in conclusion.

Because sacredness comes into being when the building is consecrated, it can also be desecrated by profane acts. If this happens, then the building must be purified and reconsecrated before religious activities can proceed there. So there are ceremonies of reconsecration. Also, when a building has undergone reconstruction, it must be rededicated.

The rites for reopening of a church are similar to those of consecration, but they also invoke angels: "Let thy Holy Angels be with us and about us, and thy Holy Spirit within us, that in all our works and ways we may glorify thy name."

Blessing, the public invocation of beneficial powers into a project, should play an important role in creating places of power. Blessings, in whatever religious tradition, can be performed at various stages of any project. Traditionally, both in Pagan and Christian Europe, it has been the norm over the greatest period of human history. Only under modernism and communism have these rites been ignored. Those schooled in modernism are sometimes puzzled by this tradition. On May 15, 1998, at Wednesbury in the English West Midlands, Father Mocciaro Nunzio, a Roman Catholic priest, conducted a blessing before a congregation of 150 people. The object of the blessing was the first new tramcar that had just been delivered from a factory in Italy for the Midland Metro, the new Birmingham to Wolverhampton tramway.

At the same time, Father Nunzio also blessed the entire line so that all who might travel on the tramway in the future should have divine protection. The press reports about the event appeared puzzled that a priest should bless a new tramline in England, as most public works are started and finished with minimal modernist ceremony. The British mass media "explained it away" as reflecting Italian practice, employed because the new tramway company had a significant Italian financial interest in it. The concept that it could have value in its own right was not present in the media accounts.

In a tradition that usually goes unnoticed, engineers building tunnels install an image of St. Barbara either over the entrance to the tunnel or in a shaft. She is the guardian saint of tunnel builders. For example, in London in January 2019 Father Alex McAllister, priest of St Thomas à Becket church, Wandsworth, blessed a statue of St. Barbara in a shaft at Dornay Street made for the construction of the Thames Tideway deep sewer tunnel. Installation of St. Barbara images to protect the tunnel workers is a widespread tradition, conducted in the United States as well as Great Britain, Australia, New Zealand, and many European countries. The images are removed once the tunneling is complete.

EVOCATIO, ÁLFREK, AND ON-LAYS

According to the oldest recorded European esoteric traditions, it is possible to take the spiritual guardian of any place away from its original locus and to transport it to another place, where it is installed with appropriate rites and ceremonies. This is called *evocatio*. It leaves the original place bereft of the spirit that once resided there, a disensouled condition described by the Old Norse word *álfrek* and the East Anglian *gast*. *Evocatio* is a Pagan incantatory formula that invites the tutelary deities of a place to leave it and come to dwell in another one. Among other uses, *evocatio* was applied by the ancients when they besieged a city. The Romans invited the besieged city's deities to migrate to Rome, where they promised they would be treated better than in their original home. The conquered city thereby lost its guardian deity and was subject to control by the Romans. Leon Battista Alberti, in his *De re aedificatoria* (1452), wrote:

> The ancients, when they were about to lay siege to any town, lest they should seem to offer any insult to religion, used to invoke, and with sacred hymns endeavoured to appease the gods that were guardians of the place, beseeching them to pass willingly over to them.

Even in time of war, the *Pax Deorum* was thereby maintained as far as possible.

Among the Romans, foreign deities were first evoked in 496 BCE, when the twin gods Castor and Pollux of Tusculum were taken to Rome. In 386 BCE, the goddess Juno Regina was enticed away from Veil, and in 292 BCE, Asclepius, god of healing, was brought to Rome from Epidauros in Greece in the form of a serpent. In 264≈BCE, Vertumnus was lured from the Volsinii, and the Great Mother Goddess Cybele was brought to Rome, along with her holy stone, from Asia Minor in 204 BCE. Much later, in turn, the cult of Jesus was brought to Rome, which became its major center in the West. The Christian custom of locating spiritual power in the dead remains of saints and martyrs enabled the concept of *evocatio* to be split. When primal spiritual power was held to reside in human bones and artifacts associated with once-living people, then it needs no longer be located in one place, but could be split up and spread through the world. Re-enacting the creation myth where the anthropocosmic giant is dismembered to make the world, parts of saints could spread Christian sanctity through the world. However, focusing upon the sanctity of bones allowed priests to ignore the resident spirits of a place. Instead of acknowledging the *anima loci,* they could bury the bones of saints on a place previously rendered *álfrek* by ceremonies of exorcism, the magical technique of *on-lay.* In such a case, the *Pax Deorum* is seriously compromised.

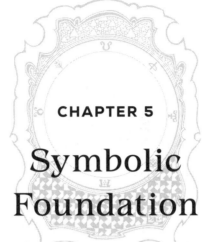

CHAPTER 5

Symbolic Foundation

Laying and Consecrating the First Stone

Mighty presences graciously grouped themselves above the stone, one of whom will often be seen hereafter in the place he blessed . . . the walls will echo to the music of his voice.
ANNIE BESANT, ON LAYING THE FOUNDATION STONE
OF THE THEOSOPHICAL SOCIETY BUILDING,
TAVISTOCK SQUARE, LONDON, SEPTEMBER 3, 1911

THE FOUNDATION STONE

The foundation stone of a building symbolizes the basis of the whole construction. If it is formed with perfect straight edges and right angles, and is laid true and level, then the whole building will also be made properly, and will stand for generations. The foundation stone is often called a "cornerstone." This is not necessarily literal, for cornerstone means the most important stone in the building, the stone upon which the whole edifice depends, both structurally and symbolically. Because of their fundamental importance, foundation stones are laid according

Figure 5.1. Foundation-stone offerings include the attributes
of the goddess of abundance, Abundantia.
(Nigel Pennick)

to symbolic rites and ceremonies. Ancient Mediterranean traditions of foundation-laying are recorded in various texts, including the Bible. The book of Isaiah (28:16) tells us: "Therefore thus saith the Lord God, I lay in Zion for a foundation stone, a tried stone, a precious cornerstone, a sure foundation." The book of Ezra (3:10) recounts, "when the builders laid the foundation of the temple of the Lord, they set the priests in their apparel with trumpets, and the Levites the sons of Asaph with cymbals, to praise the Lord . . . and all the people shouted with a great shout, when they praised the Lord, because the foundation of the house of the Lord was laid."

In former times, the foundation stone was literally part of the building's foundation. It could be a major stone, laid with great ceremony, or the smallest first brick. The meaning of its laying, as a formal beginning, is greater than its physical presence. For example, in his diaries, Elias Ashmole (1617–1692) refers to the ceremonial laying of the first brick of his new greenhouse, literally the foundation. Contemporary buildings usually have foundations of poured concrete, and hence foundation stones, when they exist, are primarily symbolic rather than structural. Some foundation stones are laid above another stone, called the "footstone." This usually has a cavity cut in it to contain foundation deposits that may include documents concerning the building, coins, bottles, and other ceremonial objects that record and empower the building's establishment. The cavity is rebated at the top so that it can be covered with a metal plate to seal it before the foundation stone is laid on top. If the building is set on the living rock, then the cavity should be cut in the living rock itself, when no footstone is needed. Ritually testing the footstone with "level" and set square is sometimes part of the foundation-laying ceremony.

It is traditional to inscribe foundation stones with symbols, sigils, or written texts. In the Christian tradition, crosses are carved on them. The foundation stone of La Consomme, Aujouleme, France, laid in 1171, had a circle inscribed at each of its four corners. The Hand of God points out the place "where it was done" at the southeast corner of the medieval church at Wissembourg in Alsace, France. More recent foundation stones include the names of officials, the date

Figure 5.2. A medieval mark-stone with a hand pointing out
"where it was done" on the southeast corner of the church of
St. Peter and St. Paul in Wissembourg, Alsace, France.
(Nigel Pennick)

that the stone was laid, and relevant sigils, emblems, coats-of-arms, and logos.

TRADITIONAL FOUNDATION-LAYING CEREMONIES

Foundation is essentially a public statement that the work has begun. In his *Die Wahlverwandtschaften* (Elective Affinities), Johann Wolfgang von Goethe (1749–1832) writes of the traditional German ceremonies of founding a house. They involve the whole community as spectators and participants in the feast that follows. The festival began with a church service, followed by a procession to the place where the foundation was prepared.

Goethe's ceremony recognizes the hidden work of the masons, because when everything is done properly, including the rites and ceremonies, all will be well. The house will stand for a very long time, while its inhabitants and the whole community will prosper.

Full form in public foundation-stone laying involves complex and sometimes spectacular ceremonies. The laying of the foundation stone of the Assembly Rooms in York, an important center of Freemasonry, on March 1, 1731, is a good example. *The Monthly Intelligencer* tells how the stone-laying ceremony was accompanied by continuous firing by the troops and the ringing of twelve bells of York Minster. In 1853, when the foundation stone of the town hall was laid in Leeds, the procession included the town officials and councilors, priests, members of the local militia, several brass bands, and the members of trade organizations, the various Friendly Societies, the Philosophical and Literary Society, the Mechanics' Institutes, and the Guardians of the Poor. The whole community, in all its aspects, was represented.

Foundation-stone laying is a time for general celebration, for then we are witnessing the birth of a new addition to the community. The stone is often laid by a notable person. The special nature of the day is emphasized by processions, music, gunfire, fireworks, flags, religious or trade union banners, flags, decorated buildings, and vehicles. The participants wear their best clothes, badges and sashes of office, official

Figure 5.3. A Masonic dedication stone, dated 1923, at Peterborough Cathedral, Cambridgeshire, England. (Nigel Pennick)

dress uniforms and regalia, or traditional ritual disguise. The procession usually begins at a nearby official building, such as a town hall or church, and its journey symbolizes a "peregrination to the center of the world," where the stone is to be laid.

CHURCH FOUNDATION-STONE RITES

Current Church of England rites for the laying of a foundation stone are conducted with hymns, prayers, and psalms that emphasize sureness and stability, such as "Christ is made the sure foundation" and the quotation from the book of Ezra about the founding of the Jewish temple at Jerusalem. After arriving on site, the bishop gives the following homily:

> Dearly beloved in the Lord, we are gathered together here to lay the Foundation Stone of a building which we humbly trust may in due time be consecrated as a House of God. And first, let us praise God's holy name for the mercy and goodness with which

he has so far prospered our work; and let us further devoutly pray that he will, of his good providence, bless all who help forward its completion; that he will protect from danger those who may be engaged in the building; and that he will bestow his blessing upon our undertaking.

After Psalm 84, a lesson, responses, and prayers that set the spiritual tone for the foundation-laying, the bishop lays his hand upon the foundation stone with the words, "Bless the laying of this stone in thy Name, and be thou, we beseech thee, the beginning, the increase, and the consummation of the work, which is undertaken to thy glory." When the stone is laid "by the person appointed thereto," he says: "In the faith of Jesus Christ we place this stone. In the name of the Father, and of the Son, and of the Holy Ghost, Amen." The bishop then declares the place to be "hallowed and consecrated for the building thereon of a house, wherein prayers and praises shall be offered." Thus, the *Pax Deorum* is established at the place. Further appropriate prayers and hymns are said and sung. One calls upon God to protect the builders of the church "and keep them from all accident and harm, that the work . . . may be brought to a happy end." Finally, the bishop ends the ceremony with a blessing of the people there.

English Freemasons have their own form of ceremony for laying foundation stones. It was used to lay the foundation stone at Freemasons' Hall in London in 1927 and must therefore be considered definitive. The ceremony is concerned more with the ritual mechanics of laying the stone than the Church of England rite, which is a more comprehensive sacred and symbolic act. In the Freemasons' rite, after assembling at the appropriate time, a Masonic official is requested to lay the foundation stone, and the stone is raised above the footstone. Next, a bottle containing documents and newly minted coins is put in the cavity in the footstone. Then, the inscription on the foundation stone is read out to the assembly. This having been done, the Masonic official is given a ceremonial trowel, with which he spreads cement on the "footstone." Next, the foundation stone is lowered in three movements.

Figure 5.4. The foundation stone of
Freemasons' Hall, London. (Nigel Pennick)

Once in place, the foundation stone is ritually hammered into place by the official with a ceremonial hammer called a *maul*. He strikes the stone at each corner, saying "Temperance," "Fortitude," "Prudence," and "Justice." The official is handed the ceremonial plumb line and tests the stone, showing it to be vertical. Next, the official receives the ceremonial "level" and uses it to prove the stone is on the level. Then a ceremonial set square is handed to the official, who tests the stone's squareness. After this, the *maul* is handed back, and the official hits the stone with it three times—first on the south, then on the west, and finally on the east side—stating that the stone is "well and truly laid." Then the stone is consecrated with libations of corn, wine, oil, and salt. Finally, the ritual ends with a prayer and benediction.

Figure 5.5a.
The Four Virtues—Temperance.
(Nigel Pennick)

Figure 5.5b.
The Four Virtues—Fortitude.
(Nigel Pennick)

Figure 5.5c.
The Four Virtues—Prudence.
(Nigel Pennick)

Figure 5.5d.
The Four Virtues—Justice.
(Nigel Pennick)

FOUNDATION-LAYING ON SPECIAL DAYS

We have documentary evidence that church foundations were laid on special saints' days. Whether the day and time were elected astrologically is not recorded. For example, the manuscript *Lives of the Abbots* tells of the laying of the foundation stone of the new abbey at Gloucester, now Gloucester Cathedral: "In AD 1089, on the day of the festival of the Apostles Peter and Paul, in this year were laid the foundations of the church of Gloucester, the venerable man Robert, Bishop of Hereford, laying the first stone, Serlo the Abbot being in charge of the work." According to William de Wanda's record, in 1220 the foundation stones of Salisbury Cathedral were laid by Bishop Richard Poore on St. Vitalis the Martyr's Day, April 28:

> On the day appointed for the purpose the bishop came with great devotion, few earls or barons of the county, but a great multitude of the common people coming in from all parts: and when divine service had been performed, and the Holy Spirit invoked, the said bishop, putting off his shoes, went in procession with the clergy of the church to the place of foundation singing the litany; then the litany being ended and a sermon made to the people, the bishop laid the first stone for our Lord the Pope Honorius, and the second for the Lord Stephen Langton, Archbishop of Canterbury, then he added to the new fabric a third stone for himself; William Longspee, Earl of Sarum, who was then present, laid the fourth stone, and Elaide Vitri, Countess of Sarum, the wife of the said earl, a woman truly pious and worthy laid the fifth.

Sometimes there are two foundation stones. In 1277, two were laid at Vale Royal Abbey in Cheshire. Six centuries later, two foundation stones were laid at the Anglican cathedral at Truro in 1880. One was at the west end and was ecclesiastical, and the other, laid by Freemasons, was at the northeast corner. Of course, the first stone laid marks the true beginning of the building, and the time it is laid contains the astrological aspects that will rule the building throughout its existence.

Figure 5.6. Medieval geometric pavement
Canterbury Cathedral England.

Traditionally, in church, abbey, and cathedral foundation rites, the bishop lays his hand on the foundation stone and calls on Jesus Christ to bless the stone in his name. In Church of England tradition, the cornerstone is laid with the following incantation: "In the faith of Jesus Christ we place this stone. In the name of the Father, and of the Son, and of the Holy Ghost. Amen." The Norwich *Registrum Primum* tells us that the foundation stone of Norwich Cathedral, laid by Bishop Herbert de Losinga in 1096, had the inscription (translated from Latin): "In the Name of the Father, and of the Son, and of the Holy Ghost, Amen, I, Herbert the Bishop, have placed this stone." Until it was destroyed in rebuilding, this foundation stone was set in the easternmost wall of the Lady Chapel.

CEREMONIAL AT BRITISH PUBLIC WORKS

The ceremony of founding the new London Bridge in 1825 is a good example of the full symbolic ritual form that an important foundation needs. On Wednesday, June 15, 1825, at about 5 p.m., the foundation stone of John (later Sir John) Rennie's new London Bridge was laid. The date had been announced by the Committee for Rebuilding the new London Bridge in May of that year. Old London Bridge was decked with flags, and many vessels, also dressed all over with flags and bunting, crowded the river. Pleasure boats, most of them with bands, brought sightseers from all along the riverside. The place for the stone-laying was the bed of the river Thames, access to which was gained by a coffer dam from which the water had been pumped.

The Duke of York and John Garratt, the Lord Mayor of the City of London, headed the entourage that came to celebrate the laying of the stone. They arrived in procession from the London Guildhall along a route that was festooned from end to end with flags and bunting and thronged by crowds. The procession was no less colorful, utilizing the whole civic regalia of the city. It included a military band, the City Watermen with their colors, the architect, judges, the music and colors of the Lord Mayor's company, the Goldsmiths, the Marshall, Bailiffs, Barge Masters, and the State Carriage accompanied by its guard of honor.

Once the officials had arrived at the coffer dam and taken their places,

> The Lord Mayor then moved towards the eastern end of the Platform, in the centre of the Coffer Dam floor, where there was a small stage covered with crimson cloth, attended by four members of the Bridge Committee, bearing the bottle for the coins, an inscription encrusted in glass, the level, and the splendid silver-gilt Trowel for laying the First Stone.

The City Chamberlain brought a purse with a set of new coins of the realm, which were put in the cut-glass bottle. This was placed in a cavity in the footstone. The City Clerk also placed a brass plaque enclosed in glass in the cavity. It was inscribed with a Latin homily composed by the Master of Oriel College, Oxford, and included the following statement:

> Nor does any other time seem more appropriate for such an undertaking than when, in a time of universal peace, the British Empire flourishing in glory, wealth, population, and domestic union, is governed by a Prince, the patron and supporter of the arts, under whose auspices the metropolis has been advancing daily in elegance and splendour.

Once the items were deposited, the ceremonial trowel was taken from its white-silk-lined leather container and passed to the Lord Mayor. It was engraved on one face with an image of Father Thames with the arms of London beneath him. On the other side was a dedicatory inscription telling of the foundation and the Lord Mayor's credentials. The Lord Mayor then said a prayer expressing the hope that in executing this great work no calamity would occur. The prayer would prove ineffective, however, for forty workers died before the new bridge was finished in 1831. It appears that the ritual was for the stability of the structure of the bridge. The welfare of workers was of little concern in those days. After the prayer, the four-ton foundation stone of Aberdeen Granite was lowered on ropes. When settled, the Lord Mayor tapped it with his ceremonial trowel and tested its horizontality with the ceremonial level. Once the stone was "well and truly laid," the Artillery Company saluted the event with a cannonade. Finally, the bands of the Artillery Company and Horse Guards played the National Anthem to bring the event to a close.

Although Masonic ceremonies are held in private today, in nineteenth-century Scotland, Freemasons played the major role in every civic foundation ceremony. Although the actual rites were conducted with full Masonic form by Freemasons, the events themselves were public ceremonies with the participation of everybody. The foundation ceremony for the new harbor at Greenock, Scotland, took place on

August 7, 1862. The members of Masonic Lodge Greenock Kilwinning No. 12, Lodge Greenock St John No. 175, and Lodge Port Glasgow No. 68 took part. According to *The Freemasons' Magazine and Masonic Mirror*, the procession was

> the largest and most imposing which has ever passed along our streets. . . . Flags were displayed from the Mid Church steeple, Customhouse, and other public buildings; all the ships in harbour were lavishly decorated with colors. H. M. S. Hogue, H. M. S. Harpy, and H. M. Cutter Harriet, were hung with bunting from bowsprit to taffrail. Ensigns were hoisted before a large number of private residences, and festoons of flags were hung across the streets. . . . A great flag was displayed in front of the theatre. Some of the house fronts were tastefully decorated with flowers, and the Gourock omnibuses displayed Masonic and other colors.

The procession to Greenock Harbour was large and took an hour to assemble before setting off at 2 p.m. It was about a mile long, and members of every imaginable trade and craft, officials of all kinds, Masonic and otherwise, marched to the place of laying the foundation stone. Every trade and order were in full regalia:

> The Foresters were headed by Robin Hood, habited in Lincoln Green, and the Oddfellows, were, as usual, distinguished by their numerous and beautiful silver emblems. The Freemasons, who turned out in large numbers, the St John Lodge particularly, made a splendid appearance, especially the Provincial Grand Lodge, whose members were decked out in the gorgeous paraphernalia kindly lent by the Grand Lodge of Scotland for the occasion.

On reaching the works, the Harbour Trustees, Members of Parliament, Harbour officials, Harbour Commissioners, Chamber of Commerce, Local Marine Board, the Sheriffs, and the Collectors of Stamps and Inland Revenue entered the enclosure, opened up right and left and halted; and the trades bodies were ranged along Clyde Street, the Ropework Quay, and Albert Quay. The Freemasons entered the enclosure and marched through the part of the procession that entered the works to the place appointed for laying the stone, headed by the Provincial Grand Lodge.

Then, at the place of foundation, the Provincial Grand Chaplain offered a prayer for divine blessing "on the great work that day formally inaugurated." The Provincial Grand Treasurer deposited a bottle in which were the various coins of the realm in gold, silver, and copper, local newspapers of the day, wine, oil, and corn. Then, the Provincial Grand Secretary read out the inscription on the brass plate to be deposited in the footstone. It told of the date, "the Seventh day of August, *Anno Domini* 1862, *Anno Lucis* 5862, and the twenty-sixth year of the Reign of Her Majesty Queen Victoria," and how

> This place was deposited in the Foundation Stone of the Harbour named The Albert Harbour . . . which Stone was laid with full Masonic Honours, by James Johnston Grieve, Esquire, Provost of the Burgh, and Acting Deputy Provincial Grand Master of the Ancient Fraternity of Freemasons in West Renfrewshire assisted by the brethren of the Provincial Grand Lodge.

The foundation deposits and commemorative plate were cemented in place by the Provincial Grand Master, who used an elegant ceremonial silver trowel made specially for the event. Then, the foundation stone was lowered onto the footstone, during which the band played the hymn tune called "The Old Hundred." Once the stone was lowered, the Grand Junior Warden ritually tested it with a plumb line, and the Grand Senior Warden did the same with a level. The Substitute Provincial Grand Master tested it with the square, and then the Grand Master, "declaring his confidence of their skill in the Royal Art, finished the work with three mystical knocks with a golden mallet. Three hearty cheers were then given by the thousands within sight of the ceremony."

Finally, the band played "The Old Hundred" once more, during which cornucopiae and silver vases were brought to the Grand Master. He took flowers and corn from the horns of plenty, and strewed them

Figure 5.7. Laying the foundation-stone of the Municipal Buildings in Glasgow, Scotland, October 1883. (Nideck)

across the newly lowered stone. Then over them he poured wine and oil from the vases. Three more cheers followed, and the band finished with "The Masons' Anthem." An engraving in *The Illustrated London News* for October 13, 1883, reproduced here, shows the laying of the foundation-stone of the Municipal Buildings in Glasgow as an enormous public gathering of witness to the ceremony. Clearly here the ritual was carried out by specialists. As a collective event, the festive ceremonial foundation of public works or buildings binds together the participants as members of society as a whole, supported by the traditions of generations gone by, and building for those yet to come.

CHAPTER 6

At the Center of the World

The Earth's Navel, the Cosmic Column, and the World Tree

The island of the lone goddess Calypso is Ogygia, "where is the navel of the sea," far removed on a "wondrous space of brine whereby is no city of mortals."

WILLIAM RICHARD LETHABY (1857–1931),
ARCHITECTURE, MYSTICISM AND MYTH (1891)

Figure 6.1. W. R. Lethaby's book *Architecture, Mysticism and Myth* (1892) contains his analysis of various symbolic themes that underlie traditional architecture. This is his drawing of an ancient Greek omphalos.

THE COSMIC AXIS
AND THE LOOM OF CREATION

The concept of the *axis mundi* or cosmic axis underlies European traditions of foundation and the symbolic layout of buildings, towns, and gardens. This axis is the result of our experience as beings walking on the earth. As we perceive it, the earth appears to be a more-or-less flat surface bounded by a circular horizon. Below us is the earth, and below the surface the dark, hidden underworld. Above us is the open, bright sky of day, and the starry heavens of night. Although we know that the Earth is spherical, rotating, and in orbit around the sun, we do not perceive movement. To us, the Earth is still, and the heavens appear to rotate above us.

To us in Europe, the sky appears to turn above us, circling around the immobile North Pole star. Our ancestors associated this axis point with the craft of spinning thread, which is accomplished by winding thread around a turning spindle. Because material accumulates as time passes, spinning thread on a spindle and the allied craft of weaving on a loom are allegories of time and destiny. To spin thread is to create. The disordered, unusable fibers of wool or flax are transformed by human skill into an ordered and usable thread. Order is brought out of chaos by realigning its materials. This requires time, energy, and consciousness. Two tools are needed in spinning—the spindle and the distaff. The spindle is rotated to spin the thread and the spun material is wound upon the distaff. European tradition views the rotating spindle as the primary symbolic model of the cosmos. The spindle operates by a rhythmic, reciprocating, cyclic motion, and from it comes an unbroken flow of thread.

The heavenly spindle, around which the fixed stars appear to rotate, is marked by the Pole Star. This is the "leading star" of navigators at sea and on land, the star toward which traditional gardeners in East Anglia orient their rows of seeds at planting time. Each year at midwinter we honor the North Star by putting an artificial star on top of the Christmas tree. The spindle is one part of the technology of weaving. Its rotating motion creates the thread that is woven together on the loom

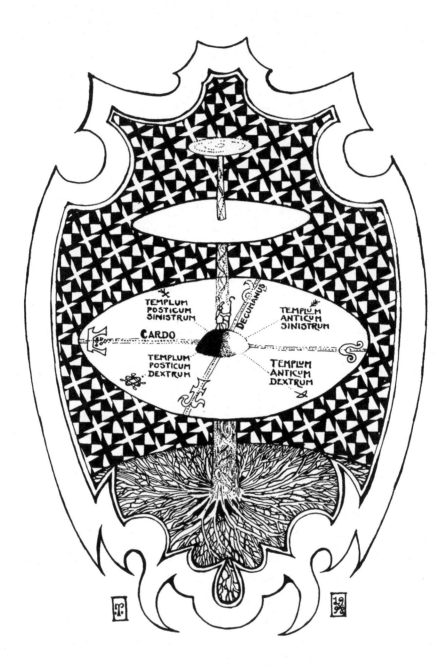

Figure 6.2. The Cosmic Axis, showing the divisions of
the Etruscan Discipline on the level of Middle Earth.
(Nigel Pennick)

to make fabric. The apparent motion of the sun through each day and year is seen as the loom of creation. In the symbolism of weaving, the sun creates the fabric of time on the loom of the Earth. Symbolically, the warp, the threads that run in a north to south direction, are laid down by the static Earth, and moving sun completes the fabric by weaving the east–west threads. The cosmic axis itself is a conceptual pillar or tube that has its origin beneath the world on which we walk, rather like a tree has its roots in the dark earth. It passes from the underworld through the surface of the earth and ascends straight toward the heavens. This splendid pillar is viewed as the stable axis that stands at the center of the world, linking above with below.

THE COSMOS OF THE ETRUSCAN DISCIPLINE

The Etruscan system of the cosmos was a complex hierarchy of central point, directions, and vertical planes. Because it was taken up by the Romans, and used in their geomantic layout of temples, towns and countries, it was of importance in later European practice. In his book, *The Marriage of Mercury and Philology,* the late fifth-century-CE Roman writer Martianus Capella described the cosmic image that underlay the Etruscan Discipline. The author describes how the gods and goddesses are invoked from their dwellings in the sixteen sectors of the cosmos to witness the betrothal. Jupiter comes from the first, along with Janus, god of beginnings. From the second comes Juno and Mars. The third sector brings other aspects of Jupiter, while the fourth brings Sylvanus, the woodland deity. From the fifth issues Vulcan, the smith of the gods. Lesser deities come forth from the other houses. The eighth house brings forth the daughter of the Sun, while the fifteenth is that of Vejovis, who is equated with Pluto, god of the underworld.

The sixteen sectors of the cosmos are further subdivided by Martianus Capella into four planes. They are viewed according to the geocentric model of the universe. The uppermost plane stretches from the aether to the sphere of the sun. It is the plane of the gods, ruled by Jupiter. Below this, between the spheres of the sun and the moon, is the region ruled by the *Dei Manes,* the underworldly spirits or daemons.

Figure 6.3. Roman altar to Jupiter,
Juno, and the Genius Loci Bad Cannstatt, Germany.
(Nigel Pennick)

The next plane occupies the region from the moon to the Earth. It is the realm of air, divided into two regions, an upper and a lower. The upper region is the aether, occupied by the *Semones* or demigods, and the lower region is the aer, inhabited by the apotheosized heroes. The lower region of aer also contains both malevolent and beneficent sprites under the rulership of Vejovis (Pluto).

Cosmic temples in Roman times acknowledged this division in the air between the aether and the aer. Temples of Vesta were circular, symbolizing the Earth, having an aperture in the roof directly above the holy flame that was the goddess. Thus, inside the temple was aer and above it, connected by the hole in the roof, was the aether. Similarly,

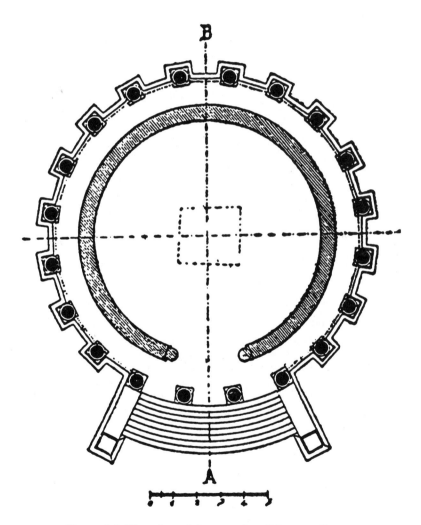

Figure 6.4. The plan of the temple of Vesta at Rome.
(Nideck)

the Pantheon at Rome, built by the Emperor Hadrian to house all of the gods and goddesses, is circular, with a round aperture at the apex of the concrete dome. The lowest of the four cosmic planes is the plane of Earth. This is ruled by long-lived spirits that include Satyrs, Fauns, Naiads, Meliae, Dryads, and so forth.

THE BARDIC COSMOS

Welsh traditions recorded in the Middle Ages envisaged the cosmos as having several "circles." These may be visualized as being stacked on top of one another along a vertical axis. This axis forms a spiritual link that connects the underworld below us, through the middle earth on which we live, with the heavenly upper world above us. According to this traditional British cosmology, at birth, death, and during other special conditions of life, spirits are enabled to travel between these worlds. In Christian terms, the axis links Hell beneath us with the Earth that is here and Heaven above, though the Christian concept of the underworld as a place of eternal punishment is quite different from Pagan and bardic ideas. Bardic teachings call the underworld *Annwn*, the middle world *Abred*, and the upper world *Gwynvyd*.

The nature of these circles or levels is described in various old Welsh texts. One, titled *Y Tri Chyflwr* (The Three States), explains: "According to the three principal qualities of man shall be his migration in Abred; from laziness and mental blindness he shall fall to Annwn; from dissolute wantonness he shall traverse the circle of Abred, according to his necessity; and from his love for goodness he will ascend to the circle of Gwynvyd." The three bardic circles symbolize spiritual progress in an upward direction, as another Welsh text tells us: "The three states of living beings: Annwn, from which comes the beginning; Abred, in which knowledge increases, and hence goodness; and Gwynvyd, in which is the plenitude of goodness, knowledge, truth, and endless life." In Brittany, traditional folk symbolism envisages the cross of Christ as a ladder linking Earth with Heaven, down which God came to Earth. Human souls can climb to Heaven by way of this cross-ladder, which is a version of the cosmic axis.

Although the bardic underworld is portrayed as a place of departed souls and unformed spirits, it is not Hell, the devilish torture-chamber of Judeo-Christian eschatology. It is closer to the Greek Pagan concept of Hades, that gloomy realm inhabited by sad, insubstantial shades. Thus, the Bards give the underworld the kennings *affwys,* the abyss; *affan,* the land invisible; and *annwfn* or *annwn,* the not-world. A Bardic question-and-answer fragment, recorded in Iolo Morganwg's *Barddas,* asks us: "Question. In what place is Annwn? Answer. Where there is the least possible of animation and life, and the greatest of death, without other condition."

In the landscape, the physical appearance of Annwn is the burial mound. Celtic folk tradition tells how sensitive people can commune with the spirits of the dead at these mounds, for they are, literally, the abodes of the dead. In his book *Gweledigaetheu y Bardd Cwsg* (1703), Ellis Wynne describes three visions of this world, death and Hell, in which the sleeping bard sees a vision of the dead, called the Children of Annwn, dancing upon the churchyard mound. It was from mounds such as this that Etruscan augurs took their omens.

From its roots in the underworld, the cosmic axis rises toward this world of living mortals, Abred. From this world, it leads onward and upward to the heavenly upper world, the Bardic Circle of Gwynvyd, the "white land." This is the bright realm of spiritual beings. On physical structures such as perrons, maypoles, and crosses it is depicted by a solar emblem, a golden orb, a gilded cockerel, or a wheel cross. They all represent the sun above the earth, symbolizing the sky god who rules the upper world. Celtic crosses in the British Isles and Marian columns in Bavaria and Austria are Christian versions of this eternal axis. In addition to having a physical reality denoting below, here, and above, the cosmic axis has a psychological meaning. The underworld roots of the axis symbolize the human unconscious, the shaft represents the ascending consciousness, and the golden top, transcendence.

In the Renaissance, as the Spindle of Necessity, the cosmic axis was recognized as a symbol of stability in the midst of change. The spindle appeared overtly in an Italian *intermezzo* (the forerunner of opera). It was performed at a festival in Florence in 1589 and titled

Figure 6.5. All our lives are under the aegis of the Three Moirai or fates, depicted here at Castell Coch, Cardiff, Wales. According to the Greek Pagan tradition, Clotho spins the thread of life, Lachesis weaves it, and Atropos cuts it. (Nigel Pennick)

The Harmony of the Spheres. The *intermezzo* was written by Giovanni de' Bardi and Ottario Rinuccini with music by Cavalieri and others. Designed by Bernardo Buontalenti (ca. 1536–1608), the staging featured an actress representing Necessity holding her spindle, enthroned with the Three Fates. Flanking them were actresses and actors representing Urania and her seven planets. Another scene of the *intermezzo* featured the Golden Mean and her Harmonies. Thus, the Spindle of Necessity was depicted at the center of all things—space, time, and the cosmos.

Figure 6.6. The Spindle of Necessity.
(Nigel Pennick)

THE NAVEL OF THE WORLD

It seems that the idea of a world center, by the Greek word for "navel," omphalos (ὀμφαλός), was recognized long ago by the ancient Egyptians. In Egypt, the world center was represented by elliptical stone that marked the middle-point of the country. It was defined as the place where the primary north–south meridian and the east–west parallel crossed each other. The center of the Egyptian Old Kingdom was Sakkara, where the navel of the world was the holy stone of Sokar, god of orientation. Ancient papyrus drawings depict it flanked by images of two birds of prey. They

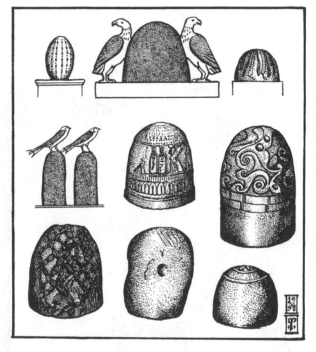

Figure 6.7. Egyptian and European omphaloi.
Top row (left to right): Contemporary representations of Greek omphaloi.
Middle row: Left and center, Egyptian omphaloi;
right, the Turoe Stone, an Irish Celtic omphalos.
Lower row: Left, the omphalos at Delphi, Greece, covered with the agrenon
(wool netting). Center, Egg-stone, Glastonbury, Somerset, England.
Right: Etruscan omphalos, Fiesole, Italy.
(Nigel Pennick)

seem to refer to a legend recorded later in Greece. During the twelfth dynasty, Egypt's center was moved. The Sakkara omphalos was replaced by a stone in the Temple of Amun at Thebes.

Later, in Greece, the more famous omphalos at Delphi was set up. This was in the sacred place of a priestess known as the Pythia. She was the oracle of Apollo, the god who, according to Plato, "sits in the center of the navel of the earth." Legend tells how the world's navel was discovered by Zeus, who, as grand geometer of the cosmos, measured the earth. From the Olympian heights, he sent forth two eagles. Zeus released one bird to the east, and the other to the west. Flying in straight lines, they met each other over Delphi, which was the navel of the world. Another legend tells how at Delphi Apollo slew with his

Figure 6.8. An ancient Greek representation of an omphalos stone on an altar, from a vessel (ca. 400 BCE) in Berlin. (Nigel Pennick)

arrow the serpent called Python so that the oracular goddess could take her place there without hindrance.

From Mycenean times, around 1400 BCE, if not earlier, the Delphic omphalos was represented in visible form by an unworked boulder regarded as an iconic emblem of the deity. Later, such an unsophisticated object appears to have been considered unworthy, so it was superseded by a finely carved stone omphalos. This too was an elliptical stone. An eagle of gold was attached to each side in the Egyptian manner. The new omphalos was carved with swags of what appear to be wool or cloth, recreating the patterns made upon the earlier stone when it was ceremonially bedecked. Several sculptured reliefs and vase paintings show the omphalos in the days when it was revered as the oracle's holy symbol, dressed with ribbons and branches. In addition to the dome-shaped omphalos stone, Delphi possessed the other image of the cosmic center, a stone pillar. Standing 50 feet (15 m) high, it was set up between 335 and 325 BCE. It consisted of a stepped base supporting a fluted column whose shaft was punctuated with rings of acanthus leaf carvings. It was crowned with three "Thyades," dancing women facing outward. These, in turn, supported a giant Delphic tripod, the image of the trifinium sacred to the threefold goddess Hecate.

The Pagan Celts, both in mainland Europe and the British Isles, set up omphaloi as their centers. There are a few Celtic omphalos stones still in existence. One important example was probably made by the Treviri tribe at Pfalzfeld in the Hunsrick, Germany. Carvings on this omphalos include a bearded human head with horns or a headdress, set within rope-work. In Ireland, there is a similar stone at Turoe in County Galway. Its form is closely akin to the famous Delphic omphalos, with spiral swathes resembling the Greek swags. Other Irish omphaloi include a cushion-shaped omphalos at Castlestrange in County Roscommon and a stone at Mullaghmast in Kildare that is the base of a broken-off Pagan pillar. Another base of a round Pagan pillar survives at Killycluggan in County Cavan. These omphalos pillars are the model from which the later makers of Celtic crosses took their inspiration.

In England, the London Stone, recently refurbished, traditionally marks the center and holds the "luck" of the city of London, while

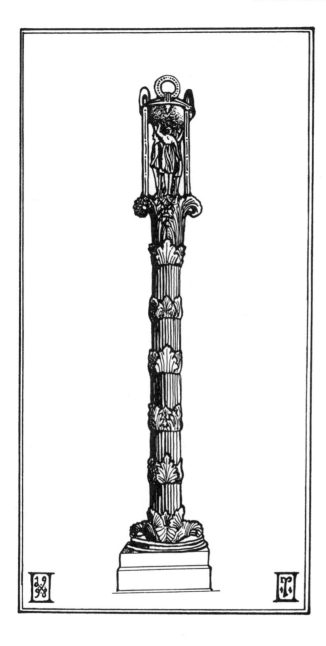

Figure 6.9. A reconstruction of the column that once stood at Delphi, Greece. (Nigel Pennick)

the same function is ascribed to the "Blue Stane" of St. Andrews in Scotland. In the Low Countries, the central points of town market-places, which in other places would be marked by a market cross, were marked by a "blue stone." Thus, the tradition of the omphalos lives on

Figure 6.10a. Cosmic Eggs on entrance to Mary Ward House,
Bloomsbury, London, England 1898. (Nigel Pennick)

Figure 6.10b. Mary Ward House cosmic egg detail.
(Nigel Pennick)

as an integral element of flourishing modern cities. The black stone in the Kaaba at Mecca, the literal as well as the spiritual center of Islam, retains the religious meaning of the omphalos to this day.

Closely related to the omphalos is the omphalion. In St. Peter's in Rome is a circular slab of antique porphyry, 8.5 feet (2.6 m) in diameter. This is the omphalion of St. Peter's. It is supposed that every Holy Roman Emperor stood upon it at his coronation or reception by the pope. The popes, too, perform ceremonies on this omphalion. Another existed in Hagia Sophia in Constantinople. It was directly beneath the center of the dome. This was called the *mesomphalos* or *mesonaos*. Other omphalia existed in the palaces of the Byzantine emperors. According to Jules Labarte, "The floor of Chalce was composed of beautiful marble mosaic; below the dome in the pavement was a large slab of porphyry, of circular form, to which they gave the name Omphalion." They were set in the floor in front of the thrones. During certain ceremonies, the emperor stood on one of these porphyry circles, and whenever he passed over one on his way through the palace, those present prostrated themselves. In front of the high altar of Westminster Abbey is the symbolic mosaic known as the Cosmati Pavement. It contains five large circles. Four outer ones, arranged in a square, are symbolic of the four elements. In the middle is a circular porphyry slab, on which the monarch stands at certain points of the English coronation ceremony. Here, as in the Roman and Byzantine traditions, the monarch is empowered when he or she is at the middle of the land.

According to this traditional viewpoint, the nature of sacred space is seen as a material manifestation of the transcendent realm of spirit centered on the cosmic axis. It is a limited, circumscribed area existing separately from, but still within, the realm of the profane outer world. Sacredness is achieved by humans who create an accurate earthly representation of the celestial archetype, effected by human transformation of the natural land into sacred space. The entirety of the cosmos is thereby represented in a reduced version at a specific place and time on Earth. The transformed natural landscape thus becomes an image of the cosmos. It is no longer just itself, but also an instance of timeless being.

Figure 6.11. Oostkerk Middelburg the Netherlands cosmic eggs. (Nigel Pennick)

Figure 6.12. Cosmic eggs on parapet of hall (1926) Heacham Norfolk, England. (Nigel Pennick)

THE COSMIC EGG

Strabo tells how the omphalos at Delphi was flanked by two eagles, the birds of Zeus, made of gold. Representations of this show the birds, presumably a male and female, appearing to guard half of a giant egg. There is a clear relationship here and elsewhere between the egg and the omphalos stone. Some representations of omphaloi show an egg-shaped stone, covered with garlands, fillets, and leafy branches—the remains of rites and ceremonies performed in honor of the holy place. At Glastonbury, an "egg-stone" was found during excavations of the Abbey early in the twentieth century. It is widely assumed to be the omphalos of that place. Occasionally, real eggs are found buried in European buildings as foundation deposits.

The egg is naturally a symbol of the creative potential of life. It is from the egg that most land animals emerge into the world, and the motif of the primordial egg from which existence emerged is a theme in creation legends. Like the navel, which is the point where each of us grew from in his or her mother's womb, the egg is the point of beginning of life. It is thus another symbol for the omphalos, the central point at which all things are founded.

In traditional architecture, an egg is sometimes suspended above the center point of a holy or royal building. Pausanias writes how at the temple of Hilaria and Phoebe in Laconia, the priestesses, called Leucippides, tended the images of the goddesses:

> One of their images was restored by a priestess of the goddesses, who, with an art not unknown in our days, put a new face on the old statue; but a dream prevented her from treating the other statue in the same way. Here is hung up an egg, fastened to the roof by fillets; they say it is the egg which Leda is said to have laid.

This ancient Greek suspended egg was continued through the centuries by later religions. In his *Coptic Churches of Egypt* (1884), Alfred Joshua Butler wrote:

Figure 6.13. The concept of the navel of the earth is combined with the grail legend in the Matter of Britain through the stories of King Arthur and the Knights of the Round Table. (Nigel Pennick)

Figure 6.14. It is considered lucky for every student at the University of Tübingen, Germany, to touch this omphalos stone before examinations or other important events. (Nigel Pennick)

The ostrich egg is a curious but common ornament in the religious buildings of the Copts, the Greeks, and the Muslims alike. It may be seen in the ancient church of the Greek convent in Kasr-ash Shammah, and in most of the mosques in Cairo, mounted in a metal frame, and hung by a single wire from the roof. In the churches, it usually hangs before the altar screen. . . . Sometimes, instead of the egg of the ostrich, artificial eggs of beautiful Damascus porcelain, coloured with designs of blue or purple, were employed. . . . These porcelain eggs are considerably smaller than an ostrich egg, but larger than a hen's egg. . . . The "Griffin's Egg" was a common ornament in our own medieval churches. In the inventory of 1383 no less than nine are mentioned as belonging to Durham Cathedral.

NORTHERN PHALLIC STONES

Before Christianity took over western Norway, many Pagan holy places had *hellige hvite stener* (sacred white stones). Because they were holy, the Christians did not destroy them, but buried them beneath churches or the ancient homesteads that were places of worship in Pagan times.

These *hellige hvite stener* are cylindrical pillars that terminate with a hemispherical finial. They are fashioned from white stone, variously marble, quartzite, or granite. Phallic in form, and measuring up to about 3 feet (90 cm) in height, they appear to have been the objects of worship of Yngvi-Frey, the chief god of the older, pre-agricultural Norse pantheon, the Vanir. At Clackmannan in Scotland there is a similar, but bigger, phallic megalith. It stands by the church, marking the former inauguration place of kings of the Picts.

Figure 6.15. A phallic megalith and accompanying Perron at the inauguration place of the Pictish kings, Clackmannan, Scotland. (Nigel Pennick)

Figure 6.16. Three pillars—standing stones at Trelleck, Wales.
(Nigel Pennick)

Figure 6.17. Stone
at Trelleck with
carving of three
standing stones.
(Nigel Pennick)

COLUMNS OF THE GREATEST AND BEST GOD

Although the form originated at Rome, Jupiter columns were erected in large numbers in the Celtic parts of the Roman Empire. Their remains have been found in Britain, Brittany, and most of France. But the largest number comes from Alsace and Lorraine in France and the German Rhineland. Over three hundred are known.

The idea of the Jupiter column came about as the result of a spiritual disaster at Rome in 65 BCE. In that year, lightning struck and destroyed the great image of Jupiter at the Capitol. In addition, the

Figure 6.18. A Celto-Roman Jupiter column at the Pagan shrine at Stein in Baden-Württemberg, Germany. (Nigel Pennick)

lightning blasted the stone tablets of the Law and an image of one of the twins beneath the Roman wolf. This heavenly blow against the most sacred images of Rome was interpreted as a disastrous omen both for Roman society and the future of the city. An official enquiry was set up at once to determine the meaning of the disaster, and to find means to rectify the bad omen. Etruscan Haruspices performed a ceremonial divination, and, as a result, the Roman augurs decided to erect a column dedicated to Jupiter at the place at which the destroyed image had formerly stood. At a ceremony in 63 BCE, a column with Jupiter's image, watching over his people, was set up. This was such a powerful protective image that it was copied all over the western part of the Roman Empire.

Jupiter, father of the gods and the people, was the seen as great architect of the universe, the sustainer of all existence. As the link between the earthly center and the father god on high, Jupiter columns symbolize this. The base of the typical Jupiter column is a square stone pedestal, the "four-god stone." This usually consists of four godly images, two female and two male. Often, the goddess Juno is on the front side; Minerva on the right; Hercules at the back; and Mercury on the left. Although this is common, there are variants. Occasionally, Apollo is in place of Mercury, or there may be an inscription on the front with or without other images.

Directly above the square pedestal there is a seven- or eight-sided section, the "seven-god stone." Above this section is the drum of the column. The seven-god stone carries divine images, generally the goddesses and gods of the days of the week. The eighth place often bears an image of Victoria, the goddess of victory. The goddesses and gods of the seven-god stone often vary. For example, a Jupiter column found at Plieningen, in the Stuttgart region of Germany, has only the week deity images of Saturn, Sol, Luna, Mars, Mercury, Jupiter, and Venus. But another, found at Schwaigern-Stetten, in the region of Heilbronn, not far away, bears images of Sol, Luna, Vesta, Neptune, Mercury, and the Gallo-Roman goddess Maia Rosmerta. The shaft itself is a tapering cylinder, often carved with patterns that sometimes resemble scales, tree bark, vine scrolls, or stylized oak leaves and acorns in a regular tesselation. The oak is the holy tree of European sky gods, of whom Jupiter is the Roman version. A few Jupiter columns have images of goddesses and gods carved on the shaft itself.

According to the canons of classical architecture, the column shaft supports a capital bearing the image of Jupiter himself. Usually, the capital is carved with conventional foliage, but some also have four heads that look out toward the four quarters. They symbolize the four seasons. Jupiter, on top of the column, is shown on horseback or in a chariot, riding down the daemon of disorder and destruction, Typhon, who is depicted as a humanoid figure with serpents instead of legs. His last moment of pain is presented as the terrified victim falls beneath the horses' hooves. Jupiter, triumphant, holds a thunderbolt in his right hand. When he is not shown overcoming Typhon, Jupiter is enthroned.

Jupiter columns are the symbolic summation of time and space, represented by the goddesses and gods of the Roman pantheon. This concept is transcendent, for in later years, when Christianity had taken over as the state religion, this scheme of portraying the gods and goddesses on a column was continued in Celtic Christianity. Celtic crosses bearing images of the figures of the threefold godhead, prophets, patriarchs, and saints are a direct continuation of the symbolism of Jupiter columns.

In the eighth century CE, the Saxons of mainland Europe revered a holy pillar or a maypole that stood at a holy place called the Eresburg. It is not known how far back in history this pillar went. Today, its site is covered by the medieval parish church of the town of Ober-Marsberg in Westphalia. The medieval Translatio S. Alexandri tells how it was a "large wooden column set up in the open. In their language it is called 'Irminsul,' which in Latin is a 'universal column.'" According to the tenth-century chronicler Widukind of Corvey, pillars like Irminsul were dedicated to the god Mars. They were set up at places sacred to the Sun. Like the Jupiter columns set up in the Roman Empire, the Irminsul symbolized eternal stability. It was a representation of the everlasting "tree of measure" (mjötvið) mentioned in Norse spiritual writings, an earthly emblem of the power of the sky god. Because it was the prime religious emblem of the Saxons, it was destroyed in the year 772 at the

Figure 6.19. Iconic image of Irminsul. (Nigel Pennick)

order of the Emperor Charlemagne, to symbolize his subjection of the Saxons to the Holy Roman Empire.

In later years, after Charlemagne, the Saxons again set up columns. But now, they were Christianized and dedicated to the Christian hero, Roland—a carving of whose head sometimes adorned the top. Some

Figure 6.20. A German "Roland" column. (Nideck)

were connected with the craft of the blacksmith, standing in the vicinity of smithies. The nineteenth-century Austrian antiquary Anton Ritter von Perger associated them with the old Germanic smith god Wieland (Wayland the Smith of English tradition). In Christian times, the most prominent pillars were crosses, some of which were elaborated into small buildings. Other pillars without crosses, topped with a sphere or a "fir cone," were set up. In England, they were often called Market Crosses, with their Scots equivalent, the Mercat Cross in Scotland.

In France and what is now Belgium, they are known as Perrons. Perrons and Market Crosses were physical markers of time and space literally at the center of community life. They were places where the rules of commerce, including weights and measures, were stated. Often,

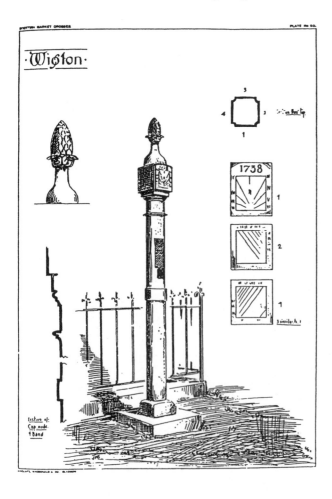

Figure 6.21. The cone-surmounted Perron-sundial of 1738 at Wigton, Scotland. An illustration by W. Small from his Scottish Market Crosses. (Nideck)

they measured time, either by the shadows they cast, or because they carried sundials. Here, oaths and transactions were witnessed, official proclamations were read, justice and punishment dispensed. When a Perron was set up, it brought with it all of the elements of civilization. At the moment of its foundation, the Perron brought the physical presence of right time and measure, law and order to the place. It was the outer symbol of the inner principle of stability and order that the cosmic pillar represents.

Figure 6.22. The Perron, Liege, Belgium, symbol of the city's liberty, reconstructed in 1692 by the baroque sculptor Jean Delcour (1627–1707) with carvings of the Three Graces. (Nigel Pennick)

Figure 6.23. Twenty-first century Perron Paternoster Square London erected in a new square near St Paul's Cathedral which replaced a modernist office development of the 1950s built on a district destroyed by bombing in World War II. It was intended to harmonize with the nearby baroque Cathedral. (Nigel Pennick)

Figure 6.24. Perron in labyrinth Hilton Cambridgeshire, England.
(Nigel Pennick)

THE THREE PILLARS

Three sacred pillars standing together are an ancient icon of holiness. At Knossos on Crete, three freestanding pillars oriented on an east–west axis stood as a sacred symbol in the Minoan shrine. According to the biblical accounts, the cross of Christ stood between two other crosses, on which the thieves were crucified. Thus, symbolically, the cross of Christ is actually the middle pillar of three. The Flemish medieval Christian mystic Hadewijch saw visions of a crystal cross set on three columns, which she interpreted as an image of eternity and the threefold personage of the godhead. In 1398, three pillars of fire appeared on the German holy mountain called Horselberg (the Venusberg of Tannhäuser). They were interpreted as an epiphany of the goddess Horsel. In Celtic tradition the three pillars appear on Breton Calvaries, where all three crosses stand upon a "holy mountain" base that represents the mount of Golgotha. Today, the three pillars are part of the mysteries of the Jewish Qabalah and symbols in the craft of Freemasonry.

TREE PLANTING

Many towns and villages in Europe have central trees, planted deliberately as markers. The act of planting a tree is analogous to laying the foundation stone of a building, except that the tree then grows itself. Like foundation stones, the time of planting trees is important. All traditional European systems of day lore include auspicious and inauspicious days for planting. For example, in his *Works and Days* (ca. 850 BCE), Hesiod tells us that the thirteenth day of the waxing month is best for planting out.

The horoscope of a tree may be seen as influencing the fortune of the place in which it grows. Certain trees have been viewed as the epitomes of the "luck" of a town or village. The now-destroyed Merlin's Oak at Carmarthen in Pembrokeshire, west Wales, was one such tree. Its associated prophecy, "When Merlin's Tree shall tumble down, then shall fall Carmarthen town," told of its spiritual sustenance of the town.

Central town and village trees are microcosmic images of the cosmic axis, supporting the stability of the heavens, and hence the physical and social order of the town itself.

The custom of planting a tree to commemorate a famous event is ancient. The linden tree called the *Murtenlinde* in Fribourg,

Figure 6.25. The Fribourg Murtenlinde (1476–1983),
as it was shortly before its destruction by a motor vehicle.
(Nigel Pennick)

Figure 6.26. Murtenlinde and Perron Fribourg Switzerland, 1983.
(Nigel Pennick)

Switzerland, was planted in 1476 as a commemoration of the foundation of a new order, the overthrow of Burgundian hegemony at the
Battle of Murten. This linden tree was a living commemoration of the
foundation of a new, stable society, ordered according to eternal laws. It
lasted until 1985, when it finally died, having been lethally damaged by
a motorist on April 13, 1983. Then, in 1985, the *Murtenlinde* was cut
down. A new tree, genetically identical with the *Murtenlinde,* grown
from a cutting, was planted nearby, but not in the middle of the street,
where the original one stood. The spirit of the old tree, and hence the
city, continues.

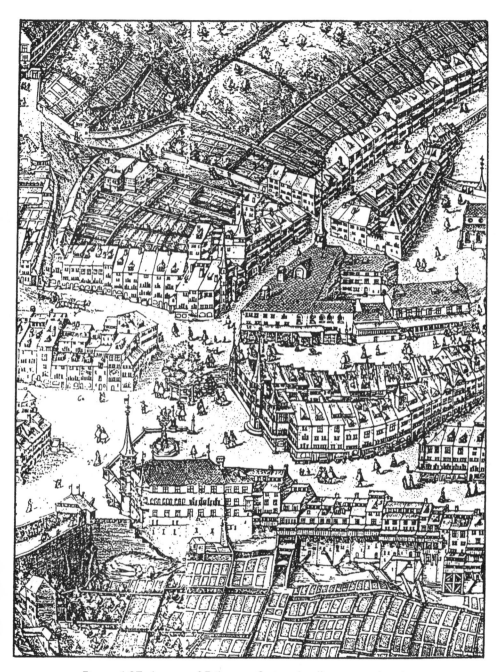

Figure 6.27. A map of Fribourg, Switzerland's center, showing
the central linden tree called the Murtenlinde (planted 1476) and,
nearby, St. George's fountain. An engraving by Martin Martini 1606.
(Nideck)

The planting of permanent trees as the central axis of a city is symbolized mythically by the legends of staves putting forth leaves at special places. It appears in the German legend of Heinrich von Ofterdingen, better known by his bardic name, Tannhäuser. He visited the goddess Venus in her palace on the Venusberg. Later, forced to do Christian penance in the shape of a pilgrimage to Rome, he asked Pope Urban IV (Jacques Pantaleon, reigned 1261–1264) for forgiveness. The pope told Tannhäuser that there was as much chance of God forgiving him as his staff bearing leaves again. At that, his staff suddenly put forth leaves as a sign that the bard was forgiven. At Glastonbury, the leaf story is told of the staff of Joseph of Arimathea and, at Stow in Lincolnshire, concerning that of St. Etheldreda. In both instances, legend tells us, a saint's cut stave grew roots when it was thrust into the earth at an important location, which then became a miraculous tree. At Glastonbury, the staff became the famed holy thorn tree, and at Stow, a mighty ash. Although the legend tells of staves thrust into the ground miraculously returning to life, they might well recall actual ceremonial plantings at precise auspicious moments. New leaves are a symbol of miraculous regeneration at a specific place and time, often as an answer to prayer. The custom of planting trees in commemoration of some notable event continues to this day.

Concerning planted trees, occasionally there are controversies over those planted ceremonially by notable people whom their opponents consider execrable. Such trees are endangered. In his text *The Madness of Extremes* (1990), the Austrian artist Friedensreich Hundertwasser comments upon this. He notes that when an "enemy" plants a tree, people want to uproot it in case anyone sees the tree's existence as evidence that the person who planted it did a good deed. Human shortsightedness prevents them from seeing that "future generations will relax in the shade of this tree." These future generations, Hundertwasser asserts, will have very different problems from those of today. They will not think it important "whether the tree was planted by a Christ or an antichrist, a Fascist, a Green, a madman, a murderer, or a Communist. They will simply be happy that it is there!"

CHAPTER 7

Space, Time, and Ceremony

The Eightfold Division of the World and the Eight Winds

The East symbolizes wisdom; the West, strength; the North, darkness; and the South, beauty.

ENGLISH MASONIC ADAGE

THE GNOMON

Although modern building practice uses different techniques, there are traditional methods that relate the dimensions and orientation of a building to the natural qualities of the place. Having found the proper location, the locator erects an upright gnomon at the omphalos. This gnomon must be of a length appropriate to the geographical latitude of the place. Then a number of concentric circles are drawn on the flattened earth, using knotted rope to maintain the correct distance. In the forenoon, a mark is made whenever the end of the sun's shadow cast by the gnomon touches a circle. Then, in the afternoon, the same is done. This is called taking the altitude of the sun's opposing limbs. By geometrically bisecting the opposing points, a true meridian or north–south line is drawn. By drawing a line between opposing marks on the circle, an east–west, or equinoctial, line, is produced at right angles to the meridional line. In the Etruscan Discipline, the meridional line is the *Cardo* and the equinoctial is the *Decumanus*. From these two lines, which intersect at the omphalos where the gnomon stands, geometric figures can be drawn that serve as the basis for any building, fair, or town intended to be erected there.

Ancient philosophy asserted the unity of all existence, the greater being reflected in the lesser. This happens when the apparent

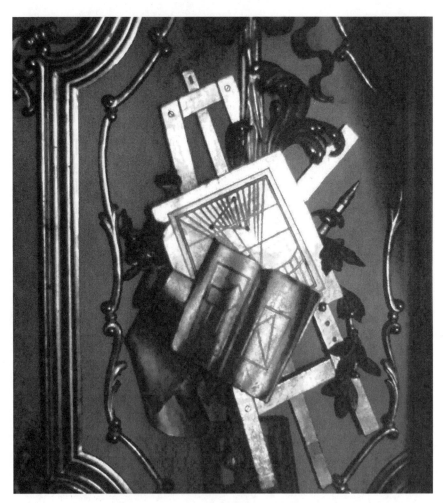

Figure 7.1. Ornamental representation of geometrical tools in the Residenz Munich, Germany. (Nigel Pennick)

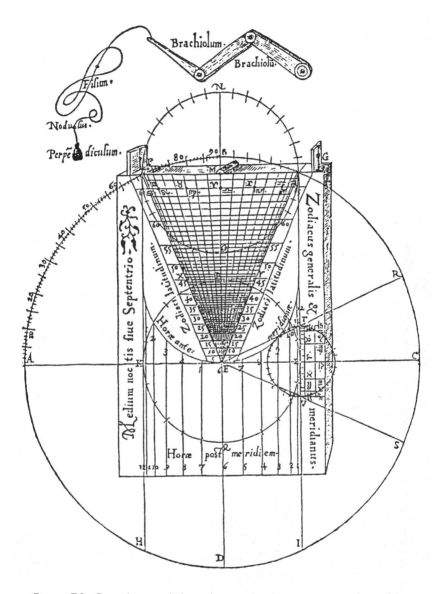

Figure 7.2. Complex sundials and surveying instruments such as this, designed by Oronce Fine (1494–1555) were taken to China by Jesuit missionaries and formed the basis of contemporary Feng-Shui instruments. Prior to the Jesuits in China, the compass circle was divided into 365 (for the days in the year) but the Jesuits' European instruments, with the conventional 360 degree division took over from the 365-fold division and Feng-Shui compasses and other surveying were modified accordingly. (Nideck)

movements of the sun are marked at any point on Earth. The recorded movements are the result of the actual geometry of the Earth, and when they are brought into visible physical form, then the implicit structure of the conditions of our lives are made explicit. The often-paraphrased Hermetic maxim, attributed to Hermes Trismegistus, the Egyptian founder of the sciences, states: "That which is in the lesser world (the microcosm) reflects that of the greater world (the macrocosm)."

Figure 7.3. Hermes Trismegistus. (Nideck)

There are two ways of seeing the apparent motion of the sun. The sundial works by taking its shadow at an individual spot on the Earth. Then the movement of the shadow denotes the movement of the sun. This is an incoming method. There is also an outgoing method, which is the more ancient tradition. This is to observe the sun directly. In the Etruscan Discipline, the augurs always took great note of the horizon visible from their chosen places. They observed the apparent motions of sun, moon, and stars over the fixed features of the landscape, the hills, mountains, valleys, rivers, and coasts.

IRISH SPATIAL AWARENESS

The Irish language is remarkably conserved from antiquity. It preserves ancient Celtic ways of understanding space. Spatial descriptions in Irish provide nuances that are not found in English. There are four main horizontal directions, the *airde* (singular: *aird*). *Thoir,* the east, is the primary direction, the most important point in the sky. The cardinal points are thus *an aird thoir* (east), *an aird theas* (south), *an aird thiar* (west), and *an aird thuaidh* (north). The four *airde* are envisaged as the front of the oriented person. *Theas,* the South, is the person's right-hand side. Behind the person is *thiar,* the west. Finally, the left is *thuaidh,* the north. The Irish language has special forms that denote going toward or coming away from an *aird.* The person is the center from which all things are, come, or go. Direction is defined by the person, not the orientation of things. Thus, in English, something coming from the East is viewed as traveling Westward. In Irish, it is coming from the East, toward the observer at the center. The Irish view is the humane view, where the human aspect is always paramount. Things and directions are not relative, but absolute in terms of the observer.

Irish perception of vertical space is also very subtle. Objects or actions above the individual have different linguistic forms from those below. Thus, there are words that describe motion upward from the individual and motion downward to the individual from above. Irish also recognizes things above the person that are not in motion. There are other words that describe motion downward from the person, and

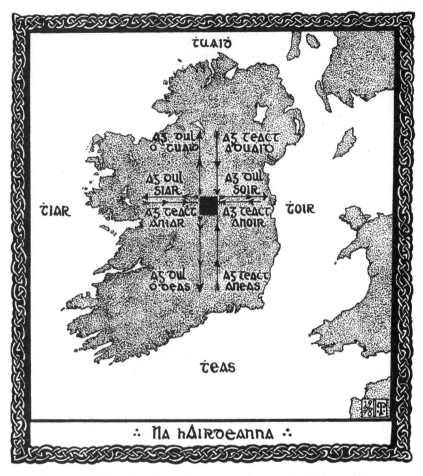

Figure 7.4. The four directions, according to the Irish tradition.
(Nigel Pennick)

upward toward the person from below. Things not in motion below the person are also recognized. The entire Irish perception of space is thus as follows:

There are four basic directions on the horizontal plane. These are perceived as possessing three natures. Firstly, they have their static form, as general orientations from a person. They also have relative motions, both incoming the outgoing. There are also two directions in the vertical plane, up and down. These, too, have a static and a moving form, toward and away from the individual, who is the central reference point.

THE EIGHT DIRECTIONS

The ancients used a fixed system of orientation to observe the celestial and terrestrial phenomena. By natural measure, they divided the circle of the horizon first into four quarters by the technique outlined above. These were drawn conceptually to the horizon in each direction. Between these meridional and equinoctial lines, the horizon was divided by further lines running to the intercardinal directions. They created thereby the eightfold division necessary for one to construct a foursquare building or enclosure facing the four quarters of the heavens. The southern quarter is the quadrant that lies between southwest and southeast; the eastern quarter lies between southeast and northeast; the northern quarter is between the northeast and the northwest; and finally the western quarter is between the northwest and the southwest. The four cardinal directions are thus the midpoints of the four quarters, the *ættingar* (sg. *ættingr*) of the Norse tradition.

These eight directions are derived directly from the physical structure of the world, the north–south polar axis and the east–west one at right angles to it. This is the essential arrangement of the Etruscan Discipline. But in addition to the fixed structure of the world, there are the variable features of the apparent motions of the heavenly bodies in relation to the fixed site. Depending on the latitude of the site, the position of the rising and setting sun at the solstices (the longest and shortest days) and on other important sacred festivals of the year will be at different places on the horizon from the intercardinal directions. Furthermore, the height of the horizon above or below the viewing point will alter the rising place of the sun, moon, or star, and unless the site has an equal height horizon called a "zero horizon" all around it, this will destroy the symmetry of sunrises and sets. On a zero horizon, a solar geometry exists in which midsummer sunrise is diametrically opposite midwinter sunset and midwinter sunrise opposes midsummer sunset.

Because the length of day varies with the season of the year, and this season is directly observable by the position of sunrise on the horizon, it is possible to mark the calendar by means of sunrise direction. This can be seen in the furniture of the most sophisticated sundials.

Figure 7.5. The wheel of the day.
(Nigel Pennick)

Between the southernmost sunrise at midwinter in the northern hemisphere, and the most northerly sunrise at midsummer, the sun rises due
east at the equinox, crossing southward in winter and northward in

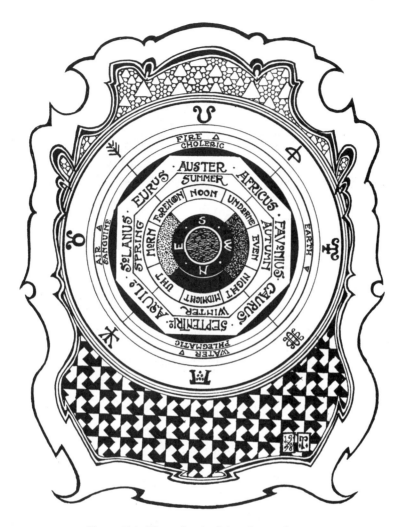

Figure 7.6. The wheel of the day and year.
(Nigel Pennick)

summer to define the two halves of the year, the dark half and the light half. Between the two solstices, the traditional rural calendar of the Celtic north marked the end and beginning of winter at the festivals of Beltane (May Day) and Samhain (November 1). In the harmonized landscapes of the past, these rising and setting points were indicated either by natural features, or by artificial markers such as standing stones or cairns.

HOROLOGII ICONISMUS.

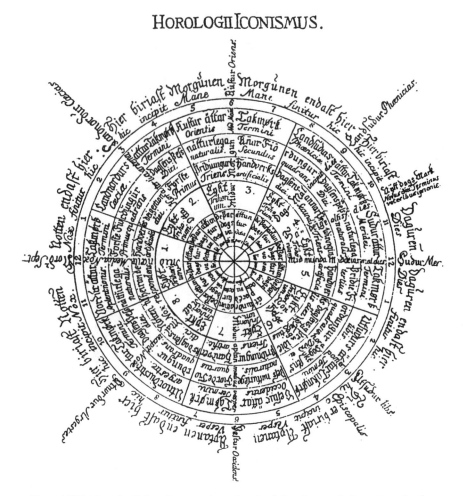

Figure 7.7. Horologii Iconismus, the wheel of the day and directions in the Northern Tradition. Drawing by S. M. Holm in Stephán Bjornasson's Latin translation of the Ryimbegla, Copenhagen, 1780. (Nideck)

As well as delimiting the places of corresponding sunrises, they denote the time of day. When the sun is rising due east at the equinoxes, that is 6 a.m. according to contemporary clock hours. When it sets due west, it is 6 p.m. When the sun stands due south at any time of year, it is twelve noon. At midsummer, the sun stands much higher in the sky than at noon on midwinter's day. At midsummer noon, the sun is at its greatest altitude, and at midwinter, its lowest. At any time of year when the sun is above the horizon, it will always be above the same horizon marker at the same time of day. At 6 a.m. on midsummer's day, the sun will stand due east from the observer, but well up above the horizon, and so on.

THE EIGHTFOLD
IN THE NORTHERN TRADITION

The apparent circle of the horizon can also be the basis for time-telling. Here, the position of the sun is not shown by a shadow cast by a gnomon, but observed directly. This is the way that time was told before the invention of the gnomon and sundial. It survived in parts of northern Europe well into the twentieth century as the primary way of dividing the day. Like the Etruscan Discipline and the eight winds of Vitruvius, the northern European way of determining direction- and time-measurement is based upon an eightfold division of space.

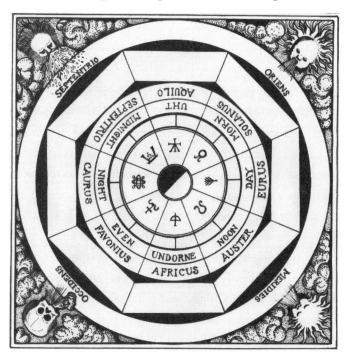

Figure 7.8. The eight winds, tides of the day, and seasons.
(Nigel Pennick)

The best-recorded examples of this eightfold system come from Scandinavia, Iceland, the Faeroes, and Shetland. The system of division of the horizon was universal, applying to time, space, and place. In Old Norse, each eighth was called an *ætt* (equivalent to the Irish *aird,* which is a quarter). As in the Etruscan Discipline, the northern European perception came from the basic fourfold division of the human. Unlike the Irish tradition, where East is the primary "facing" direction, the Norse tradition, like the Etruscan, envisages the person facing south. The four cardinal directions—North, South, East, and West—thus correspond with the human's back, front, left, and right. Between these four cardinal directions are projected four intercardinal directions, to the northeast, southeast, southwest and northwest. These eight conceptual lines to the horizon form the midpoints of the eight regions of land, horizon, and sky centered on the person. Each *ætt* then faces the corresponding cardinal or intercardinal direction. This is the same principle used in traditional building, where a foursquare structure "faces" the cardinal directions. Thus, the north wall faces north, running from east to west. The east and west walls run north–south. The eightfold division of space follows the same system.

The Norse word *ætt* and its relations is instructive in that it shows the integral nature of things that modern English tends to divide. *Ætt* can refer to a group of eight, as in the directions or a rubric of eight runes. It also has the meaning of a region of the sky, a compass direction, and a family. From this comes the word signifying one's family descent, *ættaðr,* "descended," meaning belonging by birth or family to a place (homestead), and *ættmaðr,* a "relative or kinsperson." Thus, in traditional northern European society, the land upon which one lives and one's ancestral descent are one and the same, linking the individual with the material structure of the world in which one lives. This contrasts markedly with the alienated insecurity in which many people live today, where their common ancestral heritage has long since been taken forcibly by powerful aristocratic families.

Before the introduction of the twelve-hour day from the Mediterranean region, northern European time-telling divided the day into eight *tides* (this has nothing to do with the tides of the sea). These

Figure 7.9. An eighteenth-century Finnish engraving of the World Support, according to Saami beliefs, shown as a Pietarinleikki sequence on a runestaff, standing between two sighting-pillars. (Nideck)

tides are determined by the position of the sun as viewed from any point. Each of them occupies one *ætt*. At the middle of each tide is the cardinal or intercardinal direction, the *aettingr*. Thus, the time of noon is when the sun is due south, on the aetting of south. This is at the midpoint of the tide of noon, called *middæg* (midday) in Anglo-Saxon and *Mittagsstätt* in German.

EIGHT TIDES
(with Terms from Three Related Germanic Traditions)

Tide	Anglo-Saxon	Old Norse	German
Morntide (4:30–7:30)	morgen	morginn	Morgen
Daytide (7:30–10:30)	dæg, dægtid; undern, underntid	dagtími	Tagmahl.
Midday or Noontide (10:30–13:30)	middæg, nōn	miðdegi, miðdegisskeið	Hochtag
Afternoon (13:30–16:30)	ofernōn	ofanverðr dagr	Untern
Eventide (16:30–19:30)	æfentid	aftan	Abend
Nighttide (19:30–22:30)	niht	nótt	Nachtmahl
Midnight (22:30–1:30)	midniht	miðnætti	Nacht
Uht (1:30–4:30)	uhta, uhtantid	ótta	Uchte

There were certain markers of direction and time that played an important role in the northern landscape in pre-clock times. They were in everyday use in the Faeroe Islands until the second quarter of the twentieth century. The direction called *rismál* in the Old Norse language was the rising time in summer, the point at which people got up to work (modern German *Aufstehzeit*), corresponding to 4:30 in clock time. This is when the sun crosses the borderline between the

Figure 7.10. The runes of the Elder Futhark can be arranged around the wheel of time and give corresponding meanings to solar directions. (from Nigel Pennick's *Runic Astrology*)

tides of Uht and Morn. The next named marker is at 7:30, the English Daymark, called *dægmæl* in Anglo-Saxon, *dagmálastadr* in Old Norse, and *Tagmahlstätt* in German.

In summertime, around four-thirty after noon (16:30), the time that the sun passes from the Tide of Afternoon into Eventide, is the time to stop the day's work. In Old Norse, this corresponds to what is called *eyktarstaðr*, referring to the place of the sun at this time with respect to the local landscape. The last significant marker is at 19:30, the time of the evening meal.

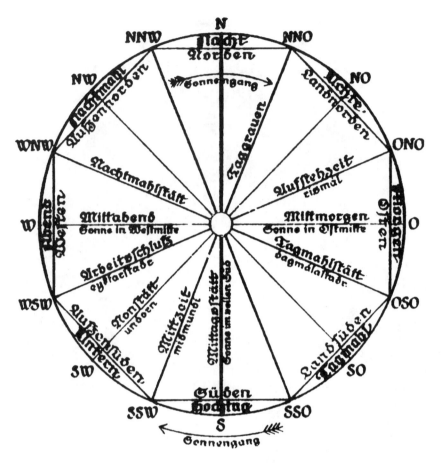

Figure 7.11. Northern Tradition showing the eight tides
of the day with corresponding solar directions, according to
Otto Sigfried Reuter, 1936.

In this ancient northern European system, the elements of place,
space, time, and human activity are integrated in one. As a universal
system, this division into eight is the basis of the year cycle celebrated by
contemporary Pagans. Paganism recognizes eight major festivals, based
upon the equinoxes and solstices and the harvest cycle. In the Northern
Tradition, they are the Autumnal Equinox (September 23); Samhain
(November 1); Yule (December 21–25); Brigantia (February 1); Vernal
Equinox (March 21); Beltane (May Day, May 1); Summer Solstice
(June 21); and Lammas (August 1).

Figure 7.12. A rare combined sundial and zodiacal clock
in the fortified monastery at Bebenhausen, south Germany.
(Nigel Pennick)

COSMIC SACRED GEOMETRY

According to some medieval symbolists, the cosmos can be considered in architectural terms. Considering the derivation of geometry, and hence all architecture, from terrestrial and celestial phenomena, this was a natural conclusion. Because medieval Christians believed that the world was created by God according to divine principles, geometry itself was seen as the underlying matrix through which God worked. According to this view, God as creator chose the numerical and geometrical ratios of the spheres, the planets, Nature, and music. By contemplating these structures and ratios, it was held that people could approach the deity who created them. Following this current of thought, the Cistercian poet Alain de Lille (Alanus ab Insulis, ca. 1128–1202/3) envisaged God to be the Architect of the World. This is the image of creation described in Masonic symbolism. It represents a different view of the relationship between the human image and the world. Instead of the concept that the world is the body of the slain anthropocosmic giant, the anthropoid God makes the world according to geometrical technique. Medieval and later depictions of God the Father in this vein show him holding compasses in his hand. He uses them to draw the circle that is the foundation of the world, recalling the ancient Egyptian foundation rite, but with the female element removed. The best-known example of this image is *The Ancient of Days,* by William Blake, the frontispiece of his *Europe a Prophecy* (1794).

The eightfold division of the Etruscan Discipline and perhaps also the northern landscape underlay the medieval European Masonic method of sacred geometry called "Ad Quadratum." It appears overtly in the designs of symbolic pavements in medieval buildings. Mosaic pavements remaining today at Westminster Abbey and Canterbury Cathedral in England, and at locations in Italy and Germany, present us with cosmological schemata expressed in geometrical form. According to William R. Lethaby, the English medieval alchemist Sporley stated that at Westminster Abbey, the circles of the Cosmati Pavement were symbolic of the four elements. In former times, the omphalos of the

Figure 7.13. The Great Architect of the Universe.
Based on *The Ancient of Days* by William Blake. (Nideck)

Westminster cosmogram carried an inscription explaining that the pavement was emblematical of the microcosm.

The sacred geometry expressed by the arrangement of tesserae in these mosaics encodes the mathematics and geometrical structure that underlies all existence. In addition to their cosmological dimension, many of the cathedral pavements of Western Europe symbolized the totality of the yearly cycle, bearing representations of the Labors of the Seasons and also the signs of the zodiac. Canterbury Cathedral's *opus alexandrinum* pavement is surrounded by roundels with the zodiacal

Figure 7.14. A Rose Mosaic designed and made by Nigel Pennick
before the entrance of a private house near Stuttgart, Germany,
founded according to proper rites, with a rose-oil container and other
foundation deposits beneath the central point. (Nigel Pennick)

emblems. The pavement labyrinth at Sens Cathedral in Burgundy had
an octagonal stone at the center surrounded by eight keystone-shaped
slabs, expressing the basic principle of the Etruscan Discipline, the
union of the eightfold horizon with the navel of the world.

Ceremonies of foundation are just the beginning points of layout
and construction over a wider area. They may be seen as the navel or
egg from which the greater organism comes into being. From the ini-
tial point of foundation, certain symbolic patterns are developed whose
form follows cosmic principles. Thus, in traditional European societies, place and time are taken into account when performing ceremonial
events. The symbolic quality of local, regional, and national gatherings,
for example, are recognized in their location and timing. Ideally, every
fair, moot, parliament, pardon, tournament, city, or royal court should
be a microcosmic reflection of the structure of the land and the people.

Figure 7.15. A medieval French engraving of the wheel of the days and the labors of the seasons, the basis of all human life. (Nideck)

PLACES OF ASSEMBLY

In the time when lords and kings progressed around their country, collecting taxes and dispensing justice, their temporary assemblies were arranged according to symbolic principles that reflected the county, state, or nation. The great hall of Tara, seat of the High Kings of Ireland, was laid out internally according to set principles that reflected the relative values of the ranks of society, and the practical arrangements of access and security. Democratic assemblies, too, ranging from local folkmoots to the Althing of Iceland and the Tynwald of the Isle of Man, had the structure of the cosmological plan of the holy city. Delegates from each of the four quarters of the land camped on their corresponding side, in places ritually appropriate to their trade, profession, or calling. For the duration of the event, held at a significant time of year, the whole area became a ceremonial replica of the kingdom. The king, or a symbol representing his authority, was placed at the very center. The Ballinderry gameboard is a representation of this layout.

THE MYSTIC PLOT

Traditions of foundation exist throughout European folk culture. According to the German researcher Otto Höfler in his *Kultische Geheimbünde der Germanen* (Cultic Secret Leagues of the Ancient Germanic Peoples, 1934), current folk customs of "misrule"—in which the normal standards of behavior are inverted—once had more formal elements. In medieval Europe, Höfler tells us, there were secret societies composed exclusively of young men which were literally a "law unto

Figure 7.16. *Opposite:* The Great Hall at Tara, seat of the High Kings of Ireland, was laid out according to symbolic principles. According to The Yellow Book of Lucan, the various ranks, professions, and trades of Celtic society were seated in corresponding parts of the great hall, according to precedence and function. 1. Charioteers and Stewards. 2. Deer Stalkers. 3. Aire Forgaill (first grade nobility). 4. King and Queen. 5. Aire Ard (third grade nobility) and Cli (third grade poets). 6. Aire Tual (second grade nobility) and Historians. 7. Aire Desa (fourth grade nobility) and Dos (fifth grade poets). 8. Fochloc (sixth-grade poets). 9. Cooks. 10. Fort Builders. 11. Champions and Cano (fourth-grade poets). 12. Sappers. 13. Board-game Players. 14. Spencers. 15. Braziers. 16. Physicians. 17. Pilots. 18. Merchants. 19. Jesters. 20. Buffoons. 21. King's Fools. 22. Flute Players. 23. Schoolteachers. 24. Goldsmiths. 25. Smiths. 26. Shield-makers. 27. Chariot-builders. 28. Conjurors. 29. Satirists. 30. Door-keepers. 31.Horsemen. 32. Harpers and Drummers. 33. Judges. 34. Doctors of Letters and their nominated successors. 35. Chief Poets and Anruith (second-grade poets). 36. Hospitallers. 37. Master Wrights and their successors. 38. Soothsayers and Druids. 39. Builders and Wrights. 40. Horners and Pipers. 41. Engravers. 42. Cordwainers. (Nideck / Nigel Pennick)

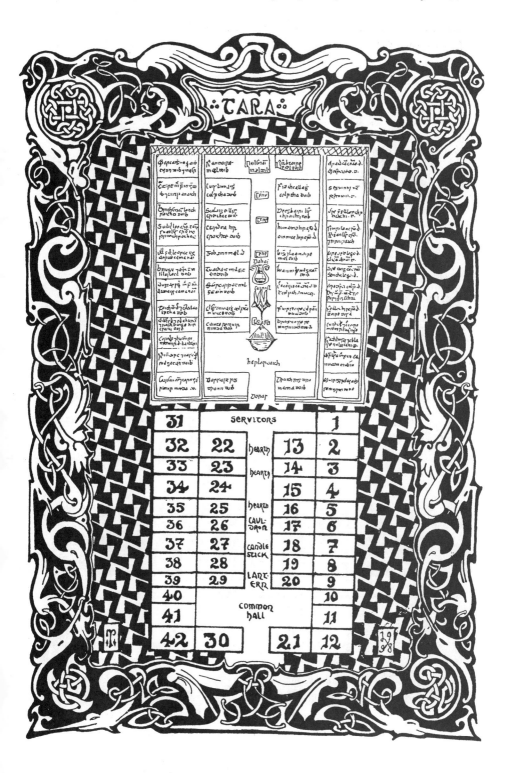

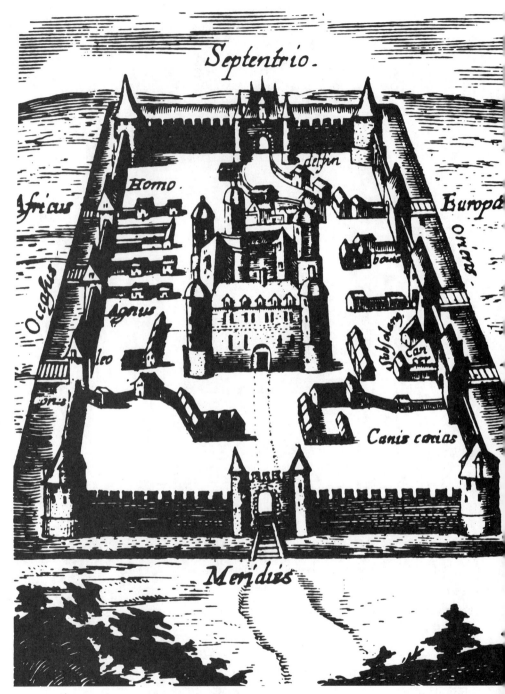

Figure 7.17. The four-square archetypal Holy City
is oriented to the quarters. (Nideck)

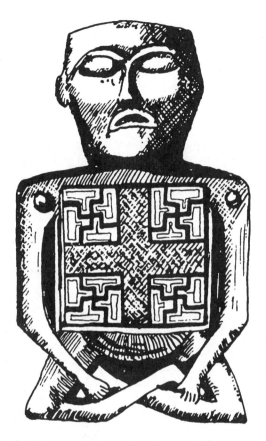

Figure 7.18. Celtic humanoid metal and enamel fitment with the body quartered in the "holy city plan." (Nideck)

themselves." They came together at night and, disguised in ritual costume, roamed the countryside. Their members were initiated, having sworn oaths of silence and anonymity. The anonymity and collective strength of these gangs enabled them to enforce standards of public behavior, to oppress their enemies and extort largesse and money from their victims. They were often the perpetrators of the summary forms of punishment called variously rough justice, skimmington, the Skeleton Army, kangaroo courts, and witch-hunts. These gangs of young men roamed about their neighborhoods at night assaulting those whom they thought guilty of transgressing their social code. The "wild horde" or "wild hunt," composed of wild people roaming at night, is mentioned in disapproving early medieval monkish writings. In England, the Whifflers, Mumps, Gullivers, and Plough Stots occasionally did this at Yuletide, on Plough Monday, and on May Day.

In Bavaria, there were groups of young men called *Haberfeldtreiben*, who branded those people they thought to have infringed village rules. In Westphalia, the secret courts known as *Vehmgericht* tried and punished or executed those deemed guilty of various offences. In medieval Germany, the gridded Mystic Plot was used by the *Vehmgericht*, the "Vehm," secret and unofficial tribunals that met at certain places in Westphalia. In later years, after the *Vehmgericht* had died out, its origin was said to be in the old Pagan priesthood, but its function makes this

Figure 7.19. The Wild Horde appears each year around midwinter in various customary guises in central Europe. Among the demonic characters of misrule are the fearsome Schiachperchten in the Perchtenläufe (Perchten processions) of Austria. These guisers appeared at Muhlbech in Austria on January 3, 1997.
(Nigel Pennick)

unlikely. The Vehm existed to uphold the Christian religion, which had been imposed upon the defeated Saxons by the Emperor Charlemagne in the year 772. The Vehm, like other secret organizations of rough justice such as the Bavarian *Haberfeldtrieben,* saw its brief as punishing so-called secret crimes. These could include the practice of magic, witchcraft, poison-making, and conspiracy with Jews to perform acts of wrongdoing. Forcible usurpation of land was also punished by the Vehm, whose members saw the maintenance of land boundaries as a particularly important task.

Each Vehmic court was composed of sixteen men, who held their office for life. Their chief was called the *Freigraf* (Free Count). There were fourteen ordinary members, called *Freischöffen.* The most junior was the *Fröhner* (Summoner). In the early days, it was stipulated that the court should be held in the open, and in daylight. It had to be *"up roder Erde gemaket"* (made on the red earth), that is, within the limits of the ancient Duchy of Westphalia, and was only held at specific locations. These special places were marked by foundation deposits. When the court was held, the place was tested by the *Fröhner* digging there. If tiles and ashes were found there, it was the right place. Then, to reconsecrate the place, the members of the Vehm threw in a handful of ashes, a piece of charcoal, and a tile. The Vehmic sigil was an eightfold pattern consisting of eight square tiles overlapping one another, symbolizing the eight directions meeting at the center and thus the court's jurisdiction over the entire land of Westphalia. The four elements of ceremony—place, time, measure, and human participants—were present, and the proceedings could take place.

Next, the *Fröhner* laid out the Mystic Plot. It was a square measuring sixteen feet by sixteen feet. The *Fröhner* first tested his Mete-Wand against the *Freigraf*'s foot, rather in the manner of Jacob Köbel's 1531 engraving (see p. 176). Then the Judgment Seat, called the *Freistuhl* (Free Seat), was brought to the site and placed at the central point. Then the court was held. Those who were charged had been kidnapped previously and imprisoned before being brought before the Vehm. Those found guilty were hanged immediately on a nearby tree.

The temporary grid upon the ground, as in the Vehmic Mystic Plot, symbolizes a spiritual building. In early English Freemasonry, the plan of the lodge in which the ceremonies were to take place was drawn in chalk on the floor of a room and erased afterward. Customarily, this Masonic tesselated pavement also measures sixteen by sixteen squares.

FAIRS

The cosmic patterns on which moots, fairs, and towns have been based, have remained long after the spiritual elements have become obscure. However, so long as the associated customs are observed, the less apparent patterns also remain present as part of the proceedings. These traditions have continued, especially at annual fairs, which are very conservative of continuity. Many European fairs held annually at the present time have an archaic provenance formalized by dukes and kings

Figure 7.20. A labyrinth with its surrounding Vebond and ceremonial entrance, laid out by Nigel Pennick in the Green Area at the Strawberry Fair on Midsummer Common in Cambridge, June 6, 1998. (Rupert Pennick)

in the medieval period, when locational principles were followed as a matter of course. Like the administrative assemblies, fairs were also laid out as microcosms, reflecting not only the country but also the eternal order of the cosmos, temporarily brought to earth at that specific place for a certain time.

Probably derived from temporary fairs, the traditional layout of market towns is part of this tradition. Relative positions are assigned on a gridded square to various trades, occupations, and pastimes. These relate to corresponding planets, directional qualities, or the deities or saints that rule them. Traditional fairgrounds are laid out according to the same principle as market towns, having rows and districts dedicated to specific trades, professions, or pastimes. In many places, these temporary rows were made permanent by the erection of buildings in place of stalls or booths. Where redevelopment has not swept away the traditional street plans, their successors stand on the same sites, preserving the alignments.

The street layouts of certain towns were derived definitely from the temporary fairs and markets that preceded them. In the old shire of Huntingdon, the old part of the market town of St. Ives sports a gridded pattern. This is derived from the layout of the early medieval St. Audrey's Fair, which is held annually in the streets of the town in the week nearest October 17, St. Etheldreda's Day. In the county to the south, Cambridgeshire, the remains of the same process exist in the district of east Cambridge called Barnwell. There we find streets called Oyster Row, Mercer's Row, and Garlic Row, which are a survival of the grid of the once-mighty Sturbridge Fair, whose plan remained unchanged for centuries. Garlic Row was the main street of the Sturbridge Fair, running north and south between the main road to Newmarket and the River Granta at a place where it was crossed by ferry by the present Green Dragon public house.

At the center of traditional European fairs, it is customary to erect a pole, known variously as the Pau, Pal, or Maypole. This marks the geomantic center, and carries the emblem of authority, such as glove or crest, symbolic of the king or queen *in absentia*. The central post is of fundamental significance in the ceremonies attending the foundation of fairs, markets, and towns. Permanent maypoles stand in most Bavarian village centers and marketplaces. The largest of them all stands in the center of the Viktualienmarkt in Munich, the Bavarian capital city. As in the sealing of the Mundus in the Etruscan Discipline, setting up the pole marked the moment of foundation of a new town in medieval Europe.

Figure 7.21. The Maypole at Wennenden, Baden-Württemberg, Germany, May 23, 1998. (Nigel Pennick)

At fairs, the setting up of the post denotes the establishment of authority in the fair for its duration. In effect, fairs are temporary towns in which law and order must be maintained. This status is reinforced in England by the royal charters that authorize and empower many long-established fairs. Customarily, the law is administered within the fair by a special jurisdiction, enforced by the Court of Pie Powder (from the French *pied poudre,* "dusty feet"). Such courts are tribunals that enforce summary jurisdiction, meting out immediate punishments to transgressors like the less public Vehm. In England, Courts of Pie Powder were held at major fairs in England until 1939, when World War II put an end to them. They were convened at the major fairs held at Bristol, Ely, Guildford, and Newcastle upon Tyne, being the last examples of traditional mobile jurisdiction under English law.

The character of fairs changed greatly in the nineteenth and twentieth centuries, but they did not cease. They became primarily concerned with entertainment, with mechanized rides and sideshows. Although the content of fairs altered significantly, their layout tradition was maintained. Fair folk customs are little known outside their close-knit community, but all specialized communities maintain knowledge of how to accomplish the required tasks, and among the people who stage traveling fairs, this includes methods of laying them out that have proved effective over generations of use.

An incident that occurred in the West Midlands of England during World War II used the showmen's locational technique to determine the site of a grave. Such a rite would have been recognized by the ancient augurs. In December 1943, Pat Collins, "The King of the Showmen," died. The *Sunday Express* (December 12, 1943) reported:

> There was a strange incident at the cemetery when the old man's son visited it accompanied by Father Hanrahan, of St. Peter's Catholic Church, Bloxwich, to select a site for the grave. . . . When he came to seek a site for his father's last resting place it was found that the Catholic portion of the cemetery was full. The adjoining land that belongs to the cemetery was specially consecrated. When Mr Collins went to select a place for its first grave, he brought his

Figure 7.22. Maypole at Wellow Nottinghamshire England.
(Nigel Pennick)

foot forward, raised it, and brought his heel down sharply on the turf, making a deep dent in it, exclaiming as he did so: "This is the spot. I want the exact center of my father's grave to be over that mark." He explained to the priest: "My father used those words and that gesture for 60 years every time that he inspected a fairground site to indicate where the principal attraction, usually the biggest of the merry-go-rounds, was to be erected. He never measured the ground, but the chosen spot was always in the exact center of the showground. It was a ritual with him."

Mr. Collins used the same means to select a grave on a greenfield site as for the location of the center of a fair. The rite of bringing down the heel to fix a place can be seen in Rugby Football, where it is called "Making a Mark." In laying out modern traveling fairs, the connection between the center of the showground, where the pole symbolizing the cosmic axis once would have stood, and the axial rotation of the merry-go-round appears to be another overtly symbolic survival amongst showmen. From this, it may be surmised that dancing around the central maypole may have been superseded by mechanical merry-go-rounds. Even if this is not the case, symbolically it works very well.

CHAPTER 8

The Meaning of the Directions

Symbolism and Nature of the Winds

Make me your door, then, south; your broad side, west:
And, on the east side of your shop, aloft,
Write Mathlai, Tarmiel, and Baraborat;
Upon the north part, Rael, Velel, Thiel.

BEN JONSON, *THE ALCHEMIST* (1610)

SYMBOLIC DIRECTION-QUALITIES

European traditions have several ways to describe the qualities of the directions. According to Norse cosmology, four dwarves—Norðri, Austri, Suðri, and Vestri—support the world. They give each direction a specific quality. According to the Judeo-Christian magical system of medieval Europe, the directions defined by this sixteenfold division and its subdivision into thirty-two were said to be ruled by various spiritual and demonic powers. The most basic division, into four, allowed the allocation of the four quarters to the qualities of the four seasons, the four archangels, the four elements, and the four humors.

Lesser powers or daemons were given command of the subsidiary directions according to their corresponding characters that related to

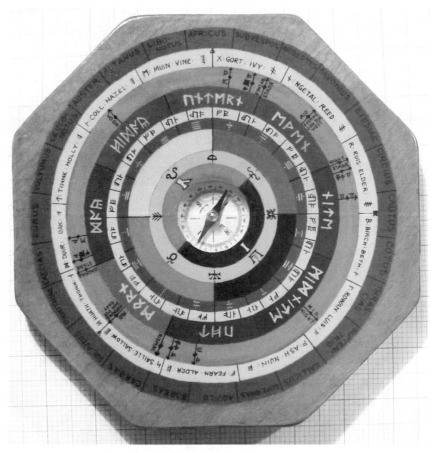

Figure 8.1. Northern Tradition geomantic compass
made by Nigel Pennick at Runestaff Crafts 1986.
(Nigel Pennick)

the seasons and corresponding four elements. Thus, according to a
sixteenth-century source, the daemon who rules the north is Rasiel;
that of the east is Pamersiel; in the south, the regent daemon is Barmiel;
and in the west, Malgaras. The daemon Rasiel, being of the north, is
regent of midwinter, midnight, darkness, coldness, and the meeting-
point of earth and water. He is called Rael by Ben Jonson (ca. 1572–
ca. 1637) in his play *The Alchemist*. The daemon Barmiel, befitting a
logical system, is the complete opposite of Rasiel, being the daemon of
midsummer, bright light, hotness. He stands at the meeting point of air

and fire. The other daemons are related similarly to the year cycle, like Rasiel and Barmiel also having their time of day. The actual "Mercurial spirits" that Jonson mentions in *The Alchemist* are angels of the Second Heaven described in the *Heptameron* or *Magical Elementals* by Pietro d'Abano (aka Petrus de Apono) (1250–1316). In d'Abano's text, among others, Mathlai, Tarmiel, and Baraborat rule the east, while Rael, Velel

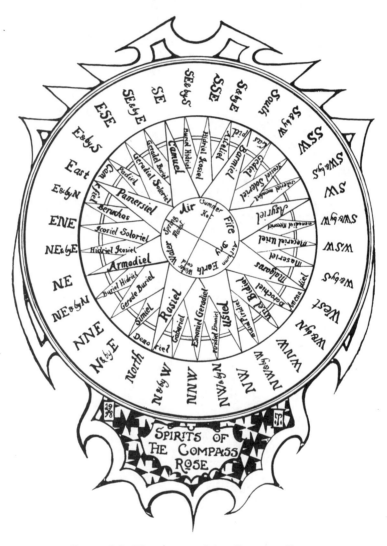

Figure 8.2. The spirits of the Compass Rose,
according to eighteenth-century English Qabalistic tradition.
(Nigel Pennick)

and Thiel rule the north. Their corresponding weekday is Wednesday, the day of Mercury, patronal god of trade and business, ideal for the proposed tobacconist's shop.

In *The Alchemist,* Abel Drugger, a tobacco-seller, consults the alchemist, Subtle, about the geomancy of his new shop, which is to be built at the corner of a street. He asks in which direction the door should face, and how it may be arranged auspiciously inside, by *necromancy* (as traditional Western geomancy was called then in England). The quotation at the head of this chapter is Subtle's advice. Jonson's comedy tells us that in his time geomantic techniques were used to determine both the external and internal layout of buildings. Orientation was only one of the elements taken into account, for Subtle advises Drugger on the appropriate astrology and building charms necessary for a successful business.

Figure 8.3. Erwin Von Steinbach, *acht ort* expresses a general principle of geometry in geomancy and architecture.

The classical demonological ascription of the directions gives them a theoretical basis. They are general, not specific, for they relate to the general qualities of the directions, such as east/sunrise/spring and north/night/winter. The European Jewish tradition from which the demonological system comes is primarily urban and not located in one place. Thus, a general system arose that worked as well in Dundee as in Cracow or Cremona, Madrid or Malta. Christian direction meanings, following their Jewish roots, are also general and applicable in the northern hemisphere. The precise, local ascription of direction quality to the winds is more directly rooted in place and cannot be transferred from one place to another like directions based on religious systems.

DIRECTION-DEFINITION IN
THE HINDU TRADITION

The gods move about like dice, which give us wealth and take it away.

RIG VEDA, TENTH MANDALA

In India during the Vedic period (ca. 1200–600 BCE), the directions possessed meanings related to the throw of dice. Dice played an important part in the royal consecration ritual, *Rajasuya,* described in the *Satapatha Brahmana.* Here, the priest lays five dice in the king's hands, reciting a prayer from the *Vajasaneyi Samhita:* ". . . you are dominant: may these five directions of yours prosper." By taking the dice, the king defined his rulership over the directions.

Another Vedic text, the *Taittiriya Samhita,* contains an invocation to the five directions: east, south, west, north, and the zenith. In this system of correspondences, where dice can be used to define a direction, there are only five possible throws. The throw *Krta* (4) defined the east; *Treta* (3), the south; *Dvapara* (2), the west; *Askanda* or *Kali* (1), the north; and *Abhibhu,* the zenith. It is unsure how the ritual dice game was played, but it seems that in ancient Indian geomancy, certain directions were chosen by the throw of dice. There are parallels with the definition of directions in Arab geomancy and the *Vintana* of Madagascar by means of geomantic figures.

The seventeenth-century-CE *Nirnayasindhu* of Kamalakara tells how Narada journeyed to Kailasa, a holy mountain in the Himalayas. There he saw the god Shiva playing dice with Parvati, his consort. According to Narada, the whole cosmos is the surface on which the god and goddess play dice. The two halves of the year, the twelve months, the days of the lunar month are likened to different plays of dice.

The two possible outcomes of the game, win or loss, are creation and dissolution, for the whole of existence is the dice game he witnessed between the god and goddess. When Parvati wins, there is a beginning in creation, but when Shiva wins, there is an end in dissolution. But, as the cosmic dice game is eternally in play, neither god nor goddess have a final victory, and there is an endless cycle of coming-into-being and dissolution.

As in all traditional cultures, the different qualities of the directions are recognized in *Vastu Vidya* (Indian geomancy). The *Grihya* sutras describe the principles of orienting doors. The *Gobhila Griha Sutra* tells us: "One who desires fame or strength should build his house with the door to the East; one who desires children or cattle, with the door to the north; one who desires all these things, with the door to the south. Let him not build it with its door to the west and with a back door." The *Matsya Purana* calls a house without a west-facing door *Nandyavartha*. One without a north door is *Ruchaka;* without an east door, *Svastika;* and without a south door, *Vardhamana*.

THE CLASSICAL WINDS

According to classical mythology, symbolically the winds are personified as the sons of Astraeus and Eos (Aurora). In the earliest reckoning, they were four in number: Boreas, Euros, Notos, and Zephyros. They were venerated all over the ancient world with rites and ceremonies conducted at fine temples. They were especially venerated at ports. According to the Greeks, Boreas, called "The King of the Winds," came from Thrace. He is the strong north wind, depicted as a powerful winged and bearded male figure. When he travels through the upper air, he is enveloped in mists.

Lower down, he makes whirlwinds of dust. His sons, Zetes and Calais, the Boreadae, were killed by Hercules and became the winds that blow for the nine days preceding the Dog Days. They are shown with long blue hair, golden scales on the shoulders, and winged feet.

Euros (Vulturnus), the east wind, is depicted as an impetuous, flying youth, with his hair streaming in the storm. He is shown sowing flowers with both hands as he passes. Notos (Notus), the Roman Auster, is the south wind, "the father of rain." He is shown as a tall being, his hair whitened with age. His clothing drips with rain, and he is depicted as pouring rain upon the earth from a vessel. Notus was considered harmful to flowers as well as human health. Zephyros (Zephyrus), the west wind, is shown as a fine youth wearing a flower-garland on his head. He is supported by butterflies' wings and is considered the consort of the goddess of flowers, Flora. The pleasant breezes called Zephyrs are considered to be the attendants of the West wind. They are depicted as young, winged boys.

The winds were under the control of Aeolus, who resided on the island of Lipari. He was under the protection of the goddess Juno. Aeolus kept the winds in caverns, sending them out and bringing them back at his will. He is the tutelary deity of wind vanes, sails, and wind-

Figure 8.4. Wyvern vane on erstwhile Red Cow pub Cambridge England. (Nigel Pennick)

mills. His musical instrument is the Aeolian Harp, which uses the winds to create the Divine Harmony.

THE VITRUVIAN WINDS

In European antiquity, the horizon was divided into 16 and 32 by the Etruscan Discipline. This was a division that described the world according to the basic geometry of the earth. In the Mediterranean region of Europe, there is also an ancient complementary system based on the winds. It seems that there were only four winds in remote antiquity, as described in the preceding section. But, like the Etruscan division, the developed geomantic description of the directions was also based on the eightfold, having eight winds. The eight winds were considered to be the most important. But because each wind had two accompanying lesser winds or "breezes," one on each side, effectively there was a twenty-four-fold division. The subsidiary breezes are shown in the illustration here taken from Fra Giocondo's 1511 edition of the works of Vitruvius.

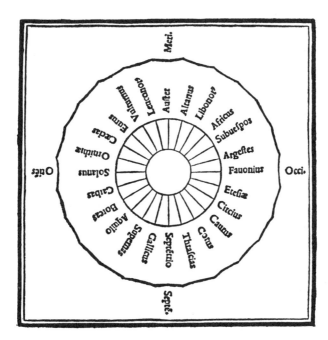

Figure 8.5. The Vitruvian winds, according to
Fra Giacondo's edition of Vitruvius, Venice 1511. (Nideck)

Figure 8.6. The Tower of the Winds at Athens,
designed by the Macedonian architect Andronicus of Cyrrhus.
The triton on top was a wind vane that pointed to
representations of the eight winds below the roof.
(Nigel Pennick)

Writers dealing with the directions of the heavens often used the names of the winds to describe them. This has led to a great deal of confusion. In the city of Athens, the Macedonian architect Andronicus of Cyrrhus built the octagonal structure called the Tower of the Winds. On each side of this building, which was oriented appropriately, was a sculpture representing the presiding genius of the corresponding wind. Beneath each personified wind were the inscribed lines of a sundial. Inside was a complex water-driven clock. The tower still exists, partly ruined, having been converted to a mosque during the period of Ottoman rule.

In his *Ten Books of Architecture,* the Roman architect Vitruvius told how around 50 BCE Andronicus set up his wind marker:

> On top of the tower, he set a conical-shaped piece of marble and upon that a Triton of bronze with a rod in its outstretched right hand. It was so designed to rotate with the winds, always stopping to face the breeze and using its rod as a pointer directly over the representation of the wind that was blowing.

Because every natural force in ancient times was personified, or ascribed to a ruling genius, spirit, or deity, the powers associated originally with the winds unfortunately came to stand for the compass directions in their own right. Vitruvius's ascriptions, however, were local, and the winds were named after their local character or the place from which they seemed to originate.

Along with the sundial, the winds are the true local definition of the geomantic nature of a place. They are truly specific, related directly to place without intervening theory. They have been recognized for thousands of years, defining the orientation of buildings in western Europe as long as 7,000 years ago. Vitruvius described the winds that he knew from his native land. He recognized that he was simplifying a complex system when he designated only eight winds: "Perhaps those who know the name of very many winds will be surprised," wrote Vitruvius, "that we set forth

Figure 8.7. Weathercosk on church at Swavesey Cambridgeshire England. (Nigel Pennick)

only eight." He defined the eight winds that became the standard description of the directions in European tradition. In the north is *Septentrio;* to the northeast is *Aquilo;* and in the east, *Solanus.* The southeast has the wind called *Eurus,* and the south, *Auster.* Then, in the southwest is *Africus;* in the west, *Favonius;* and in the northwest, Caurus.

Between the eight winds are sixteen breezes, which Vitruvius saw as subsidiary to them. To the west of *Septentrio* is *Thracias,* and to its east,

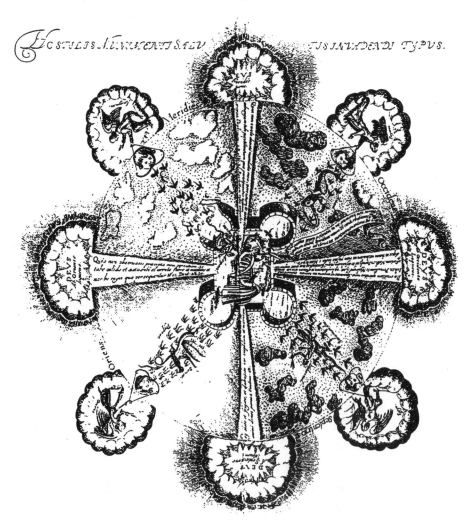

Figure 8.8. The Fortress of Health, assailed by plagues and illnesses carried by the four winds emanating from "the round earth's imagin'd corners." Engraving to illustrate the work of Robert Fludd 1629. (Nideck)

Gallicus. Supernas and *Caecias* are to the north and south of *Aquilo,* while *Solanus* is flanked by *Carbas* to its north, and to its south by the *Ornithiae,* which blow at certain times. The southeasterly wind, *Eurus,* is flanked by *Eurocircias* and *Volturnus.* Next comes *Leuconotus,* to the east of the south wind, *Auster.* On the other side is *Altanus. Africus* has *Libonotus* to its south and *Subvesperus* to its north. The west wind, *Favonius,* is flanked by *Argestes,* and, at certain periods, the *Etesiae.* Finally, *Circius* and *Corus* are immediately to the south and north of *Caurus.* Vitruvius also recognized the breezes of the day and winds related to location, an understanding recognized to this day in certain Mediterranean regions.

Vitruvius used the standard eight winds diagram as a means of orienting streets in towns. He arrived at this not by direct observation of the winds themselves, but by drawing a diagram on the ground. Its orientation was based on the erection of a gnomon to measure opposing limbs of the sun, the traditional means of finding the north–south *cardo.* When Vitruvius's work was recognized as the major source of how to design classical architecture, Renaissance architects took the names of the winds from Vitruvius's part of Italy and incorporated them in their work. In laying out the compass rose by means of sun shadows, Vitruvius confused the literal description of actual winds with a figurative use of their names to denote the directions of the compass.

A medieval understanding of the system used by Vitruvius divides the directions into four quarters, whose dividing lines are between the north–south *cardo* and the east–west *decumanus.* Thus, there are four quarters that face the four main directions of north, east, south, and west like the four sides of a foursquare building. According to this division, the half from northwest to southeast, containing north and east, is dry. The other half, containing south and west, is wet. The half between northeast and southwest, containing east and south, is hot; while the other, containing west and north, is cold. This gives each of the quarters a specific quality. The northern quarter is cold and dry; the eastern, hot and dry; the southern hot and wet; and the western, cold and wet.

To enable architects to orient streets properly with regard to

Figure 8.9. Temple of the Winds Castle Howard, Yorkshire, England.
(Nigel Pennick)

the winds, Vitruvius gave intricate descriptions of their nature and properties. "Let the directions of your streets and alleys be laid down on the lines of division between the quarters of two winds," he wrote. This, he claimed, would have the effect of blocking the disagreeable force of the winds from dwellings and rows of houses: "Therefore, the rows of houses must be aligned away from the quarters from which the winds blow, so that as they come in, they may strike the angles of the blocks and their force thereby be broken and dissipated." As principles, Vitruvius's recommendations are valid today, so long as we take our local wind conditions into account.

The Vitruvian understanding of the winds was used by Spanish locators in the American colonies. Instructions for town location, foundation, and layout issued by Spanish kings are explicitly geomantic. The main documents are those issued by King Ferdinand to the locator

Pedrarias Dávila in Mexico in 1513, to the Jeronymite Order in 1518, and instructions for the settlement of the Province of Amichel sent to Francisco de Garay in 1521. These principles were used by the "good geometer" Alonso Garcia Bravo when he laid out Mexico City.

In 1573, King Philip II codified the imperial Spanish geomantic principles. They told the founders of new towns and cities not to select places

> of great elevation, since the winds are troublesome . . . select places of intermediate elevation that enjoy fresh air, especially coming from the north and south, and if there are mountains or hills near the site, they should be to the east or to the west, and if for some reason a place of considerable elevation must be chosen, make sure that it is not subjected to fogs; if the site is by a river, it should be located to the east, so that the rising sun touches first upon the town before it touches the water . . . do not place it near lagoons in which there are poisonous animals and polluted air and water. The four corners of the Plaza face the four principal winds, because in this way the streets leaving the Plaza are not exposed to the principal winds. The Plaza should be a rectangle, prolonged so that the length is at least half again as long as the width, because this form is best for festivities with horses, and for any others that are to take place.

LOCAL WIND TRADITIONS

Although since Vitruvius's time the best architects have recognized that the Vitruvian windrose was rooted in its place of origin, the less able have applied its wind-references unthinkingly to other, inappropriate, places. In this way, they were used as far away as England, Russia, and South America, where the real winds bore no resemblance to the local conditions that Vitruvius was describing in his part of Italy. This is the same literalist problem that dogs those who would transplant a metaphysical system from one place to another, regardless of its suitability. It is prevalent today with literalist practitioners of Feng Shui, where descriptions originating in and tailored to one or another place in China are carried to totally different ones and applied there without modification. Classically, the "bad" directions in Feng Shui, appropriate for the place in which it originated and used indiscriminately by unthinking practitioners, is laughably wrong in others.

Country oral folklore and regional farmers' calendars contain much relevant local windlore. There are numerous vernacular rhymes that recall the effect of various winds. An old Scottish rhyme tells us that the direction of the wind at New Year sets the tone for the future year:

> If on New Year's Night wind blow south,
> It betokeneth warmth and growth;
> If west, much milk and fish in the sea;
> If north, much cold and snow there will be;
> If east, the trees will bear much fruit;
> If northeast, flee it, man and brute.

Another Celtic poem, *The Winds of Fate,* is similar. It tells that the wind blowing at one's birth determines one's future life, a parallel and complement to natal astrology. The first breath that a baby takes is the air of one of the winds, and this affects him or her throughout life.

> The boy who is born when the wind is from the West,
> He shall obtain clothing, food he shall obtain;
> He shall obtain from his lord, I say,
> No more than food and clothing.

> The boy who is born when the wind is from the North,
> He shall win victory, but shall endure defeat.
> He shall be wounded, another shall he wound,
> Before he ascends to an angelic heaven.

> The boy who is born when the wind is from the South,
> He shall get honey, fruit he shall get.
> In his house he shall entertain
> Bishops and fine musicians.

Laden with gold is the wind from the East.
The best wind of all four that blow:
The boy who is born when that wind blows
Want shall never taste in his whole life.

Whenever the wind does not blow
Over the grass of the plain or mountain heather,
Whosoever is then born,
Whether boy or girl, a fool shall be.

Another traditional Irish rhyme tells us of the benefits and drawbacks of each wind:

The East Wind is dry and puts fleece on the sheep.
The West Wind is generous and puts fish in the nets.
The South Wind is moist and makes the seeds flourish.
The North Wind is harsh and makes people glum.

In her *Shiela Ní Gara,* the Irish poet Ethna Carbery (Anna MacManus) wrote of the quality of the winds, with their traditional colors:

Green shears of Hope rise round you like grass-blades
    after drouth,
And there blows a red wind from the East, a white wind
    from the South,
A brown wind from the West, a grádh, a brown wind
    from the West—
But the black, black wind from Northern hills, how can
    you love it best?

In his masterpiece *The Third Policeman,* written in 1940 and published in 1967, the Irish humorous writer Flann O'Brien (Brian O'Nolan, 1911–1966) described the colors of the four winds in similar manner. O'Brien called the north wind "a hard black." The east was deep purple; the south "fine shining silver"; and the West wind, amber.

Like all folk-rhymes and songs, the traditional Scottish and Irish adages applied to specific places, even when they are no longer remembered. Often, though, they have spread widely, and are used indiscriminately in places where they are not valid. Carbery's colors of the "four winds of Eirinn" may also have originated in a certain Irish locality and been extended indiscriminately to the whole island. Even in one small country like England, variations can be enormous. For example, the "bad" direction in London is southwest, while in Cambridge, 80 kilometers (50 miles) to the north of London, it is northwest. Lancashire folk tradition knows that rain is most likely when the wind is in the southern or southwestern "haever." There, the wind can be in a "good haever," and the east is the "lucky haever." The Norse and Celtic traditions of dividing the world into eight *ættir* or airts is yet another traditional way of designating the nature of the winds that blow at any specific place.

Places close to one another can have markedly different direction qualities, so it is clearly folly to apply a foreign fixed system to describe them. Local experience and local knowledge must be respected always over abstract and imported systems of description. Primarily "good" and "bad" directions depend on the winds. The qualities and virtues of the winds at different places depend on the interaction between climate and landscape, and do not have general application. One cannot take a description of the qualities of the directions of one place and apply them elsewhere. One must take notice of local traditions and make measurements to determine the meaning of the winds.

The living tradition in Provence and the Cote d'Azur in the south of France shows the complexity of wind lore that cannot be simplified and extended generally to other places. In southern France, there is a compass rose divided into 32 winds whose meaning varies from place to place and from season to season. A wind from a certain direction in summer may bear a different name from its wintry counterpart. Also, the same wind may come from a different direction in different places, according to local topography. Provençal windmills have diagrams of the winds painted inside. A particularly good version exists in the hilltop mill at Montmajour, near Arles. The standard form of "La Rose Des

Vents" (wind rose) is a basic ideal description that in practice is far more complex. In this wind rose, the north wind is called *Tremountano;* the east, *Levant;* the south, *Marin;* and the west, *Narbounes.* The northeast direction is *Aguieloun;* the southeast, *Eissero;* the southwest, *Labé;* and the northwest, *Mistrau.*

HE'S GROUND HIM BETWEEN ~ TWO STONES

Figure 8.10. The lore of windmills lies at the heart of European location traditions. An illustration from Nigel Pennick's "The John Barleycorn Cycle." (Nigel Pennick)

Figure 8.11. Windmill Thaxted, Essex, England.
(Nigel Pennick)

The complexity of wind designation in Provence shows that the fine understanding of the winds, lost in many places today, is still a living force there. Only a local could give a full description. On the coast, the north-northeast wind is called *Mountagniero* or *Trémontano-greco*. Inland, in Arles, its name is *Trémontanobusso*. The *Trémountano* is a cold, violent wind from the mountains, a northerly on the coast. When it is less strong, it is called *Trémountanello*. The

Figure 8.12. The Rose of the Winds from Provence, France.
(Nigel Pennick)

northeast wind in Nice is called *Grégal*. In autumn, the northeast wind is *Li Rispo,* while in wintertime it is called *Orsuro.* A violent northeasterly is *L'Aguielon.*

The wind from Mont Ventoux, the Celtic holy mountain of the winds sacred to the god Vintios, where Pagan pilgrims left little ceramic wind-horns as offerings, is called *Ventouresco*. The Roman Emperor Augustus erected an altar to the winter wind *Circius* (now called *Noroit*) at Narbonne, as it "chases the clouds and purifies the air." The south wind is called *Miejour, Miejournau,* and *Mijournari.* Its "standard" name on the coast is *Marin,* and when it is fresh and soft, *L'Embat.* In summer, it is *Li Marinado.* In the days of sail, seamen watched out for the arising of the spring wind called *Suroit,* and the breezes and zephyrs coming from Africa, called *Lis Aureto.* At Cap Corse and Bastia, the Provençal sailors were aware of the strong wind *Le Labé.* On land, the character of westerlies depends on local topography. The wind called *Le Pounent* in some places is known as *Narbounés* in Narbonne and *Travesso* in the Rhone Valley.

The *Etésiens* are the periodic winds that rule the Mediterranean during a number of days. In the winter, they blow from the north, and in summer, from the south. Other winds follow one another at certain times of year. The east-southeasterly known as *L'Eissaro, Le Levant-Eissero* or *Siroco,* is followed by *L'Autan,* which is a powerful wind bringing high seas. *L'Eissaro* is also known as *Le Ven Blanc,* "the white wind," recalling the old Celtic description of winds according to color. In spring, the dry and cold westerly wind called *L'Auro-Rousso,* "the red wind," blows across Provence. The qualities and virtues of the winds are real, and recognized in Provence, whose culture embodies a subtle understanding of natural conditions. Thus, the voice of the wind in the Camargue is likened to the lowing of a cow, the *"vaco de Faraman que bramo"* (cow of Faraman, which bellows), and the most famous Provençal wind, the *Mistral* or *Mistrau,* which causes unrest, is personified as Jan D'Arle.

The traditional understanding of landscape in Provence is highly sophisticated. There are a number of traditional trades whose practice embodies detailed knowledge of how to recognize the subtle qualities of any place. The shepherds' techniques of recognizing these qualities, called the ambience of a place, have remarkably fine sensibility for the meaning of places. The traditional Provençal understanding of each place's ambience has led to a remarkable degree of harmony of buildings in the landscape. Provence provides some of the finest instances of European traditional geomancy one can experience. It is a tradition that has continued for thousands of years and lives today.

Although Provence is particularly rich in its wind traditions, all over Europe similar local designations exist. The fishing tradition of the Ammersee in Bavaria, Germany, has its own local wind designation. There are two parallel designations of the eight winds recognized there. One wind rose names the winds from their points of origin, while the other gives them functional names. Because the Ammersee is relatively small, there is much less complexity in wind naming than in the Provençal examples given above. In the functional wind rose, winds from the southeast and south are the *Sunnenwind.* In the other wind rose, the southeasterly is the *Beuberger Wind,* and the southerly, *Gebirgswind,* the mountain wind from the Alps to the south.

The functional windrose calls the northeasterly and easterly *Vorderwind* (front wind), while the westerly is *Hinterwind* (back wind). This is the *Schwabenwind,* coming from Swabia, the land to the west of Bavaria. A southwesterly is *Hochwind* (high wind), which is called *Wessobrunner Wind* in the other wind rose. A northwest wind is *Querwind* or *Zwerchwind* (crosswind). This has no designation as a wind name. To the north is the *Geradeheraufwind,* which is called *Donau,* the wind from the Danube River.

The Ammersee example, like the Provençal, shows that local winds are the primary concern of reality. Theoretical wind roses are meaningless in practical conditions and should have no place in contemporary building design. The planners who worked in Stuttgart on constructing a 109-hectare new city district where the numerous tracks leading to the *Hauptbahnhof* (main station) were put in a tunnel beneath the new development, took the local climate, including the winds, into account. The new streets of Stuttgart 21 are designed so that they do not block the local wind-flows that define the climate of different parts of Stuttgart. This is modern geomancy, in the tradition of Vitruvius and the other old builders, based upon a proper understanding of local climate and weather. The techniques exist, and they are in use. There is nothing else to do but to use them.

CHAPTER 9

Natural Measure

*Dimensions Emergent from
Nature and the Land*

*Harmony in living bodies results from the counterbalancing
of living bodies. Its concordances, its equilibrium, exactly
follows general laws according to order of nature. The great
masters who built the monumental wonders had complete
knowledge of the techniques of their art and were capable of
applying it, having taken it from its original natural sources,
because that science had continued living in them.*

Auguste Rodin (1840–1917)

PRINCIPLES OF NATURAL MEASURE

Natural Measure describes the kind of measures that were used in
Europe before the imposition of, firstly, national systems, and then,
the metric system. The origin of Natural Measure is archaic. Its units
can be detected in the earliest definable measures known to archaeology. Fragments of Natural Measure survive today in the form of the
Mile and its customary subdivisions. Natural Measure is organized in a
direct way. It is a truly user-friendly system, for it is an expression of the
natural characteristics of the world and the materials that compose it.

Over thousands of years, this way has proved the best means of dealing with the practical applications of agriculture, craftsmanship, cooking, and trade. Unlike number-based systems, Natural Measure is part of real, material things. It is not abstract, but nevertheless is based upon an interconnected set of relationships, each of which has its own particular numerical structure, compatible with one another, and, where necessary, divisible by all the main divisors.

As with other spatial and temporal divisions, the traditional European eightfold concept is paramount in Natural Measure. The eightfold division

Figure 9.1. The Canon of Measure. (Nigel Pennick)

of weight, distance, and capacity is related to the geometrical properties of the square rather than the much more recent intellectual concept of number. Dividing something equally three times, the first division being into two equal parts, the second division making four, and finally the third division making eight, links the significant numbers three and eight that is a feature of natural measure. Commonly traditional measures are based upon this natural progression. The use of the sacred number three, giving three successive divisions, thus produces eighths. The eightfold system relates the division of objects to the division of space and time, as in the Etruscan Discipline and the Tides of the Day.

MEASURING LENGTH NATURALLY

One of the most conserved ancient measures appears in multiple form in the Imperial Mile, used officially today in the United Kingdom and the United States of America, and unofficially in the Irish Republic. The unit contained within the Mile is the so-called Northern Cubit. Although the early names of this measure are unknown, the name Northern Cubit was coined by the metrologist Sir Flinders Petrie and it has stuck. As a measure, it was in use before 3000 BCE. Its spread covers the Indus Civilization, Mesopotamia, China, North Africa, and Europe. In Europe, it is associated in the main with the Teutonic nations, being brought by them to the lands where they settled. As the Ell or Elne, it was in official use in Europe as a cloth measure until the nineteenth century. Its half, the Foot, is the basis of English land measure, and is still used in the United Kingdom and some of her former colonies.

Figure 9.2. Medieval City Measures Augsburg Bavaria Germany.
(Nigel Pennick)

In northern Europe, natural measure can be taken as being based upon two related Feet—the Natural Foot and the Northern or Saxon Foot. The latter is equal to half a Northern Cubit or Ell, measuring 13.2 Imperial (British and American) Inches, 33.53 centimeters. This measure is archaic, having been found incised on a shell discovered at Mohenjodaro. Dated at around BCE 2500, the measure was accurately cut and divided into tenths. In Egypt, wooden Cubit measures of the Twelfth Dynasty from Kahun (ca. BCE 1900) bear the Northern Foot, and finely inscribed Royal Cubit rods of the Eighteenth Dynasty (BCE 1567–1320) have the Northern Foot marked next to the eighteenth Digit.

The Teutonic nations were users of this Foot, too. When they began to use it is not clear, but in the year 12 BCE, the Roman general and governor, Nero Claudius Drusus, was compelled to adopt the Northern Foot as a standard in Roman controlled provinces in the north, as it was the customary measure among the Tungri tribe in Lower Germany. This Foot, defined officially by the Romans as "two digits longer than the *Pes*" (8 Roman Digits instead of the 16 Digits in the Roman Foot) gives a value of 33.325 centimeters.

Our earliest English records of the Saxon Foot, identical with the

NATURAL MEASURE

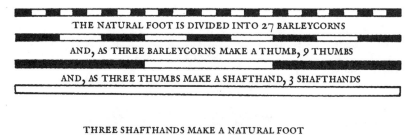

THE NATURAL FOOT IS DIVIDED INTO 27 BARLEYCORNS

AND, AS THREE BARLEYCORNS MAKE A THUMB, 9 THUMBS

AND, AS THREE THUMBS MAKE A SHAFTHAND, 3 SHAFTHANDS

THREE SHAFTHANDS MAKE A NATURAL FOOT

FOUR SHAFTHANDS MAKE A NORTHERN (SAXON) FOOT

Figure 9.3. Natural measure is based upon a simple progression of dimensions that can be used without complex mathematical or algebraic calculations. (Nigel Pennick)

Northern Foot, are primarily from land measure. It is the basis of the Rod, otherwise called the Pole or Perch, the Rood of Land, the Acre, the Furlong, and the Mile. These measures are also multiples of the Natural Foot, which was used in Celtic countries, also for measuring land. The Natural and Saxon Feet are both submultiples of the Rod. The Natural Foot is one twentieth, and the Saxon Foot, one fifteenth. This gives a ratio of 3:4 between the two feet (which is the same ration of the musical interval of a Fourth). It allows direct conversion. The Natural Foot was not confined to the British Isles, for it was long conserved in the south of France where the land measure of the *Canne,* comprising eight Natural feet, defines much land measure. In Marseilles, five *Cannes* made a *Pan,* twice the length of the English Rod.

Figure 9.4. The length of the medieval German locator's pole, measuring 16 feet, is traditionally taken from men coming out of church on a Sunday morning. An engraving from Jacob Köbel's Geometrey. (Nideck)

The Natural and Saxon Feet are both subdivided into Palms or Shafthands, three for the Natural Foot and four for the Saxon. Each Shafthand is again subdivided into three Thumbs, each of which is again subdivided into three Barleycorns. The smallest unit in natural measure is thus the Barleycorn, which measures 0.37 Imperial Inches (9.3 mm). Each Thumb thus measures 1.1 Imperial Inches (2.79 cm); each Shafthand or Palm 3.3 Imperial Inches (8.38 cms). The Natural Foot thus measures 27 Barleycorns and the Saxon Foot 36. These are multiples of the Northern Tradition sacred number, nine. Above the level of the Foot, the division becomes predominantly eightfold. The basic system is thus as follows:

One Thumb consists of 3 Barleycorns.

One Shafthand consists of 3 Thumbs (9 Barleycorns).

One Natural Foot consists of 3 Shafthands (9 Thumbs, 27 Barleycorns).

One Saxon Foot consists of 4 Shafthands (12 Thumbs, 36 Barleycorns).

One Ell consists of 2 Saxon Feet (8 Shafthands, 24 Thumbs, 72 Barleycorns).

One Fathom consists of 3 Ells (6 Saxon Feet, 24 Shafthands, 72 Thumbs, 216 Barleycorns).

One Rod consists of 15 Saxon Feet (60 Shafthands, 180 Thumbs, 540 Barleycorns). This measure is also equal to 20 Natural Feet.

One Furlong consists of 40 Rods (600 Saxon Feet, 800 Natural Feet).

One Mile consists of 8 Furlongs (4,800 Saxon Feet, 6,400 Natural Feet, 800 Fathoms).

The numbers 540 and 800 present in this system appear in Norse cosmology in a description of Odin's Hall, Valhalla. Valhalla is said to have 540 doors, from each of which emerge 800 warriors called the *Einherjar*. Thus, there are 432,000 in all, the number of Barleycorns in 800 Rods (20 Furlongs). This numerological description of the great hall and its contents demonstrates the northern European understanding of the unity of the cosmos, where seemingly different things are shown to have significant numerical relationships with one another.

NATURAL AREA MEASURE

Measures of area are derived directly from the linear Rod of 15 Saxon Feet. The Rod of Land is the area defined by a rectangle measuring one linear Rod by one Furlong, that is, 15 by 600 Saxon Feet, 20 by 800 Natural Feet. The area is thus 9,000 square Saxon Feet and 16,000 square Natural Feet. Four Roods of land make one Acre. It is an area defined as 60 by 600 Saxon Feet or 80 by 800 Natural Feet. In area, the Acre measures 36,000 square Saxon Feet or 64,000 square Natural Feet. One Acre is thus an area of 10 by 100 Fathoms, 1,000 square Fathoms.

Ten Acres make one Ferdelh or Ferlingate. This is a square Furlong, 600 by 600 Saxon Feet, 800 by 800 Natural Feet; in area, 36,000 square Saxon Feet and 64,000 square Natural Feet. Four Ferlingata make one Townyard or Virgate. Traditionally, towns were divided into four districts called Ferlings, the extent of each ideally was a Ferlingate in area. The inner part of Huntingdon, the county town of Old Huntingdonshire, is a good example in England of a Townyard of four Ferlings. Customarily, each of the four town Ferlings is a separate parish, with its own church. Finally, in land measure, four Townyards or Virgata make a Hide of land. The basic system of area in natural measure is thus as follows:

One Rood consists of 9,000 square Saxon Feet.
One Acre consists of 4 Roods.
One Ferlingate consists of 10 Acres.
One Townyard (Virgate) consists of 4 Ferlingata (40 acres, 160 Roods).
One Hide consists of 4 Townyards (Virgata) (160 Acres, 640 Roods).

ALTERATIONS AND MODIFICATIONS OF NATURAL MEASURE

When the Normans conquered England in 1066, the old Saxon and Celtic measures then in use were not altered, for King William I wished to appear to be the lawful successor of the Anglo-Saxon monarchs. Thus, William the Conqueror confirmed the new measure in his new laws: "Concerning measures and weights, they shall have throughout the whole kingdom measures most trustworthy and duly certified, and weights most trustworthy and duly certified, just exactly as the good predecessors have appointed." Successive kings of England likewise certified and ratified the existing traditional measures.

In addition to the Feet of natural measure, there were a number of other Feet used in Britain for different purposes. The Feet used in medieval Britain were the Natural Foot (25.1 cm in modern measurement); the Roman Foot (29.6 cm); the Greek Common Foot (31.7 cm); and the Saxon Foot (33.5 cm). The Natural Foot was used in land measure, mainly in Wales; the Greek and Roman Feet were used by architects and builders, while the Saxon Foot was applied to land measure, buildings, and handicrafts.

But in 1305, King Edward I, a victorious and powerful monarch who re-founded the legal system, also reformed the weights and measures of his realms, beginning the centralizing tendency toward standardization that has continued until the present day. Before reforming measure, Edward had founded many new towns according to geomantic principles located and designed by the Locators James St. George and Henry le Waleys, among others. Edward assumed the title "Rex et Bastidor" (King and founder of fortified towns), and, in his *Statute for Measuring Land,* reorganized measurement, based on a standard iron yard made for the express purpose.

The 1305 Statute stated:

It is ordained that three grains of barley, dry and round, make an Inch, twelve Inches make a foot, three Feet make an Ulna, five and a half Ulne make a Rod, and forty Rods in length and four in breadth make an Acre.

And it is to be remembered that the Iron Ulna of Our Lord the King, contains iii Feet and no more, and the Foot must contain xii inches measured by the correct measure of this kind of Ulna; that is to say, the thirty-sixth part of the said Ulna makes i inch neither more nor less; and five and a half Ulne make i Rod, sixteen feet and a half, by the aforesaid Iron Ulna of Our Lord the King.

Edward I's lawyers were forced to redefine "this kind of Ulna" (the Yard) to distinguish it from the Saxon Ell or Ulna. The Statute thus introduced the English Yard as the standard new measure, not the Rod. This was soon subdivided according to traditional principles into eight and sixteen. One sixteenth of a yard became the Nail, a measure used in British weaving and clothes making until this century. Likewise the Yard was used at Cambridge for dividing butter into ounces: according to ancient statute a pound of butter was rolled into a regular cylinder a Yard in length, then by halving, halving, halving again and so on, sixteen equal pieces—a Nail in length and weighing an ounce—were produced. This system was in use until the middle of the nineteenth century.

Edward's metrologists also compressed the Barleycorn so that three made an Inch rather than the older Saxon Thumb. This new English measure, later given the grander title of Imperial Measure, was a compromise that was intended to unify the measures of the land so that taxation and regulations could be more easily enforced. Land measure, such as the Rod, Rood, Acre, and Mile, could not be changed, as they were the basis of land ownership and the dimensions of farm and town alike.

So, the Rod was taken as the starting point and divided rather clumsily into sixteen and a half feet, or 198 inches. This is nowhere near as convenient as the Saxon division of 15 feet and 180 Thumbs. This revision produced the inconvenient measure of the Mile as being 5,280 English Feet rather than the eminently divisible 4,800 Saxon Feet. In later years, this inconvenience was one of the factors that enabled bureaucratic state authorities to abolish Imperial and other European traditional measures by the Metric System, despite it being inherently less convenient to use in physical reality but easier to calculate theoretically.

THE MEASURE OF THE LAND

In medieval times, each settlement or region had its own measure, tailored to local conditions. In Central Europe, the Holy Roman Empire was insufficiently powerful to impose a single empire-wide system of weights and measures. Instead more appropriate local systems evolved. As a result, the local legal measurements of the city are often marked on the prominent public building, most usually the main church. For example, the main entrance of the minster Unserer Lieben Frau in Freiburg im Breisgau in south Germany has the size measures for the bread of the city. These and the linear measures of Freiburg were defined by the *Locator Civitatis* of Konrad von Zähringen when the city was founded in the year 1120. In Bern, another Zähringer-founded city and capital of Switzerland, the Bernese foot and shoe are depicted under the medieval clock tower of the city along with murals depicting the foundation of the city.

In a similar way, in the early nineteenth century, the British Imperial measures were set in granite in the north wall of Trafalgar Square in London. As in the Central European tradition, the British standards at Trafalgar Square were not for ornament, but for practical reference. In the absence of reliable commercial measures, they were used well into the twentieth century to check the accuracy of measuring tools.

Among others, the engineers of the early deep underground railway lines in London—the "tubes"—used the Trafalgar Square measures. Needing pinpoint accuracy to drive their tunnels in the three-dimensional environment beneath the city streets, the surveyors at the end of the nineteenth century always worked from first principles. The tunnel builders made their own surveys between mark points, which they fixed themselves by direct observation.

In August 1898, before commencing their survey, the engineers of the Baker Street and Waterloo underground railway (now the Bakerloo Line) checked their surveyors' chain against the Trafalgar Square measures. The chief surveyor of this line, F. E. Wentworth-Shields, then made solar observations to determine his own meridian (true north–south line) on the south bank of the Thames. The "true meridian" was measured with a theodolite, by observing the sun in the morning and afternoon, and, after making the necessary corrections for changes in delineation, bisecting the angle to obtain the meridian. Based on principles that the ancient Egyptians had used, Wentworth-Shields's survey was a success and the tunnels were driven with masterly accuracy.

Figure 9.5. The street grid of Bury St Edmunds in Suffolk,
laid out around the year 1050, has two parallel main streets,
480 feet apart, the southern of which is oriented along the
axis of the abbey church.
(Nigel Pennick)

Figure 9.6. A view of laborers at the clay face digging the Baker Street and Waterloo railway tunnel, London 1890s. The wooden cross hanging from the crown of the tunnel is a survey marker that was sighted indirectly from the original meridian on the surface. (Electric Traction Publications)

THE SIGNIFICANCE OF NATURAL MEASURE

Neither ancient nor modern architects have been able to find anything else in the world which could better serve as a measure for designing the arrangement of their works than this model, man.

GERARD THIBAULT, *L'ACADEMIE DE L'ESPEE* (1628)

According to one medieval Christian symbolic idea, the cosmos can be viewed in terms of architectonic measure. This view was expressed by the Cistercian poet Alain de Lille (Alanus ab Insulis, ca. 1128–1202/3), who described God as the Architect of the World. This is the symbol taught by Freemasonry. According to this philosophy, God as creator chose the numerical and geometrical ratios of the spheres, the planets, Nature, and music. Creation's measure was defined by man, the human being's body, itself seen as the image of God. By contemplating these structures and ratios, which are within our own bodies as well as the structure of the cosmos, Christian mystics believe that people can approach the deity who created them. By using these measures, creation can be extended according to the principles. Every time we use them, we perform the act of "sub-creation," in the image of creation.

However, the literalism of number has all but triumphed over the symbolic understanding of the divine cosmos. The transition between direct experience of the world and its manipulation in abstract terms is nowhere better demonstrated than in measure, exemplified by the near-universal triumph of the Metric System over traditional measures. The craftsperson, the cook, and the dealer in materials on a direct level all need systems of measurement for immediate use, and it is clear that this means using natural divisors, two being the most obvious and wide-spread. Thus the Cooks' Measure, in use despite irrational attempts to replace it with numbers, is a practical and direct way of measuring the materials of food. Yet ours is largely a digital world of number, paper-work, computing, calculating, and everything that this alienated mode of being represents.

The craftsperson, cook, and gardener deal with physical reality, while the numerically based person manipulates mathematics. Each to his or her own, of course, but in this era of implicit universalism, there is the hidden inference that everything will one day be standardized. This is not new, for we have seen how successive monarchs attempted to standardize measures so that they could more readily extract taxes from their subjects. But since the French Revolution in 1789, a new superstition has come into being, that only the decimal system can be used to describe existence numerically. In the darkest days of the French revolutionary Terror, the day was divided into ten hours of 100 minutes each, and the Metric System was imposed upon the people as part of the program of rationalization. Since then, French revolutionary principles have had their ups and downs, but the decimalization of the world, and its expression in number, which was seen by the French revolutionaries as the only rational way to live, has grown apace.

The beautiful symbolic subtlety of the Natural Foot and its divisions, or the inherent usefulness of the spoonful, the Pint, and its multiples, contrasts with systems whose only attractiveness comes from the ease of adding figures. The saddest part of all of this is the fact that, just as the tenfold view of the world was rolling over all others, advances in computing rendered any universal system unnecessary. Contemporary technology allows the immediate and automatic conversion of one unit into another. The need for compulsory standardization is past, and we can choose whatever measure best fits what we are doing. Pluralism is facilitated by a technology based, like many traditional systems, on binary mathematics. But to those who rule, "globalization"—their word for universal standardization—seems to be the only way to go. The wish to standardize all things, even to the ludicrous extreme of altering the lengths of beds or the sizes of doors into "round figures" in Metric, has become so powerful that certain measures are no longer just unofficial but actually illegal.

In the 1940s, the modern architect Le Corbusier (Charles Edouard Jeanneret, 1887–1965) recognized the ineffectiveness of using mere Metric numbers to define measures within architecture. So he looked for a harmonic proportional system that would better measure his buildings. Accordingly, he reinvented tradition and devised a system of measuring-scales based on the height of a man, six English feet, developed through the Golden Section ratio (1:1.618). He called this measuring system *Modulor,* the "golden module." Subsequently, he used it as the basis for his buildings. In 1947, for the foundation of his famous apartment block in Marseilles, L'Unite d'Habitation, he designed the foundation stone according to traditional principles, but incorporating his *Modulor.* The stone measured 183 by 86 by 86 centimeters, and contained a recess 53 by 16.5 by 27, in which the ceremonial papers (foundation deposit), were sealed. "The great stone, consecrated eight days later," wrote Corbusier, "possessed dignity and elegance." It was laid ceremonially on October 14, 1947. Thus, the proportions of the foundation stone were a reflection of the whole future building, expressing the traditional principles of self-similarity in a new form.

CHAPTER 10

Traditional Time–Telling

Sunlight and Shadow

Fear not, my friend . . . for know, that every particular
*Nature certainly and constantly produces what is good to
itself; unless something* foreign *disturbs or hinders it. . . .
every* particular *Nature thrives, and attains its perfection,
if nothing from* without *obstructs it.*

ANTHONY ASHLEY COOPER,
THIRD EARL OF SHAFTESBURY (1671–1713),
THE MORALISTS (1709)

SOLAR PHENOMENA OF PLACE

In the natural world, the horizon around us can be seen as forming a 360-degree circle, with us at the center. Each direction point on the horizon relates directly to a time of day, which is defined as the time when the sun appears to be present there. In reality, it is the direction from which the light comes. Even during the hours of darkness, the sun is still in its corresponding time direction, but "beneath the Earth" and thus invisible. Owing to the apparent daily motion of the sun, the eight basic directions of the sun define the times of day. When we tell the time on a sunny day, as our ancestors did, we do so by noting the direction of the sun. This can be done either directly by observing the sun's position or indirectly by inspecting the shadow cast by the gnomon of a sundial. In the northern hemisphere, the most basic observation is that when the apparent position of the sun is due south, then it is noon or midday. Irrespective of the season of the year, the noonday sun always stands due south of the observer. This is almost exactly half-way between the azimuths of sunrise and sunset, and for practical purposes of determining the meridian by measuring shadows, we assume it is.

However, the azimuths of sunrise and sunset are not constant, but vary with the seasons. At the spring and autumnal equinoxes, when the length of day and night are equal, on a horizon level with the observer, the sun rises in the due east and sets in the due west. This makes the length of daylight on these two days in the year exactly half of the 24-hour cycle. On the longest day of the year, the summer solstice, both sunrise and sunset are at their most northerly positions (in the northern hemisphere, as this is discussing the European tradition). At the other end of the year, the winter solstice, the day's length is its shortest. Correspondingly, both sunrise and sunset at midwinter are at their most southerly limit. The angle of midwinter sunrise/sunset is equal in angle south of the equinoctial (east–west) line that the summer solstices are north of it. After the winter solstice, the sun rises and sets progressively northward until the summer solstice is reached. After this, sunrises and sunsets occur progressively southward until the winter solstice is reached again, and so the cycle continues. Halfway between the two solstices lie the equinoxes.

In the Northern Tradition, it is customary to observe the azimuth of the sun, whose direction indicates the tide or hour of the day. This is accomplished readily by reference to physical landmarks visible from a central viewing-place. In the traditional landscape, prominent features served as day-markers. In the main, they were natural elements of the country such as mountain peaks, hilltops, headlands, and sea-stacks. Where no suitable natural markers existed, people set up artificial markers. These included cairns of stones, standing stones, stone crosses, artificial notches in the horizon, and specially planted trees. When the sun rose, set, or stood over them, local people knew that it was then the corresponding time of day. In the parts of northern and central

Europe where this system was used, the markers were known in different places and times as a *Dagsmark*, "*Eykt* mark," *dægmælspilu*, Ward Hill, or Point-de-Jour. The tradition of using such markers continued in use in the Faeroe Islands until the 1940s. Although none of them are in use for these functions today, many of these ancient markers do still exist in the landscape. In some districts, the names of prominent features still recall their time-telling function. Where this system existed fully, the whole landscape was a means of time-telling, not only of the time of day, but of the season, and even special days, too. Because sunrises and sunsets occur at certain places corresponding with the time of year, these horizon markers also served as indicators of the seasons and festivals.

MARKING REAL TIME

There are many possible ways that we can mark the passing of time. Most of them are based upon a regular division of daily solar movement. This brings us two basic possibilities. The first is the regular division of the cycle of day and night as a whole. This is the basis of the present 24-hour clock. The other method is to measure hours as divisions of the whole period of daylight, beginning at sunrise or sunset. The first division is regular throughout the year, for the daily cycle is for all intents and purposes constant. The second system, called "temporary hours," varies from day to day, according to the length of day in the season.

In his book, *A History of the Church of the Holy Sepulchre* (1897), J. Charles Cox wrote:

> The Greek and Latin method of dividing day and night into 24 hours, though doubtless introduced into Britain during the centuries that it was a Roman province, seems for the most part to have died out with the departure of our rulers. The invading tribes that subsequently settled in England, knew little or nothing of the more civilized system, and whether Angles or Norsemen, were accustomed to the octaval division of day-night, with its subdivision into 16, which still exists in Iceland and the Faeroe Islands.

In northern latitudes, the eightfold division of the Northern Tradition is a far more practical way of dividing the day than the duodecimal system. The variation in the length of summer and winter days, and hence their subdivisions, is too great for a twelvefold system to accommodate successfully. However, the traditional eightfold system was abandoned gradually after the Norman conquest.

In the Mediterranean region, it was customary to divide the day into twelve parts from sunrise to sunset, the "temporary hours" or "Babylonish Hours." An alternative variant of this system is the "Italian Hours" division, which reckons hours elapsed since sunset on the previous evening. This system is far from ideal, for it requires complex geometries to be marked out on sundials. It has the added disadvantage of working progressively less well the nearer one gets to the poles. The further away from the equator one is, then the greater the difference in day-length between winter and summer, and the greater the variation in length of the twelve "temporary hours" of the day. It was this system that the Christian Church attempted to import into northern Europe to replace the more practical system of the eight tides.

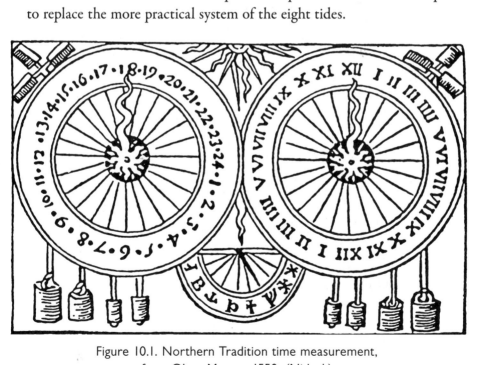

Figure 10.1. Northern Tradition time measurement, from Olaus Magnus 1550. (Nideck)

OLD SUNDIALS IN THE BRITISH ISLES

There are a number of very ancient sundials still extant on old churches in the British Isles and mainland Europe. These are called different names but are the same thing: Sexton's Wheel, Scratch Dial, and Mass-Clock. Perhaps the (translated) Anglo-Saxon name of Sun Markers is most appropriate. Their specific function, other than generally telling the time, is not known, but many experts agree that their occurrence on churches indicates that they may have had some function in indicating the times of religious services. This is why they are sometimes called Mass Clocks. Usually, they are composed of just a few lines scratched into the ashlar stone surround of a door or window, but in a few cases, they are more ornate, being fully carved dials with inscriptions. Invariably, they are vertical dials. According to the Anglo-Saxon grammarian, Ælfric (ca. 950–1021), in Anglo-Saxon England there were professional sundial-readers who bore the title *dægmælsceawere* (daymark-shewer) or *tidsceawere* (tide-shewer). These people were local time-announcers, whose duty it was to observe the dial and to tell the tides to local people.

The earliest dateable sun markers have a fourfold division of the day, while later ones tend to reconcile the eightfold division of vernacular custom with the twelvefold division derived from Mediterranean usage. In Ireland, the earliest sun markers incised on upright stone slabs divide the day into four. They date from the seventh century onward. One can still be seen in the churchyard at Kells, and another at Monasterboice. A seventh-century sundial at the church at Escombe in County Durham, England, also has a simple fourfold division. It is likely to be one of the oldest still in situ in England. Similar Saxon dials divided into four tides exist on the churches at Warnford and Corhampton in Hampshire, and at Daglingworth in Gloucestershire.

The standing stone cross at Bewcastle in Cumbria, which dates from around the year 675 CE, has a dial divided fourfoldly. It is marked by bold lines, each area of which is divided into three sections by fainter lines. Another notable ancient sun-marker, dating from between 1056 and 1066, exists at Kirkdale, Yorkshire. On the south side of the church

Figure 10.2. Ancient eightfold sundial stone, Kells, Ireland.
(Nigel Pennick)

is a stone more than two meters long that has a dial at the center of an inscription in Anglo-Saxon. The dial is divided by lines into eight sub-divisions, three marked with a cross line at right angles, and one with an elder form *Hagal* rune. Part of the inscription reads: *ÞIS IS DÆGES SOLMERCA ÆT ILCVM TIDE*—"This is the day's sun-marker at every tide."

Figure 10.3. A sundial designed and constructed by Nigel Pennick, 1998, on a private house in the Schurwald in south Germany. (Nigel Pennick)

Some of the extant ancient dials seem to have been attempts to reconcile the eightfold division of the horizon with "temporary hours," an impossible task without the refinements of geometry we see in later sundials. For instance, the *Dægmæl* Point, at 7:30 a.m. in modern terms, which was the beginning of the workday in the winter half of the year, is often marked on ancient sundials by the *Hægl* rune or by a swastika, as at Aldborough in Yorkshire. Because they were superseded by mechanical clocks and watches, the great number of carved sun-markers that probably existed has been whittled away by the ravages of time. It may be surmised that whole types or classes of sundial, which once were in general use, have been completely destroyed, and are only hinted at in surviving literature.

At the same time that monks or priests were scratching dials on walls in the British Isles, and shepherds were thrusting dods (straight sticks, traditionally of hazel or willow) into the earth, sophisticated dials and geared calculating machines were in everyday use in Constantinople, Baghdad, and Cairo. These allowed the users to calculate forthcoming astronomical events, such as on which days the phases of the moon would fall. The best-preserved of these is the so-called Antikythera mechanism, discovered in a shipwreck almost a century ago, and dated at around 80 BCE. Several other, less complex, geared calculator-sundials are known dating from then to about 500 CE. The more sophisticated machines were long the preserve of Arab instrument-makers. In their geared mechanisms, they were the direct forerunners of powered mechanical clocks.

TRUE LOCAL TIME

Despite the universal use of clock time to "tell the time," in most cases clock time does not show the true local time, that is, time defined by the actual visible position of the sun at the place where we are. Standard times, arranged in arbitrary zones, from which our clock time is taken, were set up for the convenience of transport, commerce, and politics.

Rarely does their time-telling correspond with true local time. Real time is defined by taking midday (high noon) as the primary reference point. Midday is defined as the moment when the sun stands due south. This is known as local apparent noon. Because the Earth is rotating, when we tell the time by the sun, we are seeing its apparent position in relation to our viewing point. So the time shown directly by the sun's position, or indirectly by a shadow cast by the sun, is known technically as Local Apparent Time (LAT) or True Local Time (TLT).

True local time is shown by the traditional sundial. Because any one time is localized to any specific meridian (places on a north–south line on the Earth's surface), no two places that are not on the same meridian have the same true local time. A meridian is any imaginary line that runs in a direct north–south line from the North Pole to the South Pole. When the sun stands above a meridian, the time at any place along it is true local noon. Places to the east of the meridian are

Figure 10.4. Gate of Honour with sundials
Gonville and Caius College Cambridge. (Nigel Pennick)

in the afternoon, and to its west in the forenoon. All places along the meridian itself are at noon. It follows that only the sites on the meridian, places with the same longitude, are at the mean time of the time zone that defines the meridian. Places east or west of the meridian must have different times. A place 15 degrees east or west of the meridian will be one hour behind or in front, respectively, of that meridian.

Depending on the latitude, the actual physical distance on the ground varies. But even a relatively small distance east or west of a meridian really makes a significant time difference. In the Northern Hemisphere, the further north one goes, the shorter the distance becomes. At latitude 30 degrees, the east–west distance that makes a time difference of one second is 1,316 feet (401 m); at latitude 35 degrees, it is 1,245 feet (380 m); for latitude 45 degrees, the distance is 1,075 feet (328 m); at latitude 50 degrees, it is 977 feet (299 m); and for latitude 55 degrees, it is 872 feet (266 m).

Clocks are mechanical or electronic systems that run at a precisely fixed and constant rate. Because of this, we tend to think of all time measurement as proceeding precisely and regularly like a clock. But

Figure 10.5. Sundial by "New Art" architect Herbert Ibberson, Hunstanton, Norfolk 1908. (Nigel Pennick)

because the Earth is part of Nature, and not a rigid, humanmade, mechanical structure, days measured by the sun are not regular. They vary in length at different times of the year when compared to regular clock time, and these variations are cyclic, related to the orbit of the Earth around the Sun.

Solar time, observed of course from the rotation of the Earth, is not mechanically regular like a clock. So the apparent solar motion—true local time—is irregular when measured according to human mechanistic timekeeping, Sundials, which show solar time, were not suitable for use in navigation or regular services such as railroad timetables. Because of this, official time is reckoned from a hypothetical "accurate" Sun, which moves at a constant speed on the celestial equator. This is an artificial construct, so the Sun appears to run sometimes ahead of the clock, and at other times runs behind it. As Mean Time is used universally, this means that true solar midday, twelve noon, when the sun stands due south on the meridian, is not the same as clock midday. In mid-February, the sun stands on the meridional line nearly 14½ minutes later than clock twelve noon, while in late October and early November, the sun arrives at the meridian 16½ minutes earlier than clock twelve noon.

Only on April 16, June 14, September 2, and December 25 in most years of the four-year leap-year cycle, true local time coincides with this fictitious averaged time. This fictitious hypothetical standard day is actually the basis of clock time, the Mean Time used almost everywhere on Earth. The equation of time diagram can be used to read off the difference between mean time and true solar time on any particular date.

The current disuse of true local time is a major symptom of modernity's separation of human beings from Nature. Like every other destructive usage, this was not a sudden event, but the result of a long process. The first deviation from the universal use of true local time came when weight-driven mechanical clocks were perfected. From these unnaturally regular machines came first the concepts of Mean Time and then Standard Time. The first effect of mechanical clocks was to replace the measuring of true local time by sundials with the regular

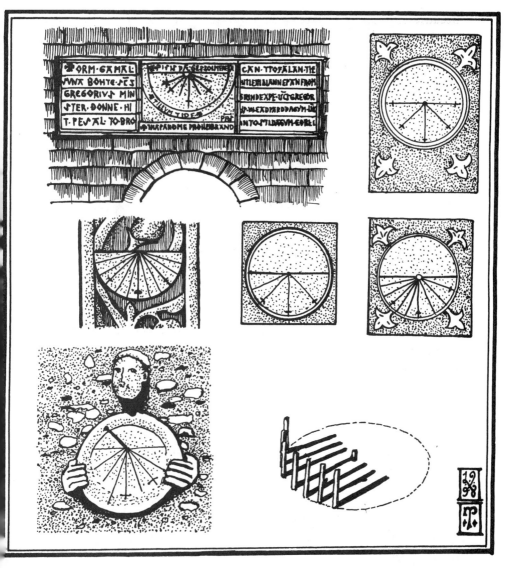

Figure 10.6. Old English Sundials.

Top line: Left, Anglo-Saxon sundial of immediate pre-Conquest date on the church at Kirkdale, Yorkshire. *Right:* Ancient dial at Warnford, Hampshire.

Middle Line: Left, sundial on the late seventeenth-century high cross at Bewcastle, Cumbria. *Center:* Daglingworth, Gloucestershire.
Right: St Michael's, Winchester, Hampshire.

Lower line: Left, Anglo-Saxon sundial, North Stoke Church, Oxfordshire.
Right: a traditional Shepherd's Dial with peripheral gnomons.
(Nigel Pennick)

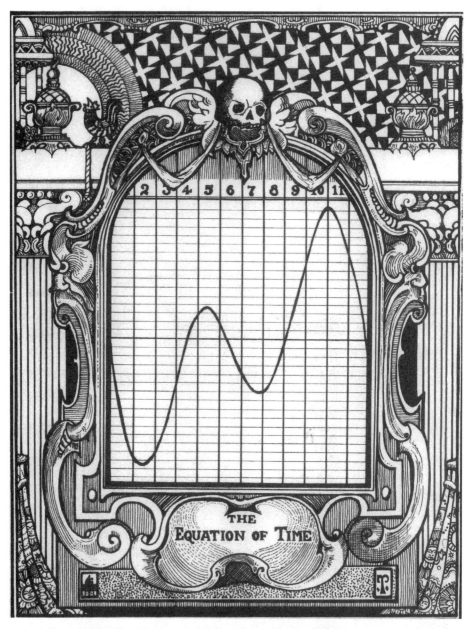

Figure 10.7. The Equation of Time. The top numbers are the months
of the year. The center line is zero and the lines each represent a
minute plus (+) above the center line and a minute minus (−) below it.
So the amount of time that solar time is running early or late
according to clock time can be read off from the curve.
(Nigel Pennick)

mechanical Local Mean Time. The apparent motion of the Sun was replaced by a mechanically regular time-reckoning. Clocks removed direct observation and, because of the cultural tendency of humans to admire regularity, soon made sundials appear inaccurate.

From the late seventeenth century, certain master clockmakers sought to make clocks that could show true local time, and the East Anglian clockmaker Ahasuerus Fromenteel (ca. 1607–ca. 1693) produced clocks with the "equation kidney" that showed true solar time. The equation kidney is a mechanical device invented by Fromanteel that has a shape based upon the mathematics of the equation of time, enabling a hand on the clock to point to true solar time on any day;

Figure 10.8. A Noon-mark sundial on the south-facing facade of the town hall at Wissembourg, Alsace, France. (Nigel Pennick)

the clock is also continuing a calendar mechanism with the month and date. One of the oldest examples of this type of clock is still working in the elegant Pump Room at Bath. But despite Fromenteel's ingenious invention, it was cheaper to make strictly regular clocks. Strictly regular clocks, or chronometers, were also needed for maritime navigation, and clockmakers strove for greater regularity rather than greater accuracy at following true local time by the Sun.

Figure 10.9. Medieval Zodiacal city clock Prague Czech Republic.
(Nigel Pennick)

With the advent of relatively fast national communication systems, such as railways and telegraphs, national time was invented. In England, where this happened first, railway companies enforced standard times based on the Mean Time at company headquarters or the accepted meridian of the capital city. No longer could true local time be used when trains started running to a timetable. Some of the earliest instances came in the 1840s, when the first long-distance railway lines opened between London and Southampton and London and Bristol. Both ran in a predominantly east and west direction, which meant that the true local time at each end of the lines were considerably different. In order to run trains, it was found necessary to draw up timetables, and these required that the time should be standardized on all parts of the company's property.

Because of these new timetabled transport links, the inhabitants of Southampton and Bristol and places in between abandoned the use of true local time and started to use London time instead. It was not long before the mean time on the London meridian, London Mean Time was made compulsory in Great Britain. For a period, this imposed national time was known as Railway Time or Parliament Time, but soon it was taken for granted, and true local time was no longer recognized.

TIME ZONES

Finally, with the establishment of the Greenwich Meridian in 1886, a worldwide system of zones was set up, partly as the result of worldwide telegraphic communication. Greenwich Mean Time was based around the zero meridian of Britain, located at the Royal Observatory at Greenwich in southeast London. From the Greenwich Meridian, further meridians at 15 degrees and multiples of 15 degrees were defined. According to this new world time system, every place within that time zone, stretching for 7 minutes and 30 seconds on either side of any designated meridian, had the same mean time.

This means that places near zonal boundaries have a Standard Time that has little connection with true local time as told from the position of the Sun. Places 7 degrees 30 minutes east of the meridian are a half-hour in front of meridional Mean Time, and those 7 degrees 30 minutes west are a half-hour behind. This is a very coarse system, to which must be added the problem that time zones are also determined by other political factors. National boundaries and other similar factors confuse the strict limits of time zones, and so any place may be up to two hours different from actual solar time, and three hours when so-called Daylight Saving Time is implemented in summertime.

Over the years, there has been another tendency, that is to absorb relatively accurate local time zones into increasingly inappropriate larger ones. This has usually taken place as the result of war or economic union. For example, Dublin, 6 degrees 15 minutes west of London, had a time 25 minutes behind London until October 1, 1916, when (along with the rest of Ireland) it was "brought into line" with London, per-haps as a result of the nationalist uprising. Until then, although it was part of the United Kingdom, all of Ireland had used Dublin time since the advent of railways.

When the Irish Free State broke away from the United Kingdom in 1921, nevertheless it kept London Mean Time. The skewed daylight in the west of Ireland, according to clock time, is noticeable to any visi-tor from Great Britain. The Netherlands used an even more accurate time zone 19 minutes and 32.1 seconds fast of Greenwich Time until 1940, when it was "rounded up" to 20 minutes. It was finally abolished in 1950, when Central European Time, based on the meridian that runs through the Baltic island of Bornholm, was imposed. When it was part of the British Empire, Aden, in south Arabia, had a time 2 hours, 29 minutes, and 54 seconds in front of that at Greenwich, and certain parts of Arabia and India still use true local time.

Most large countries, however, are divided into several separate time zones. The United States has four major zones, set up in 1883 by an agreement between the railroad companies, who devised the idea of adjacent zones with one hour's difference in time from one another. The former Soviet Union had no fewer than eleven time zones. The cen-tralized Communist regime in China, however, insisted that the whole country, including the occupied land of Tibet, must have only one. This was enforced despite the size of Chinese territory, which covers an area from around 75 degrees East to around 125 degrees East. This is over three hours difference in true local time from east to west, an absurdity in practical terms, but an example of authoritarian disregard for Nature. At the time of writing, Western Europe, excepting the British Isles, is in a time zone that is actually based upon Mean Time calculated on the meridian of 15 degrees East. The position of this meridian may be visualized as a north–south line running some miles to the east of Prague in the Czech Republic and through the island of Bornholm in the Baltic Sea.

In parts of Western Europe using Central European Time, the clocks can be giving a reading that is over an hour in front of the true local time. In the summer, with "daylight saving time," this becomes two hours and more. Almost half of the European Union—that is, the territory west of 7 degrees 30 minutes East—is using a clock an hour ahead of the proper mean time for the time zone. Unfortunately, at the time of writing, there are still those in British politics who wish to base the time zones of the United Kingdom and the Irish Republic on Bornholm mean time. The result of this would mean midwinter sunrise in the north of Scotland and the north of Ireland at around 11:00 a.m., clearly an absurd dislocation of harmony with natural phenomena. In the early 1990s, Portugal, which lies as far west as Ireland, went onto Central European Time, but the mistake became apparent when its real effects were seen, and now it has reverted to the Greenwich standard.

TIME DISLOCATION

As if this were not the only dislocation, as a consequence of two world wars, additional alterations have been made to timekeeping. Known variously as "Summer Time," "Daylight Saving Time," and "War Time," this is an additional hour added to the mean time of the time zone. It "puts the clock forward" and calls midnight 1:00 a.m., and so on. The reason for imposing these changes to clock time was originally to make the working day start an hour earlier and end an hour earlier, in order to better utilize daylight and thus save energy in lighting. Implicit in this is the assumption that people would refuse to go to work an hour earlier in the summer and keep the clock the same. It is assumed that the populace would refuse to do this, so a confidence trick was devised by the propagandists, that the hours should be changed twice a year instead, and it still works today, unquestioned by the vast majority of people.

In 1818, the English poet Samuel Taylor Coleridge made a very significant observation when he drew the distinction between mechanic and organic form. Form is mechanic when on any given material we impress a predetermined form, one that does not arise necessarily out of the natural properties of the material; on the other hand, organic form is innate—it develops from within so that the fullness of its development is one and the same with the perfection of its outward form. This applies to time. When the fabric of our existence in which we live our lives is made mechanic rather than organic, then our entire consciousness is altered. Our existence no longer arises from the natural properties to time but is forced into a predetermined form.

All of these dislocations serve to separate people both from the physical reality of the world and the realm of the sacred. The observance of sacred times, which exists to bring us into harmony with Nature, is at odds with modern commercial timekeeping. If they are to have any effect, sacred times must relate directly to local time, not the artificial time zones of reductionist science and politico-fiscal systems. So, when working with elected times for foundation we must use true local time, or our actions will be out of step with the inherent natural qualities of time.

THE ORIGIN OF MECHANICAL TIME

Clocks have their origin in mechanical astrolabes and other astronomical and calendar machines, which were used in ancient Greece and later in the eastern Roman Empire. The oldest extant example dates from around 80 BCE. In the Middle Ages, the center of excellence in their theory and construction shifted from eastern Greek Christendom into Arab-dominated Islamic countries, and the earliest ancient instruments of these kinds that still exist come from Cairo. Around the year 1000 CE, the Islamic astronomer-mathematician Al-Biruni wrote a book titled *On the Full Comprehensiveness of the Possible Methods for Constructing the Astrolabe,* in which he describes a mechanical instrument. It was a mechanical astronomical calendar that showed the phases of the Moon and its age in days, also the relative motions of the Sun and the Moon in the zodiac, that is, the day of the year and the Lunar Mansion. The machine was driven by hand, through an arbor, and was intended to be moved one day at a time. The motion is transmitted to the displays by means of gearing.

These Greek and Arab instruments were forerunners of the mechanical clocks that were developed in Western Europe. When someone successfully applied the idea of powering the ancient astronomical machines, perhaps stimulated by the invention of the windmill, a new era of time-consciousness came into being. Before power was added, Al-Biruni's mechanism showed the day of the year, the age of the Moon, and the Lunar Mansion. Because they are based on mechanical gears, each of which must have a whole number of teeth, the mechanisms are not completely accurate in recording and predicting celestial motions. But as approximations, they work well. Using this system, the year is 366.42 days long, the age of the Moon is based on the two-monthly approximation of 59 days, and the Lunar Mansion cycle is 28 days' duration. While the ancient technicians strove, with their considerable yet technically limited abilities, to reproduce in numbers celestial motions, making mechanisms that described reality, the later clock-users have tried to make the reality fit their mechanisms.

CHAPTER 11

Orientation

Facing in the Best Direction

*Run your rows north and south, with the tallest crops at the
north end of the plot.*

THE OLD FARMER'S ALMANAC

COSMIC PLACEMENT

The interaction between a chosen place on the Earth and the phenomena
of the sky observed there at a certain holy moment has been the significant factor in foundation since antiquity. The link thus made between
place and time as defined by the position of a celestial body is fixed by a
ceremonial act, generally making a mark on the Earth's surface. This act
marks the moment of the celestial phenomenon, fixing the quality of that
time in the place so long as the building may exist. The transient link of
the place to the right time was made permanent so that humans could
continue to commune with the otherworldly powers present at that fleet-
ing holy moment. Generally, the cosmological design of ancient temples
was an earthly manifestation of the otherworldly realm of the sacred.
This was brought into being around a central point, the earthly place
where the cosmic axis cuts through. This link between this world and the
otherworld preserved the holy moment within a limited, circumscribed
area separated from the profane outer world.

Figure 11.1. The Christian cosmic direction tradition in
a woodcarving in the church at Old Radnor, Wales.
(Nigel Pennick)

As the seventeenth-century English antiquary William Stukeley
wrote:

Ever since the world began, in building temples or places of religious worship, men have been studious in setting them according

to the quarters of the heavens; since they consider'd the world as the general temple, or house of God, and that all particular temples should be regulated according to that idea. The east naturally claims a prerogative, where the sun and all the planets and stars rise. The east they therefore consider'd the face and front of the universal temple.

ANCIENT EGYPTIAN ORIENTATION

In ancient Egypt, the ceremony of *Pedjeshes,* "stretching the cord" or the "Cording of the Temple," was a ritual reenactment of the moment of coming-into-being. It was the foundation ritual for temples and other significant public works. The ceremony is recorded in monumental inscriptions in temples at Abydos, Denderah, Edfu, Heliopolis, and Karnak. One of these inscriptions states:

> The Pharoah arose, attired in his necklace and feathered crown; and all the world followed him, and the majesty of Amenemhat. The *Ker-Heb* (High Priest) read the sacred text during the stretching of the cord and the laying of the foundation stone on the piece of ground selected for the temple. Then his majesty Amenemhat withdrew, and King Usertesen wrote it down before all the people.

Pedjeshes was an act of creation between the two polarities, performed by a man and by a woman. The woman is the determiner of the direction, and the man the stretcher of the cord. The enactors of this rite were the reigning pharaoh and a high priestess who personated the goddess Safeh or Seshat, "The Direction-Appointer." Each carried a club and a rod. The rods were linked together by a cord of specified length. Firstly, at the holy moment, the priestess drove her rod into the ground at the place of foundation, hammering it in with her club. Then the priestess observed the celestial body toward which the temple was to be oriented, and the pharaoh moved into line, marking the place, stretching the cord.

Then the pharaoh made a circle on the ground with the rod.

Figure 11.2. The ancient Egyptian rite of "stretching the cord." (Nigel Pennick)

Figure 11.3. Making the foundation mark can involve hammering a peg into the ground as the first act. Here, an ancient Greek Lekythos preserved at Paris shows two satyrs hammering the head of the earth goddess Gaia back into the earth. (Nideck)

Returning to the place of orientation, he hammered his rod into the ground. Then the priestess pulled her rod from the ground, and, stretching the cord, drew a circle on the ground around the pharaoh's rod. This interaction between male and female, in which the female is first static, with a moving male, then moving with the male static, is symbolic of the cooperative creation that comes about through the coming-together of the polar opposites.

These moves traced a vesica on the ground whose main axis was at right angles to the orientation. From this, the geometry of the future temple was laid out. In one part of the temple of Luxor, one may still see the orientation line chiseled into the subfloor, which once was covered with the finished flooring-slabs. Orientation toward a celestial body is recorded in another inscription: "The living god, the magnificent son of Asti, nourished by the sublime goddess in the temple, the sovereign of the country, stretches the cord in joy, with his sight toward the āk of the constellation of the Bull's Foreleg, he establishes the temple-house of the Mistress at Denderah, as took place there before." This refers to the two goddess temples at Denderah, one dedicated to Isis and the other to Hathor. This ancient Egyptian rite used direct observation to determine the proper orientation at the proper instant of time.

SPATIAL ORDER
IN THE ETRUSCAN TRADITION

The division of sacred space in the Etruscan Discipline is according to a regularized radial principle. The division refers to the heavens or to a determined area of the earth. The principles of reflectivity and self-similarity apply according to the Hermetic maxim, "As above, so below." Thus, the earthly area can be the landscape from horizon to horizon; a smaller defined area like a city, temenos, or temple; or an even smaller area like the surface of the liver of an animal sacrificed for divinatory purposes.

Etruscan orientation uses the four cardinal points: north, east, south, and west. Alternate points are connected by lines, giving a cross whose arms are oriented north–south and east–west, intersecting at the central place where the observer sits, facing south. The north–south line is the *Cardo,* and the east–west, the *Decumanus.* The circle is divided by these lines into two in two ways. The north–south *Cardo* divides the circles into an eastern region, the *Pars Familiaris,* and a western region, the *Pars Hostilis.* The *Pars Familiaris* is the side of the ascending light from midnight through sunrise to noon, when the sun is increasing in power during the day. In divination, this is the region of good fortune. To the west of the *Cardo* is the *Pars Hostilis,* the region where the sun is in decline from noon, through sunset, to midnight. In divination, this is the region of bad fortune.

The east–west line divides the observer's field of vision. The half north of the *Decumanus,* outside the observer's vision, is called the *Pars Postica,* the posterior part. The half in front of the observer, to the south of the *Decumanus,* is the *Pars Antica.* The area of good luck is thus to the observer's left, where the sun rises, and the area of bad luck correspondingly to the west, the direction of sunset.

This fourfold division is further subdivided by intercardinal lines into eight, and then again into sixteen. Each of these sixteen directions is ascribed a divine power and corresponding symbolic principles. Generally, the southern *Pars Antica* is the region of terrestrial and nature deities. Here, the gods of sea and sun rule with the Lares, Earth, and the Etruscan god Eth (equivalent to the Roman Vulcan). This is an area of lesser good fortune in divination. To the west of south is the area of freedom, ruled by the god Fufluns (Bacchus). Next is the sixteenth ruled by Selva (Silvanus), while the following sectors are under the regency of the earthly deities of fortune and fate. In divination, this is the region of lesser bad fortune.

In the northwestern quarter, the gods of fate and the infernal regions rule, carrying over from the region south of the *Decumanus.* In the northwest is the region ruled by the god Vejovis (Kronos-Saturn). The last sixteenth on the west side is ruled by Night, Nocturnus, and the Guardians of the Gates. Across the divide of midnight to the northeast are the great celestial deities that correspond with Jupiter, Juno, Mars, and Minerva. To diviners, they reside in the quarter of greater good fortune.

In his textbook on surveying, the Roman locator Hyginus Gromaticus wrote:

> The limits were not established without taking the celestial system into account, since the *Decumani* were laid out according to the sun, and the *Cardines* according to the celestial axis. For the first time, the teachings of the Etruscans established this system of measurement. These divided the earth into two parts according to the pathway of the sun. They called the part located in the north, right, and that in the south, left. From east to west because the sun and moon are directed in this way. The other line led from south to north and they called the parts on the far side of this line *Antica* and they called the parts of this side *Postica*. And from these terms the boundaries of the temples also came to be described.

Roman customs of laying out sacred space came directly from the earlier Etruscan traditions. In Etruria, temples were generally oriented to the south or southeast. The *Pars Antica* corresponded to the façade and colonnade of the temple, whist the *Pars Postica* represented the inner sanctum, the *Cella*. These Etruscan principles laid the basis for classical European geomantic layout, whose principles still appear from time to time in new developments.

In his *Ten Books on Architecture,* the Augustan Roman architect Vitruvius recorded the general principles for the orientation of Pagan temples:

> The direction towards which temples of the immortal gods should face is to be determined on the principle that, when there is nothing to prevent it and the choice is free, the temple and the holy image located in the *Cella* (sanctuary) should face the western quarter of the sky. This will enable those who approach the altar with offerings or sacrifices to face the direction of sunrise when looking towards the image in the temple, and thus those undertaking vows will look towards the quarter from which the sun emerges.

In his *De Aquae Ductu Urbis Romae* (On the Aqueducts of the City of Rome), the Roman engineer Frontinus tells us that "architects have written that it is right for the temple to be oriented to the west." Pliny's *Naturalis Historia* (Natural History) asserts that temples should face south. Varro, in his *De Lingua Latina* (On the Latin Language), agrees: "When one looks south for the seat of the gods," he states, "the west is to one's right. I believe it is for this reason that the omens on the left are better than those on the right." In *Antiquitates Romanae* (Roman Antiquities), Dionysus of Halicarnassus states that temples are oriented eastward. Livy, Plutarch, and Servius also favor the east.

INDIAN FOUNDATION TRADITIONS

In India, as elsewhere, various rites and ceremonies have to be performed at various stages of the work of building. There are copious texts on this in Tantric works and texts originating with the Pratishtha class. The *Agamas* and the *Hayasirsa Pancharatra* contain the *Shilpa Shastra,* and the *Puranas* tell of the architectural prescriptions for the worship of various goddesses and gods. Time, geometry, dimension, and form are directly related to building. The *vastu* (building place) is recognized as the body of a being named *Vastu-nara* or *Vastu Purusha*. It is seen as a demon struck down by the gods. Each of the various victorious gods presses down part of the demon's body into the earth.

The parts of the demon, located on the earth, are thus occupied by the divine powers represented by the gods. They are present in the corresponding parts of the building, once erected, and must be acknowledged. The demon, and thus the ground plan of the building, is divided up by a grid. Generally, according to the Northern School of *Vastu Vidya,* temples are on an 8 × 8 grid of 64 squares, and houses on a 9 × 9 grid of 81 squares. The Southern School recognizes up to 256 squares. The ground plan squares determine the proportional geometry of the building.

An ancient Indian Sanskrit text, the *Manasara Shilpa Shastra,* describes techniques for laying out the foundation geometry of temples. Having discovered the right place to start, we must set up a gnomon at the center of the site. The gnomon must measure 12, 18, or 24 *Angulas* in length. There are three kinds of *Angula* measure, which are used according to the context. The standard *Angula* is based upon the human body, being the breadth of the finger of the master laying out the site. From this center, using knotted rope to maintain the correct dimensions, we draw a circle whose radius measures twice the height of the gnomon. We mark the two positions of the sun when it is the same height above the horizon in the morning and the afternoon on the circle. Then we draw a line between them. This is an east–west line, the equinoctial axis. We drive a wooden peg into the ground at each end of this axis. Then, we draw equal-radius arcs centered on the two pegs. Now we have made the geometrical figure known in European tradition as a *vesica piscis*.

Next, we draw a line between the extreme ends of the vesica. This is a true meridian (north–south line). It cuts the original east–west line a little to the north of the center of the original circle. Having made the cross, we draw a new circle of the same diameter as the original one. This is the "Indian Circle." From this circle, we make an east–west vesica in the same way as the first one. Lastly, we join up the four points where two vesicas intersect with straight lines to form a square, the basis of the grid upon which the temple will be constructed.

The actual foundation geometry of the temple depends upon the time of year of the foundation. The distance between the placement of the gnomon and the second center is dependent on the height we choose for the opposing limbs of the sun. The higher the sun in the sky, the longer the distance between the two points. Although the original point where the gnomon is placed is omitted in the final geometry, in a real sense it is the place where the ground was broken first.

Geometrical ground plans of Hindu temples are Yantras, sacred sigils that are considered to be gathering points or nuclei of spiritual force. According to Tantric practice, devotees fix their meditative concentration upon these points. Yantras are envisaged as sacred sigils of specific spiritual beings called Devatas, whose actual images are not present. Tantric Yantras represent the subtle bodies of the Devatas. They have a corresponding sound, for when any Mantra is chanted, it activates the power inherent in the respective Yantra. The appropriate response is present in the person who chants the Mantra, thereby unifying the individual with the infinite.

MEDIEVAL CHURCH ORIENTATION

Jews, Christians, and Muslims all orient themselves when they pray. In prayer, Jews are supposed to face Jerusalem while Muslims face Mecca. These locations are the omphaloi of their corresponding worlds. In Jerusalem is the Rock, the omphalos of Judeo-Christian cosmology, where the mosque called the Dome of the Rock stands witness to the seventh religion whose holy buildings have occupied that site. At Mecca, the Islamic holy of holies is marked by the meteorite called the Kaaba. Because the Christian religion is a complex syncretization of both Jewish and European Pagan ideas, Christians have a less well-defined version of orientation. Some claim that orientation symbolically means facing toward the center of the world, the *Compas* at the tomb of Christ in Jerusalem. Others believe that due east is the proper direction, because Christ will emerge from the east in glory at the Second Coming.

Early Christian buildings followed Jewish and Pagan tradition in having a westward alignment—an occidentation. The original Church of the Holy Sepulchre in Jerusalem, the Christian omphalos, built by Emperor Constantine, faced west. But this did not last. Orientation, alignment toward the east, goes back to the early years of the Church as an official body. The *Apostolic Constitutions* of the year 472 CE ordered churches to be built to a rectangular plan with the head to the east. Continental medieval writers like Guillaume Durand, who wrote on the "Symbolism of Churches and Church Ornaments" in book one of his treatise *Rationale divinorum officiorum* (Rationale for the Divine Offices), state that churches should face due east. Durand himself complained that some faced solstitial sunrise. Many medieval churches, especially in northern Europe, are oriented roughly eastward, but certainly not on the equinoctial line. Rare examples where one is equinoctial, like Salisbury Cathedral, are notable for that reason. Seemingly, the reason for the variation in church orientations is recorded nowhere in the canonical writings of the church.

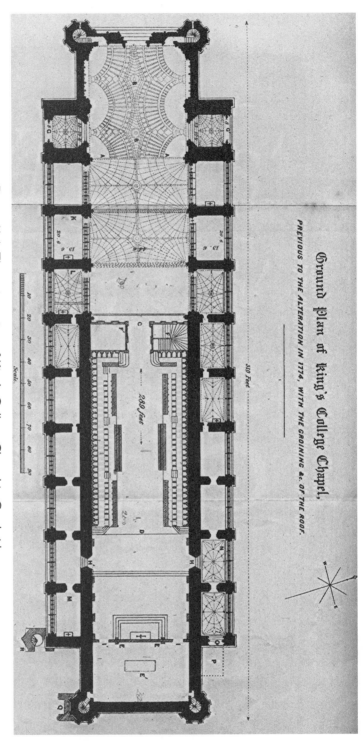

Figure II.4. The orientation of King's College Chapel in Cambridge. (Nideck)

It has long been known by antiquaries that at least some churches are oriented toward sunrise on their patronal festivals, the day of the saint to which the church is dedicated. This may be a continuation of Pagan tradition, for certain stone circles, most notably Stonehenge, are oriented on significant sunrises. However, this transmission, if indeed it happened, cannot be proved historically. Fortunately, there are thousands of medieval churches in Europe whose dedications are known. Some are certainly equinoctial, though this may be an orientation for the day of the Annunication of the Blessed Virgin Mary, at the spring equinox in medieval times. As seen from the sundial on the south side, the Frauenkirche in Munich, founded in 1468, is close to a true east–west orientation. Salisbury Cathedral, whose foundation stone was laid on April 28, 1220, is oriented "between the equinoxes," due east–west. If a church is founded facing the rising sun on its saint's day, then the sun will rise directly in front of it on every subsequent saint's day. In the long run, as the calendar drifts away from the sun as the result of accumulated inaccuracies and the precession of the equinoxes, the orientation will be lost. But this is a very long process.

Figure 11.5. Stonehenge, Wiltshire, England.
(Nigel Pennick)

MAGNETIC ORIENTATION

The earliest reference to a magnet is from the Roman poet Lucretius (ca. 58 BCE), who tells how the lodestone draws iron toward it. It was long known by blacksmiths that an iron bar, hammered in a north–south orientation, would become magnetized. The earliest reference to the magnetic compass, however, is by the Englishman Alexander Neckham, in 1187, when it was being used in navigation. It is possible that the magnetic compass was used in medieval church orientation. There are a number of medieval churches in England whose orientations could have been determined with the magnetic compass. Chichester Cathedral's orientation is related to magnetic north–south at the time of its foundation, 1108. European compasses of the 1400s were marked out with a blue cross for the cardinal points, and a red cross for the intercardinals. The east was marked by a cross, which may

Figure 11.6. During the Iron Age, the ancient European smiths discovered that when one hammers hot iron in a north–south direction, it becomes magnetized. (Nideck)

indicate the use of the compass for finding the direction of Christian prayer, or perhaps for architectural orientation.

Around 1500, a fleur-de-lys was adopted to indicate north. In England, the earliest known printed compass card dates from 1551. On a voyage in 1553, Stephen Burrowes (1525–1584) noted that the Earth's magnetic poles were not the same as the terrestrial ones. The variation was calculated by Dr. Gillebrand of Gresham College, Oxford, and a record of it has been kept ever since. In 1600, the English scientist Sir William Gilbert (1540–1603), discovered that the Earth is a vast magnet, with its magnetic poles near the terrestrial poles. When the Earth's magnetism is used to define an orientation, then the time of measurement is built into the building. It is a means of preserving one of the conditions of existence of the moment of foundation. Whether or not it was used in medieval times for orientation, in later years the compass was used geomantically in Europe. In 1735, the grave of the English antiquary Thomas Hearne was oriented by compass, and in 1811, the main axis of Regent's Park in London was aligned on magnetic north.

DISRUPTION AND RESTORATION OF ORIENTATION IN BRITAIN

At the Reformation, certain fundamentalist Protestants deemed all Church tradition either Catholic or Pagan. To them, both were equally distasteful, so they strove to abolish every custom that had no biblical precedent. Even orientation was to be abolished. In practice, there were few deliberate misorientations, but in Cambridge, the Chapel of Emmanuel College was an example. In 1584, the fanatical Protestant Sir Walter Mildmay set up a new college in the buildings of a former Dominican Priory that had been suppressed in 1538. To defy Catholic practice, he made the chapel, which was oriented properly, into the dining hall. The old dining hall, oriented north–south, he made the chapel. The chapel was criticized at the time for its misorientation, and it was never consecrated. In the 1660s, a new chapel was built, designed by Sir Christopher Wren, and oriented properly.

Figure 11.7. An eighteenth-century engraving of the chapel of
Emmanuel College in Cambridge. Designed by Sir Christopher Wren,
this properly oriented chapel replaced the misoriented north–south
one of Sir Walter Mildmay. (Nideck)

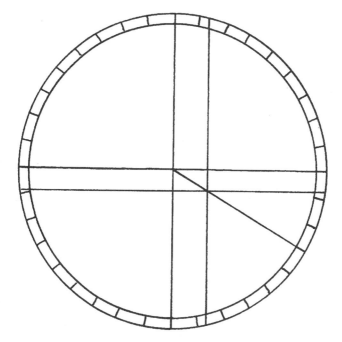

Figure 11.8. Determining the qiblah,
the direction of Mecca, according to the Indian Circle method.
(Nigel Pennick)

Because much knowledge of church orientation had been destroyed by the Reformation and later Cromwellian puritanism, seventeenth-century English antiquaries attempted to piece together the tradition once more. One of them was Silas Taylor, alias Domville, a captain in Cromwell's Parliamentary army.

Taylor built up a fine collection of ancient manuscripts. During the Civil War, his detachment looted the cathedral libraries at Hereford and Worcester, and his knowledge of orientation probably came from ancient ecclesiastical writings. One manuscript, sold at his death in 1678, had the passage:

In the days of yore, when a church was to be built, they watched and prayed on the vigil of the dedication, and took that point of the horizon where the sun arose from the East, which makes that variation so that few stand true, except those built between the two equinoxes. I have experimented some churches, and have found the line to point to that part of the horizon where the sun arises on the day of that Saint to whom the church is dedicated.

Scottish Masonic tradition, recorded in William Alexander Laurie's 1859 book *History of Free Masonry and the Grand Lodge of Scotland,* tells:

On the evening previous, the Patrons, Ecclesiastics, and Masons assembled, and spent the night in devotional exercises; one being placed to watch the rising of the sun, gave notice when his rays appeared above the horizon. When fully in view, the Master Mason sent out a man with a rod, which he ranged in line between the altar and the sun, and thus fixed a line of orientation.

The English poet William Wordsworth (1770–1850) was involved in choosing the location for St Mary's Church at Rydal in the English Lake District. The chapel has a remarkable location, chosen with exquisite sensibility for the form of the landscape and traditional English church geomancy, "How fondly with the woods embrace this daughter of thy pious care," wrote the poet. In 1823, Wordsworth wrote two poems dedicated to Lady Le Fleming, the chapel's founder, who laid the foundation stone in July that year. It was consecrated by the bishop of Chester, Dr. Blomfield, on August 25, 1825. Wordsworth poems are titled *On Seeing the Foundation Preparing for the Erection of Rydal Chapel, Westmorland,* and *On the Same Occasion.* They were published in 1827.

In a note to the second poem, Wordsworth wrote:

Our churches, invariably, perhaps, stand east and west, but why is by few persons exactly known; nor, that the degree of deviation from due east often noticeable in the ancient ones was determined, in each particular case, by the point in the horizon, at which the sun rose upon the day of the saint to whom the church was dedicated.

He tells of this in the poem:

Then, to her Patron Saint, a previous rite
Resounded with deep swell and solemn close,
Through unremitting vigils of the night,
Till from his couch the wished-for Sun uprose.

He rose, and straight—as by divine command,
They, who had waited for the sign to trace
Their work's foundation, gave with careful hand
To the high altar its determined place.

Research into orientation of churches is fraught with difficulties. The date of foundation must be known accurately, and then the position of sunrise calculated in the old Julian Calendar. Sometimes, the foundation stone was not laid on the saint's day. Then again, church dedications have often been altered over the years, and other, local geomantic factors may play their part. In the 1950s, the Reverend Hugh Benson attempted to gain useful statistics by studying British church orientations systematically. A good proportion of churches he studied did conform to the patronal day sunrise orientations, but by no means all of them.

The problems of the meaning of orientation are explicit at Cambridge, where the details of the foundation and dedication of King's College Chapel are a matter of record. In 1853, J. Rigg of the Cambridge Antiquarian Society determined that King's College Chapel, founded by King Henry VI on March 25, 1446, has an orientation that corresponds with sunrise on March 22 in that year. Its patronal days are March 25 and December 6, Our Lady and St. Nicholas, respectively. The foundation stone, however, was laid by the king on neither day, but on St. James's Day, July 25, 1446, which causes problems as to whether the orientation was determined on the day of foundation, or that of laying the foundation stone.

There are a number of possible explanations for this orientation. The chapel of King's College was founded in the middle of an existing town, the king having demolished an old church, St John Zachary,

Figure 11.9. Roof Ridge orientation of King's College Chapel
Cambridge England. (Nigel Pennick)

and houses to clear the site. If the founders viewed the rising sun over
the roofs of the houses to the east, then the orientational difference
may be explained. Another possibility is that the foundations were
prepared on March 22, and the orientation fixed from staging over
the rooftops. The new chapel may have followed the general orientation of the old St. John's church. Or, perhaps the actual accuracy
of observation was never so precise. When we compare Christian
church orientation with the traditional Islamic rule-of-thumb methods of finding the direction of the Kaaba at Mecca, which is called
the *qiblah,* are certainly less accurate than a three-day difference of
angle in a Christian chapel. They are not considered a hindrance to
ritual correctness in Islam. The psychological need for accuracy of
a greater order may have originated in the Renaissance, a worldview
that had not arrived in England in 1446. Recorded instances of electional astrology in England are post-medieval.

THE DIRECTION OF MECCA

Place, time, and orientation are integral parts of Islamic practice. The times of prayer must be determined according to the place. This is done by direct observation of the heavens. According to custom, all Muslims must pray toward Mecca. Finding the direction of the *qiblah* readily at different places was a problem tackled by Islamic astronomers. Various techniques were arrived at. Among others, the medieval astronomers Abu Rayhan al-Biruni and Ibn al-Haytham (known in medieval Europe as Alhazen) published geometrical techniques for finding the *qiblah*.

The modern Iranian mathematician Sardar Kabuli used the Indian Circle to determine the direction of Mecca. The Indian Circle is a circle divided into sectors of ten degrees, quartered into right angles, laid out on the earth at the place where the mosque is to stand. It is oriented by taking the opposing limbs of the sun, as in the foundation technique described in the Indian *Manasara Shilpa Shastra*.

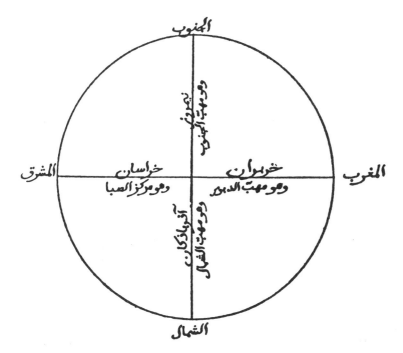

Figure 11.10. An Iranian Ather-al-Baghyah showing the meridian, Nimruz. (Nideck)

If the longitude of the place of prayer is greater than the longitude of Mecca, one should mark the difference between the two longitudes from the point in a westerly direction on the Indian Circle. If the longitude of the place is less than that of Mecca, the same is done in the easterly direction. From the point found thus, a line parallel to the north–south meridian is drawn. If the latitude is greater than Mecca, the difference is marked toward the south of the east–west equinoctial line, and if less, to the north of it by the corresponding amount. From this point, draw a line parallel to the equinoctial line. Connect the intersection of these lines with the center of the Indian Circle. This line is aligned upon the *qiblah*. Although the level of accuracy is limited, this is practically the best one can do and, according to Islamic commentators, is legally valid as the direction of Mecca.

MERIDIANS

Before 293 BCE, when the first sundial was erected in Rome, noon was proclaimed by a crier when the sun appeared between the Rostra and a place called the Station of the Greeks. At that moment, the sun was due south, and it was the middle of the day, the "meridian." Meridian markers appear to be the origin of wider markings on the land, such as overall geodetic surveys, and the point from which the sun was viewed, the omphalos, became the center.

Iranian tradition asserts that their primary meridian—Nimruz—was the center of the Old World. Before the discovery of the Americas, Persian geometers believed that the Eurasian-African landmass (the world) covered a whole day. This idea appears to date from around the year 800. The general principle was that when the sun was due south at Nimruz, the whole world was in daylight, for the sun was setting in Japan and rising on the west coast of Africa. The name Nimruz meaning literally "half-day" thus had a double meaning, marking both the midday point in Birjand, eastern Iran, and the conceptual midday point of the world. The southern Iranian province of Sistan is still called Nimruz locally because of its central geographical location.

Meridians were laid out on the ground wherever astronomical

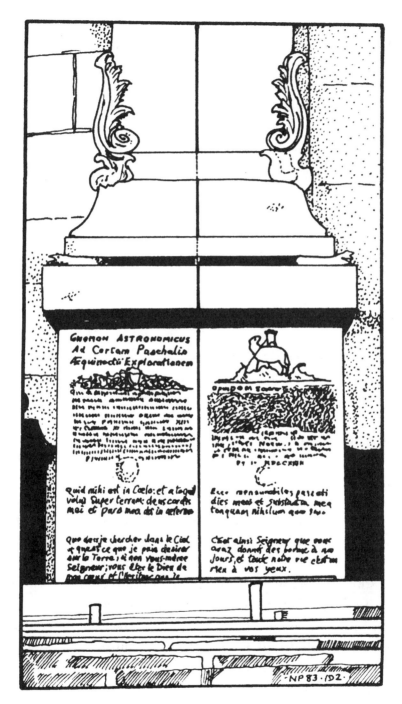

Figure 11.11. The meridian of France, marked on the wall inside the Church of Sainte-Sulpice in Paris. (Nigel Pennick)

observations were made. Ancient meridians can be seen still in several medieval buildings in France. At Chartres Cathedral, a white pane of glass in an otherwise colored window allows the rays of the sun at midday on Midsummer's Day to strike a brass tab in the pavement. It marks the instant of the sun's apex. At Tonnerre, a brass lemniscate (figure-of-eight) shape in the floor tracks the position of the midday sun throughout the year. The great architectural symbolist William R. Lethaby (1857–1931) noted that "Even now" (1891), "in some of the French cathedrals—Bourges and Nevers for instance—diagonal lines may be seen right across the floor graduated into a scale of months and days."

The meridians of Islamic observatories such as those at Maraghah and Samarkand were laid out during the same period that the medieval cathedrals were built in Europe. The design of sacred buildings, and the grid that underlies those built according to geometrical and harmonic principles, is always related directly to the perceived structure of the world, and its interactions with celestial phenomena. When rays of sun are projected onto such a grid, the various portions of it have a specific geometrical relationship to a time of day and the time of year. By these means, a harmonious relationship with the universal order can be created. The geomantic layout of the Piazza of the Italian town of Pienza (consecrated in 1462) is based on this principle.

The prime meridian of the world is located in England. It is the meridian of Greenwich, laid out on the site of the old Royal Obervatory, founded in 1675 by electional astrology. Before founding the observatory there, Hyde Park and Chelsea were considered as meridional points before Greenwich was finally chosen. In 1851, a new meridian was established by Sir George Airy at Greenwich, nineteen feet to the east of the original one established by James Bradley, the third Astronomer Royal. In 1886, this, the revised Greenwich Meridian, was adopted as the prime meridian of the world, and all time zones on Earth reckoned with regard to Greenwich Mean Time (GMT). An International Date Line was set up on the other side of the world opposite to the Greenwich Meridian. This is the marker of midnight GMT, the point at which the date changes from one day to the next, and where the new year begins. At that moment, it is noon GMT on the previous day. On four days of the year, according to the equation of time, noon GMT coincides with noon Local Apparent Time, when the sun is actually due south on the Greenwich Meridian. These are April 16, June 14, September 2, and December 25 in most years, depending on the cycle of Leap Year days. This applies to all meridians from which Mean Time is derived.

National meridians exist in most European cities. Some are public monuments. In Prague, the meridian of Bohemia is laid out in brass in the old marketplace between the town hall and Tyn church. In Paris, the meridian of France was defined in 1727 and marked in the

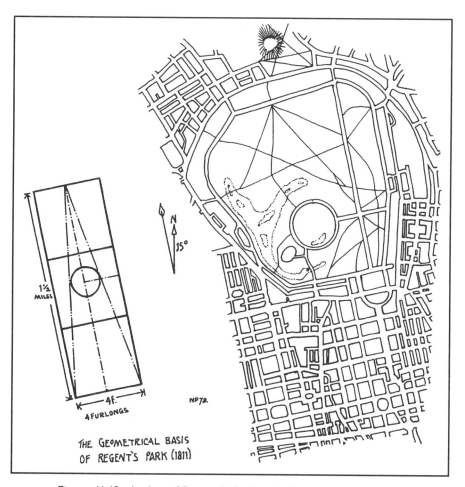

Figure 11.12. A plan of Regent's Park and the associated streets in London, laid out in 1811 by John Nash (1752–1835) on a grid aligned on megalithic north–south. (Nigel Pennick)

Church of Saint-Sulpice in Paris by the clockmaker Sully. The meridian of Portugal is at the Royal Observatory in the Tapada royal park in Lisbon. Its time is 36 minutes and 44.7 seconds "slow" of GMT. Mean time on the Paris meridian is 9 minutes and 20.9 seconds "fast" of GMT, while the Amsterdam meridian is 19 minutes and 32.3 seconds "fast." The Icelandic meridian at Reykjavik gives Mean Time 27 minutes, 40 seconds "slow" of GMT. In Latvia, Riga's meridian is 1 hour, 36 minutes, and 28.2 seconds "fast" of Greenwich. European meridian traditions were exported to the American colonies by Spanish geometers. Before joining the universal time zone system, Argentina based Mean Time on the meridian of Cordoba, 4 hours, 16 minutes, and 48.2 seconds west of Greenwich, while in Uruguay, the meridian in the metropolitan cathedral at Montevideo marks noon as 3 hours, 44 minutes, and 48.9 seconds "slow" of Greenwich.

Gradually, the meridians lost their time-telling meaning. In the western part of the British Isles, there is actually over half an hour difference in real time by the sun. When it is noon at Lowestoft in East Anglia, it is only 11:23 on the Isle of Barra in the Western Isles of Scotland. But Greenwich Time was adopted in Edinburgh and Glasgow and most of Scotland on January 29, 1848. Before that, Glasgow clocks were set 121 minutes behind Greenwich Time. In Oxford, the clock on Tom Tower in Christ Church College was furnished with two-minute hands, one for GMT and the other for Oxford Mean Time. To this day, Oxford time is acknowledged publicly. At 9:05 p.m. GMT (9:00 Oxford Mean Time), Great Tom, the seven-ton bell, strikes 101 times to commemorate the original founder-members of the college. By 1855, 98 percent of public clocks in Great Britain, however far west of London, showed GMT. Dublin, then the second city of the United Kingdom, kept its own time, 25 minutes and 21.1 seconds behind Greenwich. GMT was legally enforced on the whole of Great Britain, including the Isle of Man, in 1880. At the same time, Irish Time was also enforced on the whole island of Ireland, that of the Dublin Meridian.

France adopted Greenwich Mean Time on March 11, 1911, but the Paris Mean Time signal was transmitted from the Eiffel Tower by radio until June 30 of that year. France went over to Central European Time, one hour ahead of Greenwich, during the German Occupation in 1940, and kept it. Belgium adopted GMT in May 1892, and Spain in January 1901. Now, although it is west of Greenwich, most of the Iberian Peninsula uses Central European Time (CET), one hour ahead of GMT. Germany and Austria adopted Central European Time on April 1, 1893. Italy followed on November 1 in the same year. Denmark took CET up on January 1, 1894, and Sweden and Norway a year later. Until the Revolution, Russia used Pulkova Time taken from the meridian at St. Petersburg as the standard time. Pulkova Time is 2 hours, 1 minute, and 18.6 seconds "fast" of GMT. Certain places in Europe still have public clocks that tell Local Mean Time. Tom Tower at Oxford has already been mentioned. Another place is the Basilica Birnau on the north shore of the Bodensee (Lake Constance) in Germany. This baroque monastery has three sundials that show Local Apparent Time (Real Time), and various clocks including a tower clock that shows Central European Time and its "daylight saving" addition, a "moon clock" (lunar dial), and a clock that shows Local Mean Time. At Birnau, it is therefore easy to compare all three kinds of time measurement.

Figure 11.13. A baroque sundial on the wall of the monastery at Birnau, on the north shore of Lake Constance, Germany. (Nigel Pennick)

CHAPTER 12

The City of the Omphalos

Cosmic Centers and Symbolic Street Plans

For all things are come to be something out of nothing: And every creature hath the center, or the circle of the birth of life in itself.

JACOB BOEHME (1575–1624),
MYSTERIUM MAGNUM (1624)

KARLSRUHE

Karlsruhe is a flourishing modern city situated in the west of Germany. Important as the seat of the supreme court of the German Federal Republic, the city is also the center of German nuclear research and is much admired for its pioneering innovations in urban transportation. Karlsruhe was founded in 1715 by Markgraf Karl Wilhelm von Baden-Durlach (1679–1738). His surveyors laid it out to a remarkable plan, which exists to this day. Karlsruhe is laid out as a radial city, based upon geomantic traditions of the New Jerusalem made explicit in Rosicrucian, Qabalistic, alchemical, and Masonic works of the period immediately following the Thirty Years' War.

The layout of Karlsruhe is the epitome of European geomancy. Its key is the Qabalistic *Lehrtafel* (teaching painting) *of Princess Antonia,* an impressive symbolic painting made in 1673. It was painted as an aid to teaching mystical principles, and for contemplation. It is kept in the Holy Trinity Church at Bad Teinach, to the south of Stuttgart. The *Lehrtafel* was painted for Antonia, Princess of Württemberg (1613–1679), according to the spiritual principles determined by Johann Valentin Andreae, and developed by the Württemberg Christian Qabalists Johann Jakob Strölin and Johann Schmidlin. This painting is extremely important to the design of the later Karlsruhe, both in its exoteric form and its esoteric content.

The lower part of Princess Antonia's mystic painting is the key to the layout of Karlsruhe. The artist has depicted a garden with figures, at the center of which is Christ, who holds a cross, his right hand raised in benediction. He is standing on a rock in the center of a pool from which radiate fifteen visible watercourses that terminate in a circle of water. It is clear from the geometry that a sixteenth remains unseen behind the Christ. Between the streams are flower beds, each with its own specific plants.

Around the circle's circumference stand twelve human figures, each carrying or accompanied by a number of symbols linking the twelve signs of the zodiac with the twelve tribes of Israel and other archetypal aspects of existence. They stand by trees, which, beginning at the figure to the right of the Christ, going sunwise, are laurel, cypress, willow, fig, cedar, fir, olive, apple, pomegranate, almond, palm, and oak. Entering a gap in the hedge in which this symbolic garden is set, is the green-dressed Princess Antonia herself. We see her from the back. She is accompanied by a sheep and carries symbols of devotion. In one hand is an inverted anchor, and in the other is a flaming heart.

Above the twelve- and sixteenfold Christ garden is a representation of Solomon's Temple at Jerusalem, fronted by the pillars Boaz and Jachin. Sacred figures and symbolic creatures abound, laid out according to a sacred geometry that reflects the Qabalistic Tree of Life. The position of female figures in the painting mark the Sephiroth and bear relevant symbolic attributes. The Christ figure, at the center of the radial garden, is in the position of Malkuth. To the left of the Temple

Figure 12.1. The Lehrtafel (teaching table) of Princess Antonia (1617–1679) at Bad Teinach in Württemberg, Germany, contains, among much other symbolic spiritual themes, a representation of Jesus in a twelvefold zodiacal garden with the twelve tribes of Israel, the Temple, and in the distance the Camp of the Israelites and the New Jerusalem. Each signifies a particular manifestation of the general divine principle of the world. The layout of cities like Karlsruhe is in the same tradition as this remarkable exposition of qabalistic principles.

as we look at it is, in the distance, the Camp of the Israelites; while to the right is the New Jerusalem, partially circular, with a central castle from which radiate streets.

We are fortunate that time has been kind to this painting, having passed unscathed through five highly destructive wars fought between France and Germany. Despite its size (over 9 feet [3 m] high), this symbolic painting was designed to be seen only by the princess and her esoteric circle, for it encapsulates the esoteric ideas and principles current within courtly circles in that region at that period. This was the era following the Thirty Years' War, when Protestant and Catholic armies fought a war whose ferocity and destructiveness was unmatched in Central Europe until the apocalypse of the 1940s. Subsequent to the war, intellectual discourse was held as to the meaning of that sectarian frenzy to humane existence. Philosophy sought to integrate what had previously been seen as distinctly different opposing systems. Catholic, Protestant, Jewish, and Pagan philosophies were examined for their common points within the Perennial Philosophy.

Princess Antonia's painting is arranged like a triptych, which, when closed, shows the world's women, led by the princess, being brought to salvation. Jewish, Pagan, Muslim, and Christian women queue together for admittance to the heavenly city, to which all will be allowed entry. The laying-out of Karlsruhe forty-two years later, a tolerant city with both Protestant and Catholic churches, and a significant Jewish community, was the culmination of this synthesis.

THE HOLY CITY PLAN

In terms of new, freshly planned cities, the European tradition furnishes us with several sorts of forerunners for Karlsruhe. Of course in the old Roman Empire, most cities had been planned according to the Etruscan Discipline, laid out knowingly to a scheme that was perceived as a microcosm of the world, divided usually into four quarters. Centuries later, the plan reappeared in certain Anglo-Saxon towns such as Wareham, and among others, the free cities of what is now south Germany and Switzerland, including Fribourg, Freiburg-im-Breisgau,

Figure 12.2a. Eighteenth-century map showing the gridded street plan (top center) aligning street and abbey church.

Figure 12.2b. Abbey gateway tower shows aligned street visible through it. (Nigel Pennick)

Figures 12.2a/b. The Holy City of Bury St Edmunds, Suffolk, England was a place of pilgrimage that contained the relics of the martyred East Anglian king, Edmund (killed by the Danish army in 869). Laid out around the year 1050, it is a grid of streets whose churches are oriented along the east–west alignments. The cross that stood in the marketplace was destroyed in the Reformation, and the Abbey lies in ruins.

Villingen, Rottweil, and Bern. Founded in the twelfth and thirteenth centuries by the Zähringers, these settlements also had a form of the cross-shaped Holy City plan, in the case of Bern modified to take account of the terrain.

The focal points of these cities, at significant crossroads, are fountains, usually ornate structures protected by saints or Our Lady. Similarly, the Bastides, built under King Edward I of England in France and Wales as defended new towns, had a strict gridded pattern that reflected the new order on the land introduced throughout his territories by the powerful king. German settlements in Prussia, Silesia, and the Baltic countries were built in a similar manner.

As with the Germanic settlements, the laying-out of Edward I's towns coincided with the introduction of new laws, weights, and measures. The center points of these towns were marketplaces, the center being marked by a cross or market hall. A classic example of such a layout in Wales is Llanidloes, where the market hall stands on pillars at the center of the four streets, with gaps in the end walls that preserve the street's continuity. As new towns, these settlements were peopled by craftspeople and tradesmen recruited specifically by the monarch's agent, the Locator Civitatis. Inducements—such as freedom from taxation, or better living conditions—were offered to would-be inhabitants.

Later, in the Renaissance, cities were drawn up as more strictly geometrical ideal plans, and remained as drawings or prints, but a few were actually translated from plan to reality. Those that were realized came into being as the result of the individual willpower of aristocrats, reflecting order on both the earthly and cosmic levels. But among those physically built, there was nothing strictly comparable with Karlsruhe either in design or scale. Earlier symbolic towns and cities were surrounded by defensive walls that restricted their structural links with the surrounding country. Karlsruhe did not need them.

Many of these cities harked back to the Roman camps and cities laid out according to the geomantic principles of the Etruscan Discipline. But, as with all developments from an original, they added diagonal streets to the strictly rectilinear Roman model. Typically, such towns were laid out as squares with an eightfold street plan that ran from the corners and the middle of each side, meeting at a central square. Among these towns were Villefranche-sur-Meuse, a royal foundation of 1545; Henrichemont, also in France, founded by the Duke of Sully in 1608; the defended town of Christianshavn in Denmark (1617); the Huguenot town of Neu-Isenburg, laid out in Germany in 1699; and Frampol in Poland (1705). Other urban forerunners of Karlsruhe include the heptagonal town of Coevorden in the Low Countries, and the Venetian town of Palmanuova, laid out on a ninefold radial plan in 1593. Exactly one hundred years later, the Italian town of Grammichele was laid out by the Duke of Butera as a hexagon with six radial streets. In London, a cosmological street layout was made at Seven Dials, where seven streets radiate out from a pillar bearing seven sundials. But Karlsruhe, with its 32-fold division of the land, raised the art to a higher order entirely.

Figure 12.3. The plan of the town of Grammichele, Italy. (Nideck)

THE FOUNDATION OF KARLSRUHE

The date of the first marking of the ground at the future Karlsruhe was January 28, 1715. Markgraf Karl Wilhelm was hunting in his forest on this day when he took a rest, and then, it seems, decided to make a new foundation there. It appears that the central point of the future Karlsruhe (literally "Karl's Rest") was actually determined by the royal foresters, and this gives us another element of European geomancy incorporated in Karlsruhe's layout. In the sixteenth century, Matthaus Oeder prepared a map of the forest of Dresden Heath that shows eight radial lines, each called *flügel,* a "wing," emerging from a central point. Other models for Karlsruhe include the symmetrical radial roads that existed earlier, radiating from many settlements in Belgium. They include the radial pathways in many forests in Germany, France, and England.

There appears also to be a connection with the traditions of the central meeting place of foresters, such as the Speech House of the Forest of Dean, which is in use today by the Free Miners of the forest. A further element of foundation comes from hunting. As mentioned above, there are many hunting foundation legends in Celtic and Germanic tradition, for churches, monasteries, and cities.

Immediately Karl Wilhelm decided to build at the place chosen by the foresters, and on January 28, 1715, trees were felled and the center marked. The prince's engineer laid out the future Karlsruhe as a radial arrangement, with 32 equally spaced straight roads or rides coming from the central point, where the tower of the palace was to stand. Cutting these straight rides were two circles, one small and incomplete because the wings of the palace were built across it; and one larger, a complete circle that encompasses the whole palace complex and defines the boundary of that and the original town.

The Schloss, or palace, of Karlsruhe is located at the very center of the city. The foundation stone for the tower that marks the center was laid on June 17, 1715. This omphalos was marked by a 165-foot-high tower that can be seen as the sight-point of all the streets radiating out from it. The final knob was set on top of the tower ceremonially on November 20, 1716, less than a year and a half after the foundation

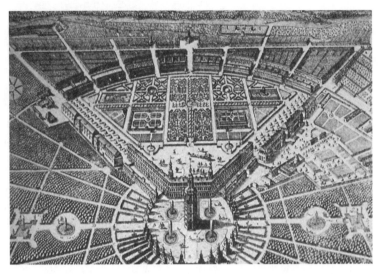

Figure 12.4. Karlsruhe, laid out in 1715, is a radial city whose focal point is the tower of the palace at its center. Some of the radial lines run many miles out into the surrounding countryside.

stone was laid. The palace's master builder was Heinrich Schwarz of Hamburg, and the engineer was Karl's employee, Jacob Friedrich Batzendorff, who is most probably the real architect of the whole city. This central tower, which was the symbol of the state, set upon the Markgraf's foundation stone, is the literal center from which 32 straight lines were laid out radially across the land.

From the tower, the main axis of Karlsruhe is meridional, running southward from the palace. Originally called Carlsgasse (Karl's Lane), this was the main street of the city. It reproduces the classical location of power in the Northern Tradition, in which the lord sits in the north, with his subjects to the south of him. Originally, the line was short, terminating at a church. Later, the church was demolished, and a granite-faced pyramid was erected on the site as a monument to the city's founder. At Yuletide every year, a large Christmas tree is erected on the alignment behind this pyramid. The axis was extended southward as the city expanded, but when it reaches the present Luisenstrasse, it diverts eastward. The principal entrance of the city's main railway station, a little further south, is on the alignment.

Figure 12.5. The central tower of the palace in Karlsruhe (1715), from which the city's geometry originates. (Nigel Pennick)

Figure I2.6. The meridional main street of Karlsruhe, looking southward along the main axis from the top of the central tower. (Nigel Pennick)

THE MIDDLE CHAMBER

Karlsruhe is one of those rare places where the symbolic and the physically real come together in one place, and they interact with an unusual intensity at different levels of being. One such symbolic reality was in the person of Karl Wilhelm himself. He was literally the father of the city, for once the city was built and inhabited, he sired a substantial number of children there through many love affairs with various female subjects. A number of his daughters by these liaisons were housed in rooms in the tower and performed in a choir that occasionally entertained him. The upper part of the tower also functioned as an observatory. Although it is only open to visitors during the hours of daylight, it gives a wonderful view of the sky, and on a sunny day, those who know how can tell the time of day by the sun from the tower. Of course, this is no coincidence, being inherent in the design and layout of Karlsruhe. In 1763, on the instructions of the French king, the astronomer Cassini (César-François de Cassini de Theury) used the tower for some important observations.

Not just the location of this octagonal tower is significant, but also its symbolism. According to Masonic tradition, the upper part of the central tower can be viewed as a representation of the Middle Chamber of Solomon's Temple. In the biblical book of Kings (1 Kings 6:8) we are told: "The door for the middle chamber was in the right side of the house: and they went up with winding stairs into the middle chamber, and out of the middle chamber into the third." At Karlsruhe, the entrances to the tower's spiral stairs from both inside and outside the palace are to the right of the direction of approach. When we reach the "middle chamber" at the top, we can then step outside to walk around a balcony to view the earth and heavens. Here, from the omphalos, we can view the manifest principles emanating from the intellect of the Great Architect of the Universe.

On the day he laid the foundation stone, June 17, 1715, Markgraf Karl Wilhelm instituted a new order of knighthood that contained thirty-one knights, with himself at the head. Thus the order on the land represented by the city was reflected in the aristocratic order.

The town itself was laid out around nine main streets, four on either side of Karl's main one at the center. A plan of 1716 names these streets, as it does the others, after the knights of Karl's order, though later they were renamed. A ninefold division defines the original city as a triangle whose apex measures 101 degrees 15 minutes (9/32). Also, the main axis is cut at right angles by an east–west street named after the Holy Roman Emperor, Kaiserstrasse. It gave Karlsruhe a triangular form, its apex coinciding with the center point of the palace tower. Today, this is the main shopping street of the city, a pedestrian precinct through which trams run.

In a real way, Karlsruhe represents the principle of maintenance of order in the land through chivalry. In this way, the city reproduced the Round Table of King Arthur, for the 32 radii included one for the "king," as though the knights were sitting in a circle around the perimeter as at the legendary Camelot. Karl's true seat was the throne at the center point of the tower and city, over the foundation stone. To the north of the palace, the main axis and the other radial rides ran through the parkland and forest, which was not built upon. Despite almost three centuries of change, seven lines are still in existence in the forest of the Hardtwald, to the north and east of the Schloss. Their vistas are visible from the tower, especially in wintertime when there are no leaves on the trees.

LINES ON THE LANDSCAPE

The longest line still traceable runs for around 8.5 miles (14 km) on the ground. After it peters out, its alignment can be followed on the map to a pilgrimage church at Waghausel, 16 miles (26 km) out from the center. On the other end of this line is the mountain peak of the Eichelberg. Another line, toward the Imperial Cathedral at Speyer, burial place of Holy Roman Emperors, exists for 5.5 miles (9 km) on the ground, but has no trace further out. Another of the radii runs to the mausoleum where the founder's family are buried.

Old maps and city plans show that the main north–south axis was aligned through the pyramid in the main square and an obelisk further down onto a hill with a church on top. This church no longer exists. The granite pyramid, which is a notable feature of the marketplace, is a memorial to the founder. In the original plan, the town church stood on this site, but extensions to the town swept it away. Today, other memorials are arranged at intervals along this main meridional axis. Ultimately, the axis aligns upon mountains in the south about 45 miles (70 km) away. Another line—the most northwesterly extant, for sadly Highway U 14 has destroyed the others—runs through a church that faces on the main square. A fragment of this alignment exists to the north in the street plan of a new settlement. Subsequently, as the city expanded, a number of new churches were built further out on the radial lines.

Set up as a central image of secular and divine authority, Karlsruhe is a remarkable center of intellectual power that remains today. Although the palace is now a museum, having been burnt in an air raid in World War II and subsequently restored, the center of power has remained within the circle. To the west of the palace stand the modern buildings of the Supreme Court of the German Federal Republic. To the east, also within the original circle of the palace complex, is the part of the University of Karlsruhe that contains the faculties of economics and mathematics. To the north of the Schloss, and visible from the tower, is the central nuclear research facility, which is served by the only tramline in Europe where passengers without a pass are forced to get off before the last stop. Thus, the foundation by Markgraf Karl Wilhelm is still truly a center of political power, as the founder intended.

The eighteenth century was a period when esoteric knowledge was not only discussed and developed, but actually brought into physical reality. At places like Karlsruhe and Bath, symbolic architects recognized and used such knowledge. This period of tolerant pluralism developed a symbolic system that recognized the commonality of seemingly different belief systems. In 1733, for example, one in eight of Karlsruhe's population was Jewish, while the remainder were classed as either Catholic or Protestant Christians. All lived together in peace, citizens of the new town whose form reflected the Heavenly Jerusalem. By expressing modernity in terms of eternal principles, the founder of

Karlsruhe sought to bring order out of chaos, to reconcile principles that might be in conflict. Such is the true nature of order on the land.

Karlsruhe was founded at precisely the same period when speculative Freemasonry was being organized in England. The first Grand Lodge was founded in London in 1717. Operative Masonry was still very much alive in German-speaking countries. As the center of western German operative Masonry, the Strasbourg lodge (now in France), L'Oeuvre de Notre-Dame, is still in existence today.

Inspired by Stonehenge, but also, perhaps by Karlsruhe, was the Circus at Bath, designed by the "druidical" architect John Wood the Elder, and begun shortly before his death in 1754. This has three radiating streets coming from a circular center, unprecedented in England at the time. The houses are replete with numerological significance and bear many symbolic emblems from the alchemical and Masonic traditions.

An hour's drive from Karlsruhe, close to Stuttgart, former capital of the kingdom of Württemberg, is another example of this cosmological planning, with significant straight lines on the landscape. A remarkable alignment laid out in 1764 is connected with the pleasure palace of Duke Eugen of Württemberg called Schloss Solitude. This palace was designed in the late Baroque style known as Rococo, and its internal decorations by Philippe de la Guêpière are remarkably fine. However, the geolocation of this palace is a most intelligent piece of landscape design. Rising openly in a commanding position, it is the secular equivalent of the spectacular location of baroque monasteries and pilgrimage churches that exist in southern Germany, Austria, and the South Tyrol. The line that runs from Schloss Solitude is a straight road to Ludwigsburg that is 8 miles (13 km) long. According to an inscription beneath the palace, contemporary with its construction, the road was laid out in French *pieds du roi,* the old French geodesic measure that, among other things, was used at the Church of Saint-Sulpice in Paris to measure the Meridian of France.

At the other end of this Württembergish line, northeast of Stuttgart, is the town of Ludwigsburg. Like Mannheim, though of a later date, Ludwigsburg is laid out on a raster into which the major alignment enters at an angle related to the corners of the grid. The dukes—and later, kings—of Württemberg would travel along this road ceremonially in carriages in summertime, and by horse-drawn "parade sledges" of remarkable symbolic beauty in the snowy wintertime. In a real sense, this was a royal road. Between Schloss Solitude and Ludwigsburg is Weilimdorf, where the road runs up and over the crest of a hill.

Although Ludwigsburg is visible from Schloss Solitude, when one is on the road ascending this hill, it is not possible to see Ludwigsburg. Similarly, on the other side, Schloss Solitude is obscured. Such niceties of orientation are common in German baroque geomancy and show a masterly understanding of landforms. It is probable that these alignments were laid out by the military engineer Colonel Jakob von Scheler (1726–1784). A parallel in England is the laying out of the grounds of Stowe by the military engineer Charles Bridgeman (1690–1738).

It is clear that the designers of Schloss Solitude, like those of Karlsruhe, had the intention of making the palace and its gardens symbolic of Paradise on Earth. In Württemberg, they followed the ideas of the court painter Nicholas Guibal (1725–1784). According to his symbolic system, there are four planes of existence expressed in the schema of Schloss Solitude. An image of the tutelary goddess of the land, Virtembergia, stood on top of the palace as the focus of the alignment. Below her, the building bore twelve statues of the twelve princely virtues that reflected the twelve tribes and zodiac figures of Princess Antonia's painting at Bad Teinach. The main central white hall of Schloss Solitude still has allegorical paintings of "the country's prosperity thanks to its Prince's virtues of love and art," complete with allegories of Württemberg's cities, rivers, treasures, and industries on the sculpted balustrades around the palace. Finally, the actual country itself lying around the princely seat completed the fourfold symbolic schema.

CHAPTER 13

At the Right Time

Favorable Days in the Calendar

Living virtuosly is the same as living in harmony with the processes of nature.

DIOGENES LAERTIOS

GOOD AND BAD DAYS

Many traditions teach that some days are good and some are bad. Their origins are various, but they became established and played an important part in the lore of beginnings and creating places of power. Bad days were easier to take note of than good ones, and so they are better understood today as days when it is inadvisable to begin a project. The ancient Greeks had a system of good and bad days counting through the lunar month. The month was divided into three periods, the waxing month, the mid-month, and the waning, defined by the phases of the moon. The good and bad days were recorded by Hesiod in his *Works and Days* (ca. 850 BCE). "Note the days that come from Zeus," wrote Hesiod, ". . . the thirtieth day of the month is best for one to oversee the work and give out supplies. Avoid fifth days: they are harsh and terrible."

The first, the fourth, and the seventh of each month were Greek holy days, while the eighth and ninth were considered especially good for human activities. The eleventh was good for sheep-shearing, and the twelfth for harvesting fruit. The twelfth was the day for women to set up their looms and begin to weave. The thirteenth day of the waxing month was a day to avoid sowing seed, but it was the best day for planting out seedlings. The fourth day of the mid-month was a good day for a girl to be born. The sixth day was inauspicious for plants and the birth of females. It was a good day for a boy to be born on, however. Animal castration was carried out in mid-month according to special days. Kids were gelded on the sixth, pigs and cattle on the eighth, and donkeys on the twelfth. The twentieth day was auspicious for the birth of wise men. In addition to these days, there were prescriptions for conducting or not performing certain activities on specific days.

The ancient Roman calendar, on which the European tradition is based, was similar. It contained "lawful days" (*fasti*) and "unlawful days" (*nefasti*). The *fasti* were days when the courts of law were open, and *nefasti,* ill-omened days on which no action was taken. Some days were partly good and bad. A *nefastus parte* day was only half "unlawful," and the *endotercisi* had a "lawful" middle part with "unlawful" beginning and end.

Whatever the origin of this system was, it had a profound effect upon later times. Whenever a time to start something was considered, these days were taken into account. The *dies Ægypticae* (Egyptian Days) were lucky and unlucky days observed in calendars coming out of Alexandria. As with the Roman *fasti* and *nefasti,* it was considered unlucky to begin any activity on some of these days, while on others only certain doings were allowed. In medieval Europe, the Egyptian Days or "Black Days" were marked on calendars and almanacs as generally unlucky days. They traveled widely, appearing throughout western Europe, including on Swedish runestocks and in Scottish abbey calendars.

A Swedish runestock of 1710 in the collection of the Royal Society of Antiquaries of Scotland is marked with the following Egyptian Days:

January 1, 2, 4, 29.	July 9.
February 11, 17, 18, 29.	September 10, 18.
March 1, 4, 14, 16.	October 6.
April 10, 17, 18.	November 6, 10.
May 7.	December 11, 18.

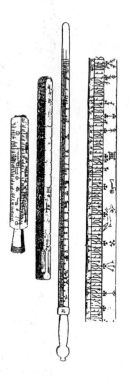

Figure 13.1. Medieval runic calendars from Germany and Scandinavia. (Nideck)

As recognized in northern Europe, the Egyptian Days were not standardized, and other days appeared. The contemporary understanding of the *dies Ægypticae* ascribes the following as Egyptian Days:

January 1, 2, 4, 15, 17, 29.
February 8, 10, 11, 17, 18, 26, 27, 29.
March 4, 14, 16, 17, 20.
April 7, 8, 10, 16, 17, 18, 20, 21.
May 3, 6, 7, 15, 20.
June 4, 8, 10, 22.
July 9, 15, 21.
August 1, 19, 20, 29.
September 2, 4, 6, 7, 10, 18, 21, 23.
October 4, 6, 16, 24.
November 5, 6, 10, 15, 29, 30.
December 6, 7, 9, 11, 15, 18, 22, 28.

Figure 13.2. Runic calendars were used in Scandinavia until the eighteenth century when a change in the calendar from the Julian Calendar to the Gregorian made them no longer functional.

SAINTS' DAYS

In parallel with the Egyptian Days, the days ascribed to certain Christian saints and the episodes in Christian sacred history were important in choosing times to begin projects. According to medieval Christian ideas, each and every human activity has a patronal saint. He or she may be envisaged as the personification of the qualities, knowledge, skills, art, and activity needed to practice that calling successfully. Thus, St. Christopher is the patron of travelers, Crispin of shoemakers, and Cecilia of musicians. The Christian saints took over the functions of Pagan guardian goddesses and gods. Some personify general principles, while others are located in specific places. Thus, St. Barbara (the old Germanic goddess Barbet) is a general saint who saves those who die without receiving the Catholic sacraments. St. Genevieve is invoked generally against disasters, while St. Agatha is specific, protecting Sicilians against eruptions of the volcano Mount Etna.

As with the older Pagan deities that preceded them, there are innumerable Christian saints associated with individual places. Most of them have special days on which they are venerated. The days of both general and specific saints are considered significant when choosing the day to begin something. Patron saints' days are particularly auspicious for ventures connected with the saint's area of influence. But an appropriate saint's day may only be chosen if other factors are also auspicious. Egyptian Days are, of course, ignored in Christian date determination, as certain saints' days fall on them. But the astrological configuration, the phase of the moon, and the day of the week are considered significant.

THE DAYS OF THE WEEK

The seven days of the week, each day influenced by an astrological "planet," originated in Babylon but, perhaps under Christian influence, were transmitted to the whole of Europe, including parts that were Pagan. The days of the week are named after the corresponding planetary deity. Monday (Moon-day) is the day of the Moon. Tuesday is the day of the Germanic sky god Tiwaz (the Norse Tyr), who is the

Figure 13.3. Apotheosized beings,
such as Our Lady here, ascend the cosmic axis
to the heavenly upper world. (Nigel Pennick)

northern equivalent of the god of war, Mars. Wednesday is Woden's day (the Norse Odin), who is equated with Mercury, god of travel and trade. Thursday is the day of the thunder god Thunor (Thor), who is the parallel of Jupiter. Friday is the day of Frigg, equated with the love-goddess Venus. Saturday is the day of Saturn, while Sunday is sacred to the Sun.

Northern European traditions ascribe certain qualities to each day. Some days of the week are bad for certain things and good for others. The day of the week on which one is born is deemed significant A traditional English rhyme tells of the fortune of babies born on different days. They contain the attributes of the planetary deities of the corresponding day, with a Christian gloss that the "Sabbath" (Sunday) is the best

> *Monday's Child is fair of face,*
> *Tuesday's child is full of grace,*
> *Wednesday's child is full of woe,*
> *Thursday's child has far to go.*
> *Friday's child is loving and giving,*
> *Saturday's child works hard for a living.*
> *But the child that is born on the Sabbath Day*
> *Is blithe and bonny, good and gay.*

There are many folk traditions that tell of omens associated with specific days of the week. An English tradition, which recalls the ancient arts of the *Fulguriator* (a priest who interprets and propitiates lightning), tells us that: Monday's thunder indicates the death of unmarried girls and women. Tuesday's thunder promises plenty of bread. Wednesday's thunder brings death to harlots, whores, and other bloodshed. Thursday's thunder (the day of the thunder god) brings no misfortune. Friday's thunder brings the slaughter of a great man, and other murders. Saturday's thunder brings pestilence and plague, and great death. Sunday's thunder tells of the death of judges and learned men.

According to English folk tradition, getting married on different days of the week is held to bring corresponding results: "Monday for wealth, Tuesday for health, Wednesday the best day of all. Thursday for losses, Friday for crosses, and Saturday, no luck at all." In the Christian tradition, weddings should not be performed on Sundays. As most weddings are held on Saturdays at present, traditionalists may ascribe the high failure rate of contemporary marriages with the "no luck at all" promised by this day.

In German builders' lore, it is considered bad luck to begin building on a Monday. A chimney must not be started on a Friday. Friday is generally a bad day for starting things. Traditionally, British fishermen will not begin a voyage on a Friday. Friday the thirteenth of any month is considered particularly unlucky. An old East Anglian adage ascribes extreme qualities to Friday: "Friday's the day will have its trick, the fairest or foulest day of the week."

Connected with the planetary days of the week are the planetary hours. According to medieval tradition, the astrological planets rule in order throughout the week. Beginning at midnight on Sunday, the planetary hours begin with Jupiter ruling from midnight to one a.m. The next hour is ruled by Mars, and the following by the Sun. From three until four, Venus rules. After the hour of Venus comes that of Mercury, then the hour of the Moon and finally Saturn, between six and seven. Following Saturn, the sequence begins again in the same order: Jupiter, Mars, Sun, Venus, Mercury, Moon, Saturn, and so on through the week until the last hour of Saturday is ruled by Venus. Then the cycle begins again. These hours are used in ceremonies that relate to the powers signified by their corresponding planetary goddess or god. Each is most powerful on its own day.

In folk tradition, the eight points at the middle of each of the eight Tides of the day are special times. People born at these times, called the Chime Hours, are said to have the second sight. In the 24-hour clock, these Chime Hours are 03:00, 06:00, 09:00, 12:00, 15:00, 18:00, 21:00, and 24:00 hours.

FAVORABLE TIME OF YEAR

The bread of yesterday, the meat of today, and the wine of last year will produce health.

THE BOOK OF IAGO AB DEWI

European building tradition recommends founding buildings in the springtime. In his *De re aedificatoria,* Leon Battista Alberti (1404–1472) cited the Roman engineer-architect Frontinus to the effect that it is best to build from the beginning of April to the beginning of November, with a break in the hottest part of summer. According to the Masonic expert George Oliver in his *Cyclopedia of Freemasonry* (1867):

> The masonic days proper for laying the foundation-stone of a Mason's lodge, are from the 15th of April to the 15th of May; and the 18th of April has been pronounced particularly auspicious, because nothing can be more consonant with reason and propriety, than to commence a building in the early spring, that the workmen may have the whole summer before them to complete the undertaking advantageously, in order that they may celebrate the cape stone with confidence and joy.

In 1448, Sir John Wenlock laid the foundation stone for the new Queens' College in Cambridge. It was laid at the southeast angle of the old chapel of the former Carmelite Friary that stood there. The date was April 15. Four hundred years later, in the nineteenth century, railway engineers counted ground-breaking as equivalent of laying the foundation stone of a building. In England in 1853, the first sod of the Somerset Central Railway was dug at Highbridge, near Burnham-on-Sea, by the company chairman. The date was April 18. While it is common sense to begin building in the springtime, when longer days and better weather are coming, there is also the symbolic element of spring as a time of beginnings, a natural time for growth to start. In harmony with nature, the building also grows.

CHAPTER 14

Principles of Electional Astrology

Choosing the Correct Time for Rites and Ceremonies

And, as the cock crew, those who stood before
The Tavern shouted—"Open the Door!
You know how little while we have to stay,
And, once departed, may return no more."

RUBÁIYÁT OF OMAR KHAYYÁM
(TRANS. EDWARD FITZGERALD)

ELECTIONAL ASTROLOGY IN HISTORY

According to traditional astrological belief, the planetary aspects present at anything's or anybody's beginning denote or influence the character of that thing or person. They also affect its future because future positions of the planets and so forth are related to their position at the beginning. The positions of the heavenly bodies at the moment of beginning are the thing or person's inceptional or natal horoscope. Electional Astrology is concerned with setting up and diagnosing charts that will give the most favorable astrological aspects to any project.

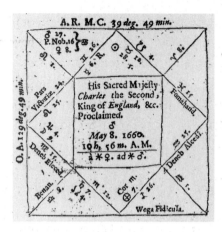

Figure 14.1. Elected Inceptional Horoscope of King Charles II, 1660.

The most appropriate time is "elected," and the venture is timed to go ahead at the right moment.

The use of electional astrology is wide. It ranges from laying the foundation stone of a new building, setting up a new company, opening a shop for the first time, getting married, or crowned king, or even the most appropriate time to make a play for something. To elect a time, the astrologer examines the aspects for the best possible chart within the time allotted for the event. The chart that appears best is called the Election Chart. When an Election Chart is used to lay a foundation stone of a building, it also becomes its Inceptional Chart.

In ancient times, building was conducted in harmony with cosmic cycles. Just as migration, animal breeding, sowing, planting, pruning, and harvesting involved procedures that had to be performed at the right time, so the making of buildings also required proper timing if success was to be assured. Important moments of time were marked by the position of the stars. In ancient Egypt, for instance, the heliacal rising of Sirius heralded the rising of the River Nile. Similarly, buildings, temples, and cities could rise when the proper celestial omens were seen.

Babylonian cities were considered to reflect the heavenly stars and constellations on Earth. The city of Assur corresponded with the star Arcturus, Sippara to the constellation of Cancer, and Nineveh to Ursa Minor, its plan "delineated in distant times in the writing of the heavens of stars." Babylon, Bab-Ilani, the "Gate of the Gods," corresponded with the constellations now called Cetus and Aries. When certain planets were visible in these zodiacal signs, then they were held to have an influence upon life in their corresponding cities. It is perhaps from this esoteric correspondence that the idea of electional astrology came about.

Electional astrology arose as a means to begin an enterprise on a day and at a time when the heavens were in the most auspicious configuration to promote growth and success. The actual aspects depended entirely upon what the enterprise was. An auspicious moment for one enterprise may be disastrous for another. Astrologers can choose an astrologically helpful time to begin any enterprise. The earliest recorded examples include coronations, foundations, and military actions. The foundation of the city of Antioch (Antakya, southeastern Turkey) on May 22, 300 BCE by King Seleucus I Nicator appears to be the first recorded example of electional astrology in action. The city of Apamea in northern Syria was founded by the same king in the same year, so it is likely that electional astrology was used there, too. Although they are rare, there are Roman holy stones and stelae bearing the dates they were set up. A Roman stela erected at a crossroads

Figure 14.2. Roman stele Quadrivium goddesses of crossroads, Stuttgart Germany. (Nigel Pennick)

at Bad Cannstatt, now part of Stuttgart, has an image of the guardian goddesses of the four directions and an inscription recording its erection on December 29, 230 CE.

ASTROLOGY AND
THE WESTERN CHURCH

As history points out, the first observers and investigators of the disposition and courses of the stars were our forebears the Patriarchs, who, inspired by the Lord God and their knowledge of geometry and the assistance of mathematical instruments, measured and defined for us the firmament and the courses of the stars.

ADRIAEN METIUS (1571–1635),
*ON THE INVESTIGATION OR
OBSERVATION OF THE STARS* (LEIDEN, 1621)

Although, according to "gospel truth," the three Wise Men used astrology to find the baby Jesus, the Christian Church has always had an uneasy relationship with the stellar art. Many influential Christian commentators have likened it to other forms of divination unlawful to believers. They have not considered astrology to be a superstition because it did not work; almost to a man, they believed in the accuracy of astrology. Their opposition came from the doctrine that everything that happens only happens because God wills or allows it (hence "acts of God" as a term for natural disasters). According to this idea, it is not the place of human beings to preempt the acts of God by foreknowledge through divination or astrology. Its corollary is that, because astrology allows humans to predict God's actions, it must then have been invented by the Devil as a means to undermine the authority of God.

In his conversion from Pagan to Christian beliefs, the church father Augustine of Hippo (354–430 CE) condemned everything in which he had once believed. Among the common practices he denigrated was astrology. In *The City of God,* Augustine wrote:

Figure 14.3. Fountain with column of Mary and Jesus
Schwaebisch Gmund, Germany. (Nigel Pennick)

God is the Lord of both stars and men. But what kind of rule over men's actions is left to God if men are necessarily determined by the stars? . . . There are some men who prefer to say that the stars rather signify than cause men's fate, that a particular position is like a form of words which causes us to know, but does not cause, what happens in the future. This view was shared by men of no mean learning. However, this is not the way that astrologers usually speak.

Because astrology had a Pagan origin, and appeared to give people knowledge of things that only God should rightfully know, certain churchmen took the view that astrology was unchristian. They chose to ignore the reality that almost all of the practices of the Christian church were also taken from earlier Pagan usages. Roman Catholic Canon Law (*Corpus Juris Canonici*) actually prohibited the use of astrology to choose auspicious times to perform actions. But many Christian kings and popes ignored this doctrine and employed astrologers.

Astrology figures in the semi-legendary histories that compose the Matter of Britain. In his *History of the Kings of Britain* (1136), Geoffrey of Monmouth (ca. 1095–ca. 1155) wrote of a magician who served King Edwin, who reigned in Northumbria from 617 to 634 CE. He was called Pellitus and came from Spain. He was "very knowledgeable about the flight of birds and the courses of the stars." The fourteenth-century chronicler Matthew of Westminster, in his *The Flowers of History,* records this story under the year 633 CE. According to Matthew, King Edwin defeated Cadwallon, king of the Britons, in battle, and then laid waste the provinces of Demecia, Menevia, and Venedocia. Cadwallon fled to Ireland, but each attempt he made to re-invade Britain was preempted by Edwin, whose astrologer, Pellitus, told him when and where Cadwallon would attempt to land. Solomon, king of Brittany, advised Cadwallon to kill the Iberian magus, Pellitus. Cadwallon sent his nephew, Brian, to York in disguise, and he assassinated the astrologer with an iron staff as he was giving alms to the poor. Unable to use astrology anymore, Edwin was unable to prevent the British king from landing at Exeter. Joining up with Pagan Mercian forces under King Penda, they defeated and killed Edwin in battle at Heathfield.

Pope Sixtus IV (Francesco Della Rovere, reigned 1471–1484) used astrology to decide the time for all of his important appointments. Rodrigo Borgia (Pope Alexander VI, 1492–1503) consulted the astrological prophecies of Cardinal Bianco. When he received news of his election as pope, having bribed the conclave of cardinals to vote for him, Guiliano Della Rovere (Pope Julius II, 1503–1513) was at Bologna. He consulted an astrologer to find out the most auspicious time for his journey to Rome and his enthronement. The astrologer

Figure 14.4. St Paul's Cathedral and other monuments, built in the golden age of masonic electional astrology, stand as representatives of the refounded New Britain marked by the restoration of the monarchy on May 29, 1660, after Cromwell's tyrannous rule. (Nideck)

Luca Gaurico (1475–1558) was employed by Guilio de' Medici (Pope Clement VII, 1523–1543) and Alessandro Farnese (Pope Paul III, 1534–1549) for astrological elections, among other things. In 1552, Gaurico published his *Tractatus Astrologicus*. Later, he was killed in the papal library when a heavy book fell on his head.

Not every pope favored astrology, however. As with the other mantic arts, there were occasional churchly edicts attempting to suppress it. In 1586, Felice Peretti (Pope Sixtus V, 1585–1590) issued a Papal Bull condemning astrology. Another came from Matteo Barberini (Pope Urban VIII, 1623–1644) on April 1, 1631, after several astrologers had wrongly foretold his death. In France, ordinances against astrol-

Figure 14.5. St Paul's Cathedral, London. (Nigel Pennick)

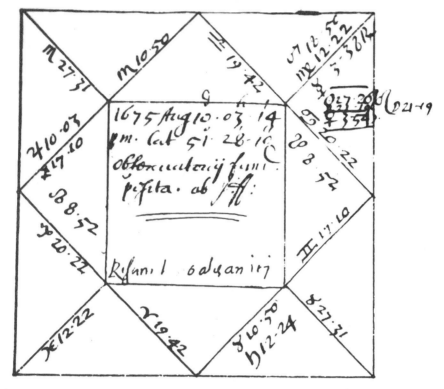

Figure 14.6. The Astronomer Royal John Flamsteed's elected chart for the foundation of the Royal Observatory at Greenwich, August 10, 1675. (Nideck)

ogy were enacted in 1493, 1560, and 1570. Published at Lyon in 1621, the *Opuscula* of the French Jesuit Julius Caesar Boulanger (1558–1628), attacked astrologers who elected the horoscopes for the foundation of cities. The Church of England priest John Vaux (ca. 1575–1651) was suspended in 1633 for his astrological activities, and occasional attacks are made by fundamentalists on astrology today.

THE ELECTIONAL ASTROLOGY OF CITIES

Despite the opposition in principle to electional astrology by monotheists, in practice it was held to be a useful technique. The inceptional horoscopes of cities were sought as a means to predict forthcoming fortunes and disasters, and new cities were founded with the best possible prognoses. In 300 BCE, Antioch was founded at the most auspicious moment. Nearly three centuries later, Gaius Julius Hyginus, the Emperor Augustus's librarian, wrote a work, now lost, on the foundation and topography of Italian towns. Another recorded instance of electional astrology was noted by Ilario Altobelli, the historian of the Franciscan order who wrote of the founding of the city of Venice around noon on March 25, 421 CE.

Pagans, Christians, and Muslims alike have all used elected times for urban foundations. In Islamic tradition, selecting propitious moments for performing important activities is called *ikhtiyarat*. The Iraqi city of Baghdad was founded in the year 762 CE at time elected by Caliph Mansur's state astrologer, Nambakht. Sagittarius was in the ascendant. The Caliph laid the first stone at the appointed moment. The foundation was auspicious, for Baghdad went on the become one of the world's most important centers of learning and experiment, especially in the fields of geodesy, alchemy, and astronomy.

The Emperor Theodosius (reigned 375–395 CE) was renowned in medieval tradition for his patronage of geometers. Telling of geometry, the medieval English poem *The Court of Sapience* says:

> *Eke Theodosius in hys maner*
> *With philosophres sate ful lustely,*
> *Of that scyence tretyng ful craftely,*
> *As good Euglyd, and many clerkes moo.*

> (Theodosius, too, in his manor
> Sat eagerly with philosophers,
> Discoursing on that science skillfully,
> As good Euclid had done, and many scholars more.)*

Medieval astrologers reckoned that the foundation day of the Italian city of Bologna from May 22, the day it, according to legend, was founded by the Emperor Theodosius. The astrologer Ludovicus

---

*Modern English translation by Michael Moynihan.

Vitalis published annual horoscopes for the city in the years 1506–1540. Then, in 1543, Pope Paul III commissioned Luca Gaurico to elect the time to lay the foundation stone of a new building in Bologna. It was described as "the third restoration of the city." The ceremony was timed by Vicentius Carpanatius, who observed the sky with an astrolabe

Figure 14.7. Studies serve for delight, for ornament, and for abilities.
(Nigel Pennick)

and announced when the exact moment had arrived. At that instant, Cardinal Eunius Verulanus of Albano ritually laid the marble foundation stone, which bore the mark of Alessandro Franese. In 1575, the local meridian was laid out in the church of St. Petronius in Bologna by a priest–astronomer, Ignatius Dante.

Astrological histories of the human race were written by the Muslim astrologers Mashallah ibn Athari (740–814) and Abu Ma'shar al-Balkhi (787–886), the latter of whom was the most famed medieval Islamic astrologer. In his *De re aedificatoria,* Leon Battista Alberti

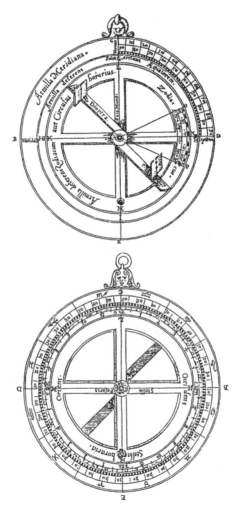

Figure 14.8. A medieval European astrolabe. (Nideck)

refers to Lucius Tarutius, who worked out the inceptional horoscope of Rome. This he did by drawing up the horoscopes of major disasters, then rectifying the chart until it was the best possible fit. In 1664, Francis Bernard, later doctor to King James II, claimed to have done the same for London. First, he determined the horoscopes of major disasters, such as the fires of London. He began with the seventh recorded great fire of London that took place in 1212, when London Bridge and Castle Baynard were destroyed. Using the same technique, Bernard also worked out the horoscope of Amsterdam. He claimed to be able to predict with an accuracy of a week when fires would occur in the future. According to Patrick McFadzean in his *Astrological Geomancy* (1985), the ascendant of London is 17 degrees Gemini, and Liverpool 18 degrees Scorpio. It seems that this knowledge was taken into account for timing of the Masonic Service held at the Anglican Cathedral in Liverpool on July 21, 1924, during the week of consecration services. Its ascendant was 18 degrees Scorpio.

ELECTIONAL ASTROLOGY IN FOUNDATIONS

The foundation of churches, abbeys, and cathedrals on auspicious saints' days has been mentioned above. Certain saints' days are astrologically appropriate in their own right, for example, All Souls' Day, November 2, when the sun is in Scorpio. This is a particularly appropriate day for consecrating cemeteries. King's College Chapel in Cambridge, founded by King Henry VI in 1446, has an Inceptional Chart that was most probably elected. The chapel, which was constructed according to a complete system of symbolism and sacred geometry, has both the Sun and Moon in Leo, appropriate for its royal name and connections. Three other planets are also in Leo, reinforcing the regal associations. Like all charts, that of King's College Chapel is not perfect, for the Moon's south node—Cauda Draconis—is conjunct Mars. This can mean that the project will never be fully completed, and that is the case at King's. Only the chapel was built out of all the buildings planned by Henry VI, and that was never finished, for the interior was never painted in the vibrant symbolic colors stipulated by the king.

Perhaps influenced by Rosicrucian ideas, or just carrying on medieval custom, electional astrology played a significant role in the foundation of colleges and churches in post-reformation England. The foundation stone of the west range of Caius Court—in Gonville and Caius College, Cambridge, was laid at 4:00 in the morning on May 5, 1565. There can be no reason for laying a stone before sunrise unless the time was particularly auspicious.

When he was Gresham Professor of Astronomy at Oxford University, Christopher Wren (1632–1723) lectured on the truth of astrology. St Paul's Cathedral, Wren's masterpiece, rebuilt after the ninth great fire of London in 1666, is the epitome of cosmic symbolism. Until recently, Wren's ceremonial measuring rod, covered in green velvet and about a fathom in length, was on show in the crypt of St Paul's.

In his Masonic *Constitutions* of 1738, James Anderson (1684–1739) wrote: "London was re-building apace; and the fire having ruined St Paul's Cathedral, the King with Grand Master Rivers, his architects and craftsmen, Nobility and Gentry, Lord Mayor and Aldermen, Bishops and Clergy, etc. in due form levelled the footstone of the new St Paul's." The foundation stone of the new St Paul's Cathedral in London, in June 1675, was laid by the master Mason Thomas Strong, and the second, above it, laid by King Charles II. The stone laid by Strong was the footstone, which contains a cavity wherein the foundation deposits are laid. Wren's epitaph in the cathedral describes him as the founder of the city, "for the public good."

Another of Wren's great public buildings was certainly started at the right moment. The time of laying the foundation stone of the Royal Observatory at Greenwich was elected by the Astronomer Royal, John Flamsteed. The stone was laid ceremonially at 3:14 p.m. on August 10, 1675. The horoscope still exists. The chart shows the Sun in the ninth house, appropriate for the furtherance of astronomy, signifying philosophical and scientific exploration. Sagittarius, the ruler of the ninth house, was rising at 3:14 p.m., and Jupiter, the sign's ruler, is also in Sagittarius. Close to the observatory, the foundation stone of the Seamen's Hospital at Greenwich was laid jointly by Sir Christopher Wren and John Evelyn at 5:00 p.m., June 30, 1696. The time was fixed exactly by John Flamsteed, the Astronomer Royal, at the Royal Observatory nearby.

The Sussex businessman Samuel Jeake elected the date for founding his storehouse at Mermaid Street in Rye. Jeake laid the foundation stone at noon on June 13, 1689. He used a radical election from his own horoscope. Noon on this day was the exact moment when Mercury, signifying commerce, was in the identical position as the moment he was born. The moon was in the twelfth house, propitious for a place of storage. To record the elected time, the building's horoscope was carved upon a stone. This was set into the front wall of the warehouse, and there it remains today.

Colonialists sometimes used local auspices for founding their missionary churches. The foundation stone of the Protestant cathedral in Antananarivo, Madagascar, was laid on August 10, 1884. This was one of the most auspicious days of the year according to the indigenous Malagasy system of chronomancy known as *Vintana*. Later Christian commentators denied any electional intention in the founding of Madagascar cathedral. Although there is no overt information on the use of electional astrology for founding Church of England churches, the horoscopes of many English cathedrals founded since 1880 appear to be favorable elections. In 1911, the noted astrologer Alan Leo elected the date and time for laying the foundation stone of the headquarters of the Theosophical Society in Tavistock Square, London. It was laid with full Masonic form by Annie Besant on September 3, 1911.

ELEMENTS OF TIMING

The time that we choose to do anything is affected by many factors, operating on different levels. If we fail to prepare, then we must prepare to fail in our actions. Ideally, to be in harmony with the cosmos and to maintain the *Pax Deorum,* any action should have the following components. It should be at the right place, with the place prepared properly. Then, the spiritual powers of the place will be in accord with the action. It must be performed by the right person, ritually purified according to appropriate sacred rites. He or she should conduct the right action at the right time. Only when all of these components are in harmony will the action be successful.

The appropriate moment to perform an action is the matter of electional astrology. The position of an elected time in the solar cycle is defined by the calendar. Any time chosen must be on a certain day of the year, and that day will be in a certain season. The quality of this day is defined by many factors. The weather in some countries is unpredictable, and bad weather may make it inauspicious to start for an enterprise even when the astrological factors are favorable. The Masonic recommendation of beginning in the spring is based partly upon this practical consideration.

Certain days are important culturally, because they are festivals. These include festivals of two kinds: those on fixed days in the calendar, and those that move. Fixed-day festivals include Pagan festivals like Lammas and Samhain, fixed Christian saints' days and Church festivals such as Christmas Day. The Church also has movable festivals like Easter and Whitsun, whose dates are the result of complex calculations involving sun and moon. In addition, the British state has public holidays called "Bank Holidays" held on the nearest Monday to certain dates. An undertaking started on any of these days will partake of their wider qualities.

The actual time of day is also important. Day length varies with time of year. Morning is a time of beginnings and evening, decline. Noon marks the high point of the sun, and midnight the low point when the calendar day ends, and the next one begins. Each specific Tide of the day has its own quality, as does each planetary hour. At any moment, the planets themselves stand in a certain relationship to the place where we are. According to astrology, they have specific influences upon certain aspects of existence. They are important in an elected chart, for their positions may help or hinder the enterprise. The quality of the time is also dependent on the phase and age of the moon. The position of the moon in the houses and signs is also of significance. The angles and the houses in the mundane sphere contribute their influence on the nature of the time we choose.

The phase of the moon and its speed can be used to accelerate an undertaking. This is also possible by choosing the ascendant. The rising sign employs a fixed sign for endurance, a cardinal one for action, and a mutable sign for flexibility. It is the task of the astrological geomant to take all of these factors into account when electing a chart for the foundation and other key events in building. The astrological geomant will rarely have the luxury of a perfect chart, and so any shortcomings must be dealt with by creative means. This is the essential skill of electional astrology.

MUNDANE AND RADICAL ELECTIONS

Ancient astrology based its electional charts on the mundane charts active at the time the election was needed. The ruling factor in traditional mundane horoscopes is the previous conjunction of Jupiter and Saturn. Previous eclipses are also taken into account. These factors form the mundane chart, and electional ascendant ought not to be afflicted there. It is fortunate if the significator, the planet that rules the subject of the election, is ruler of the sign containing either the Sun or the Moon.

Electional astrology across the world often relates the horoscope of the house with that of the resident. This is done in the Eastern geomancies of Feng Shui, *Yattara,* and *Vastu Vidya* as well as in certain African traditions, such as the *Vintana* practiced in Madagascar. It is part of European house astrology, too. According to these traditions, the individual's natal horoscope is related to the inceptional horoscope of the building in which he or she intends to live. In the case of existing buildings, there is either a good match, or not. When a house is to be started, however, there is the opportunity to harmonize as nearly as possible the horoscopes of the individual and the building. This is one of the aims of electional astrology. While aiming for a "perfect fit," this is rarely possible.

If the individual's horoscope is not favorable, then no election can reverse it, and it is no good attempting to elect a time based upon his or her chart. The individual is thus doomed to a difficult existence. If the birth (radical) chart is favorable to the elected purpose, then the elected chart should be based on the radical chart. It must be calculated carefully. The astrologer must make sure that radical electional charts do not set off any serious afflictions of the birth chart. The house that rules the matter in hand in the natal chart should be fortified, being well placed and unafflicted. The elected aspects should not afflict the Moon and angles in the radix. They should have a strong, well-placed position in the radix.

It is important that we choose the sign on the ascendant of the radical chart to be on the electional chart also, so long as it is not afflicted. Providing that they occupy auspicious positions in the natal chart, the signs on the tenth and eleventh radical cusps are good ascendants. It is fortunate to put the lord of the radical ascendant in an angle or succedent house on the elected chart and oriental of the sun. This is done whether or not it is benefic or malefic. It is considered unfortunate to move the radical ascendant counter to the Earth's rotation.

Ephemeral (or horary) elections are based upon the positions of the planets at the time when the election is made. They do not take either the mundane or radical horoscopes into account. Ideally, these should be the basis of elections. When an election needs to be made in a hurry, and there is no time to wait for the moon to have a good aspect, there are means to get the best out of a poor chart. If the moon is applying to a malefic, then the malefic is made lord of the ascendant. This is done even when this is afflicted, so long as the main significators are as free from affliction as they can be. When the moon is weak or afflicted, it must be placed in an angular or succedent house, ensuring that there is no aspect with either the ascendant, or its lord, neither the the lord of the house ruling the election, nor any other significator. For rapidity, the moon can be placed in a cadent house having no aspect to the ascendant. It should have a benefic rising or be in good aspect with the rising degree.

GENERAL CONSIDERATIONS IN ELECTIONAL ASTROLOGY

In general, it is important to fortify the ascendant in an elected chart, also its lord and the dispositor of its lord. Sun or moon should not be in the ascendant, with the exception of the Sun in Aries or Leo, and then only when well aspected. In addition, the fourth house, the lord of the fourth house, and its dispositor, should be fortified. The fourth house signifies the conclusion of the matter, and thus it is most important that this house is beneficial. The cusp of the house ruling the matter in hand must be strong and unafflicted. It is also essential to fortify the Moon as well as the house and planets that refer to the matter in hand. It is more important to fortify these than the fourth house or ascendant.

The Part of Fortune and its depositor need to be fortified. It can be in a cadent house but should neither be separating from aspect with the Moon, nor occupy the second, sixth, eighth, or twelfth house from Fortuna. Fortuna is dignified when (in descending order of significance) in Taurus, Pisces, Cancer, Leo, Libra, Sagittarius, Gemini, and the first thirteen degrees of Virgo.

Traditionally, the major planets—Mars, Jupiter, and Saturn—are said to be oriental when the Sun is passing from a conjunction with them toward opposition. In modern astrology, the planets Uranus, Neptune and Pluto are added to the original three major planets used in earlier electional astrology of beginnings and foundations. The Sun is oriental when it is in the fourth, fifth, sixth, tenth, eleventh, and twelfth houses. The Moon is oriental when waxing from new moon to full moon. Mercury and Venus, the minor planets, are oriental when they are behind the Sun in the zodiac. When it rises or sets after the Sun, a planet is occidental. The major planets are occidental when the Sun is passing from opposition with them to conjunction. The Sun is occidental in the first, second, third, seventh, eighth, and ninth houses. The Moon is occidental when it is waning from full moon to new moon.

The Moon is most significant in elected charts. If possible, the Moon should be put in a house that rules the main matter of the election, or at any angle other than the ascendant. A strong moon is best elected in Cancer, Taurus, Virgo, or Pisces. It is good if the place of the previous or new moon is dignified and well placed in the election. When in the elected chart the dispositor of the previous new or full moon is oriental, and is in its own sign, the election will be beneficial providing it is trine or sextile to the place of the lunation. If it has no aspect, then it will be ineffective. The lord of triplicity that contains the Moon as the previous lunation is important. It should be well aspected with the significators in the election, or in reception. This is when two planets are each in the sign ruled by the other, and the effect is similar to that of a conjunction.

The first twelve hours after full moon are "combust hours," bad for starting any project. The following 72 hours are favorable when the Moon is well aspected at the beginning of the thirteenth hour after full moon. The following twelve hours are "combust hours" again, and so on. This cycle of 12/72 is repeated throughout the whole month. The Moon is weakened in Scorpio and Capricorn. It is at its lowest strength from 15 degrees Libra to 15 degrees Scorpio. This period is the *Via Combusta*. When the Moon is coming away from a conjunction or opposition with the Sun, the next lunar aspect is significant in the chart. Retrograde planets should be avoided.

Electional astrology describes ten ways in which the Moon can be weakened in a chart. It is weak when conjunct, square, or in opposition to malefics. When it is slow in motion, traveling less than 13 degrees 11 minutes a day, it loses strength. It is weak when "combust" or within 12 degrees of the Sun, especially when approaching it. After separation, the first 5 degrees are the worst. It is also weakened when it is within 12 degrees of opposition with the Sun, especially when approaching it. Within 12 degrees of the Dragon's Head and Tail, the Moon's nodes, it is weakened. It is weak when cadent or in *Via Combusta,* also in latter degrees containing malefics. The Moon is weakened when it is in fall in Scorpio, especially at the exact position of the fall, 3 degrees Scorpio. It is also affected adversely when in detriment in Capricorn, Aries, and Libra, which make bad aspects with the Moon's own sign, Cancer. When the Moon is "void of course," when it does not make a major aspect before leaving a sign, its influence is weakened.

ELECTED FOUNDATIONS

When the Moon is in Aquarius, it is a good moment to commence building, also when Aquarius is rising, and the Moon, Venus, and

Jupiter are in favorable aspects to the rising degree. The basic principles of an elected chart for the foundation of a building involves fortifying the ascendant and its ruler; the Moon and its depositor; and the planet to which the Moon is aspected. The significators ought not to be below the horizon when a foundation is laid. The only exception is the Moon, when it is in the third or fifth house and well aspected by a significator or benefic above the horizon. The Moon should be waxing, both in speed and light. It should be in aspect with its depositor, and the ascendant should be aspected by its ruler. The Moon should not be aspected by Saturn or its south node, but it is good if it is applying to Jupiter.

With Cauda Draconis, the Moon's south node, it is best when it is in the twelfth house. But it ought not to be in ascendant or the second or fourth house. The fourth house is the worst. Because of this potential difficulty, the second and fourth houses and their lords should be fortified. If the building is tall, the tenth house and its lord should also be fortified. Mars should be in a sign ruled by Venus, and in good aspect with that planet. Mercury should be angular and its dispositor placed strongly. The same applies to the Part of Fortune. If a less favorable chart must be elected, then fortify the Moon, the ascendant, and the second and fourth houses with their rulers. Put the Moon in good aspect or conjunction with Jupiter. Jupiter should be in the second house where possible. Fortify the planet in the sign containing the Moon.

When electing the chart for laying the foundation stone of a church, it is customary to fortify the ascendant and the ninth house, along with their lords. Also fortify the Moon, Part of Fortune, and planets here along with their dispositors. Fortify the tenth house and its lord. Jupiter should be in good aspect to the ascendant, and in its own sign or another that is favorable, also in a beneficial house. Any planets in aspect with the Moon should also be fortified, along with the planet exalted in the ascendant.

STAGES OF RITUAL IN BUILDING

As described in previous chapters, laying the foundation stone is one of the most important ceremonies of building. It is traditional to take great care over electing the time when this is to take place. The instant of laying the foundation stone fixes the birth of the building: it creates the ambience of the building and determines its future history. Other important stages in building construction can also be elected, though it is usual for them to be celebrated with rites and ceremonies when they are reached as a natural process of the building. Most commonly celebrated is the completion of the roof in the Topping-Out ceremony. Entering the building formally for the first time is another important stage in the life of the construction. At that moment, the person or people who must use the building are affected by both the building's own ambience and the quality of the time. If at all possible, the time of entry must be tailored to the individual's radix. Indian *Vastu Shastra,* a parallel with the European tradition, calculates the horoscopes of various stages in the construction of the house: laying the foundation stone, digging the well, fixing the roof beam, and the individual's first visit to the building.

SPECIFIC ELECTIONS

In the Christian tradition, the naming ceremony of baptism is ruled by Jupiter. Bad aspects of Mars and Uranus should not be present, and the fifth house, ruling children, ought to be favorable. The process of buying somewhere to live is primarily under the rulership of Mercury, though Venus is money's ruler, and Saturn controls long-term investments. The fourth house is important in house-buying. The planets in the fourth house can affect the transaction beneficially or adversely, depending on what and where they are. Saturn can bring difficulties and delays, for example. Moving into a new dwelling-space is difficult if the new place has not been built specially. When it is possible to establish the horoscope of the house, then this must be harmonized as well as possible with that of the new occupant. As this is rarely the case, the move comes under the rulership of Mercury. The Moon and the rising sign are significant. Capricorn, referring to travel by land, is significant here.

In any case, even when it is not possible to elect an appropriate time, a ceremony of Entering the Building should be made when moving into a new dwelling-place. If appropriate ceremonies are not conducted, then an inappropriate ambience may be established in the place, leading to disharmony and conflict.

Electional astrology has always proved useful to those founding schools, colleges, or universities. As with other enterprises, it is essential that the aims and objectives are established with great care before any action is taken. Mercury is the ruler of learning, corresponding with the mutable zodiac signs of Gemini and Virgo. Gemini is a sign of interpersonal communication, while Virgo rules practical skills. Schools and colleges are founded to practice and teach both types of human skill. According to Roman astrological geomancy, Gemini is ruled by Apollo, the god of eloquence, divination, the fine arts, and music. Virgo is ruled by the goddess of the abundant harvest, Ceres, who taught humans the art of tilling the ground, of sowing corn, reaping it and, finally, making it into bread. The Mysteries of Eleusis, the most holy rites of ancient Mediterranean Paganism, were sacred to Ceres. Mercury in Gemini is considered the best for founding places of learning that are primarily intellectual in intent. Where practical skills are also taught, that is, where the core European tradition is to be maintained, then Mercury in Virgo is preferable. Where the "great and useful arts" are to be studied, then Mercury could be in Aries, ruled by Minerva. This could bring problems concerning aggressive applications of skills taught there, if not handled with great care.

The establishment of any new place of learning should be defined with appropriate symbolic ceremonies that embody the nature and meaning of the enterprise, calling upon the appropriate spiritual qualities to empower and sustain it. The electional astrology of places of worship is perhaps the most studied of all. It is clear that historically the foundation dates and times of many temples, churches, mosques, and synagogues have been elected. According to Christian tradition, as in baptism, the ruling planet for the foundation of churches is Jupiter. In modern astrology, Neptune has been added. Like many medieval Christian founders, who used significant saints' days, founders of new Pagan places of worship tend to choose Pagan festivals from the Eightfold Year or the calendar of a specific pantheon. It is possible, however, to elect the best moment of any otherwise fixed day, though the auspices may be in no way good. Followers of Asatru or Odinism may use runic astrology.

Places of ceremonial or ritual drama and performance have various rulers. The martial arts are ruled by Mars in Aries, while Venus controls the arts of ceremony and pleasure. The moon in Leo or Libra will bring general satisfaction to performer and audience alike.

RITES AND CEREMONIES

Rites and ceremonies are symbolic re-definitions of archetypal events. Foundation rites, for example, are re-enactments of the moment of creation. Such rites are examples of *anamnesis,* the recalling of things past. They re-call or re-present an event in the past so that it becomes operative here and now by its effects. In performing such rites and ceremonies, we become as one with those who have performed them before, and those who may perform them again in the future. We are thus part of a great unbroken chain of human endeavor that stretches back to the earliest times of human civilization.

The European tradition of building has a series of customary rites and ceremonies that define and empower each stage of construction and use of a dwelling place. Ideally, the dates and times of them all should be elected astrologically. First of all comes choosing and taking possession of the site. Next comes the defining of the boundaries, and then the ground-breaking ceremony. After that, the foundations are prepared and the foundation stone is laid along with the foundation deposits. Ceremonies are performed during the construction of the walls, erecting the doorframes and floors. Any religious or spiritual signs, sigils, or symbols are empowered ritually as and when they are erected. Finally, when the roof is completed, a Topping-Out ceremony is performed, and finally, a completion ceremony. Lastly, the ceremony of moving-in takes place.

In all parts of life, rites and ceremonies allow members of the family or community to participate at times when they are not physically involved with the activities. They are joyful, festal events in which every-body is included. Ceremonial foundation and construction of buildings are the means through which each individual can develop a personal bond with a place and the other people who live there. Harmony and good fortune are the result.

> *Keep within the Compass,*
> *And then you will be sure*
> *To avoid many troubles*
> *That others may endure.*
> OLD ENGLISH ADAGE
> FROM NORTHAMPTONSHIRE

Appendix 1

ZODIAC SIGNS AND ASSOCIATES

Sign	Planet	Color	Stone	Day	Number	Deity
Aries	Mars	white/red	diamond	Tuesday	9	Minerva
Taurus	Venus	blue/green	sapphire	Friday	6	Venus
Gemini	Mercury	yellow	emerald	Wednesday	5	Apollo
Cancer	Moon	violet	agate	Monday	2 & 7	Mercury
Leo	Sun	orange	ruby	Sunday	1	Jupiter
Virgo	Mercury	dark yellow	sardonyx	Wednesday	5	Ceres
Libra	Venus	blue	chrysolite	Friday	6	Vulcan
Scorpio	Mars	dark red	opal	Tuesday	9	Mars
Sagttarius	Jupiter	purple	topaz	Thursday	3	Diana
Capricorn	Saturn	gray-green	turquoise	Saturday	8	Vesta
Aquarius	Uranus	pale green	amethyst	Saturday	4	Juno
Pisces	Neptune	gray	bloodstone	Thursday	7	Neptune

Appendix 2

THE EGYPTIAN CALENDAR

Month	Zodiac Sign	Beginning
Thoth	Virgo	August 23
Paophi	Libra	September 22
Hathor	Scorpio	October 22
Choiakh	Sagittarius	November 21
Tybi	Capricorn	December 21
Mechir	Aquarius	January 20
Phamenoth	Pisces	February 19
Pharmuthi	Aries	March 21
Pachon	Taurus	April 20
Payni	Gemini	May 20
Epiphi	Cancer	June 19
Mesore	Leo	July 19

Followed by 5 Epacts, unallotted days.

Appendix 3

Ruling Signs of Cities

Aries: Florence, Krakow, Leicester, Marseille, Naples, St. Louis, Utrecht, Zaragoza.

Taurus: Bologna, Dublin, Leipzig, Parma.

Gemini: London, Leuven, Nuremberg, Paris, Turin, Versailles.

Cancer: Amsterdam, Bern, Cadiz, Istanbul, Lubeck, New York, Philadelphia, Venice.

Leo: Bath, Bristol, Chicago, Cremona, Damascus, Detroit, Miami, Prague, Rome, Taunton.

Virgo: Basel, Baghdad, Cheltenham, Corinth, Heidelberg, Jerusalem, Los Angeles, Lyon, Toledo, Washington D.C.

Libra: Antwerp, Frankfurt-am-Main, Lisbon, Piacenza, Siena, Vienna.

Scorpio: Baltimore, Cleveland, Cremona, Frankfurt-am-Oder, Ghent, Liverpool, San Francisco.

Sagittarius: Avignon, Budapest, Cologne, Naples, Narbonne.

Capricorn: Boston (Mass.), Modena.

Aquarius: Bremen, Hamburg.

Pisces: Regensburg, Seville, Worms.

Glossary

Ætt: Direction or eighth of the horizon according to Northern Tradition geomancy.

Ad Quadratum: Sacred geometry using the square as the fundamental form.

Ad Triangulum: Sacred geometry using the equilateral triangle as the fundamental form.

Aird (pl. Airde): Irish "quarter" of space.

Álfrek: Land from which the spirit has been driven out (Old Norse).

Ambience: The overall combination of qualities of a place—physical, psychological, and spiritual.

Angula: Sacred measure in Vastu Vidya (q.v.).

Anima loci: The "soul of place."

Anno Domini: The "Year of the Lord," the year in the Christian or Common Era (CE) calendar, supposedly dated from the birth of Jesus Christ.

Anno Lucis: The "Year of Light." Masonic year-reckoning from the beginning of the world, 4000 BCE. Dates in this system are sometimes inscribed on foundation stones.

Anthropocosmic Giant: The mythic giant who is slain and whose body becomes the world, or the foundation of buildings.

Augury: Mediterranean European system of divination of omens, good and bad places.

Axis Mundi: The world axis, linking the underworld with the middle world and the upper world.

Bellarmine: A brown or gray salt-glazed bottle with a bearded face below the neck. Used in East Anglian house-protection tradition.

Brandubh: Celtic board game, symbolic of the world.

Cardo: The meridional (north–south) line dividing the eastern side (left) from the western side (right) of the land in the Etruscan Discipline (q.v.) and later quartered town plans.

Conjunction: An aspect of two or more planets within the same degree of longitude.

Compas: The center of the world at the Church of the Holy Sepulchre in Jerusalem, according to medieval Christian cosmology.

Consecration: The ceremony of setting up a place as sacred.

Cosmic Axis: Axis Mundi (q.v.).

Crannog: An artificial island in a lake (Celtic).

Dægmælspilu: Horizon landmark over which the sun rises or stands at a division point of the day, viewed from a recognized center.

Dagsmark: Dægmælspilu (q.v.).

Decumanus: The east–west line dividing the northern from the southern half of the land in the Etruscan Discipline and later quartered town plans.

Dei Manes: Underworldly spirits or demons.

Dod: A willow stick, put in the ground as a sight for lining up plough furrows, boundary ditches, and traditional English shepherds' sundials.

Egg-stone: An egg-shaped stone set up as an omphalos (q.v.).

Egyptian Day: Unfortunate day in Medieval European tradition.

Eightfold Year: Contemporary Pagan year cycle of eight festivals, comprising the two solstices (q.v.) and equinoxes (q.v.), and the four Fire Festivals (q.v.).

Einherjar: The chosen warriors of the Norse god Odin, who live in Valhalla and number 432,000.

Electional Astrology: The art of choosing a time that has the appropriate astrological qualities for the purpose required.

Enhazeled Field: A piece of consecrated ground delimited by a fence of hazel staves.

Epact: Unallotted day in the Egyptian calendar.

Equinox: 24-hour period when daylight and darkness are of equal length.

Etruscan Discipline: The technique of detecting and interpreting omens in the landscape for the location and foundation of temples and human habitation. Originating in the Etruscan culture (before 700 BCE) and later used by the Romans. It is the basis of European geomancy.

Evocatio: The spiritual technique used to take a divinity from one place to another.

Exorcism: The removal of spiritual power or psychic influences from an object, person, place, or building by means of ritual.

Eykt-mark: Horizon-marker denoting west-southwest, around 4:30 p.m.

Fas: An auspicious day in the Roman calendar.

Feng Shui: Literally: "wind-water." Chinese geomancy, including symbolic landscapes, astrological geomancy, orientation, and placement. Today, there are around sixteen different variants of Feng Shui practiced.

Ferdelh: An area of ten acres.

Ferlingate: Ferdelh (q.v.).

Fire Festivals: Four festivals of the Pagan year: Beltane (May 1), Lammas (August 1), Samhain (November 1), and Imbolc (February 1).

Fixed Signs: Taurus, Leo, Scorpio, and Aquarius.

Foot-stone: A stone on which the foundation-stone (q.v.) is laid. It usually has a cavity in which foundation deposits (q.v.) are placed.

Foundation deposits: Objects buried beneath or within a building as a magical or commemorative act.

Foundation-Stone: The stone laid as the symbolic beginning of a building.

Gast: Land from which the spirit has been driven out (East Anglian tradition).

Genius Loci: The resident spirit of a place.

Geomancy: The theoretical and practical art of making human artifacts in harmony with subtle factors of location.

Goafstead: Threshing floor in a barn.

Haever: A "quarter" of the heavens, according to the Lancashire tradition.

Indian Circle: A circle divided into ten-degree sectors, used in Indian and Islamic geomancy.

Kaaba: The holy center of Mecca, toward which Muslims pray.

Lapis Manalis: "Ghost Stone," that covers the Mundus (q.v.).

Level: Builders' tool used to check horizontality.

Limites: Roman boundaries, usually ditches.

Locator Civitatis: Medieval official commissioned to find the site for a new city, design it, and recruit people to live there.

Maul: Masonic ceremonial mallet used in foundation-ceremonies.

Meridian: A straight line drawn southward from any point in the northern hemisphere, marking the midday point, when the sun is at its highest in the day.

Mundane: The area of astrology that deals with the world in general.

Mundus: Pit in which foundation-deposits are laid beneath the central point in the Etruscan Discipline (q.v.).

Mutable Signs: Gemini, Virgo, Sagittarius, and Pisces.

Natal: The area of astrology dealing with the horoscope of an individual's birth or the beginning of an enterprise.

Nefas: An inauspicious day in the Roman calendar.

Nimruz: Literally: "half-day." The Iranian meridian, said to mark the midpoint of the Eurasian-African land mass.

Northern Tradition: The pre- and para-Christian spiritual way of Europe north of the Alps, the common core of Celtic, Germanic, Scandinavian, and Baltic traditions.

Omphalion/Omphalia: A stone or circular pavement placed at the center of a city, temple or church, representing the center of the world but not considered to be literally the center.

Omphalos: The Navel of the World, taken as its literal center point, as in the Omphalos of Delphi, divined, according to legend, by Zeus.

On-lay: A spiritual power laid upon a place whose original spirit has been driven out by exorcism.

Opposition: Two or more planets placed so that they confront one another across the zodiac, separated by 180 degrees.

Orientation: Lining up a person or structure toward a specific direction.

Ostenta: Omens.

Padas: Scared squares in Vastu Vidya (q.v.).

Part of Fortune: The nodal point in the chart that is an equal distance of zodiacal arc from the ascendant as the moon is from the sun.

Pax Deorum: "The Peace of the Gods," the state of harmony and balance within the world when human activities are conducted according to natural, that is, divine, principles.

Pedjeshes: The ancient Egyptian foundation-ritual of "stretching the cord."

Perron: Stone pillar or more complex structure located in a town square or at crossroads marking the center and often bearing symbols of authority.

Pes: A Roman foot measure.

Planetary Cycle: Periods of thirty-six years, sequentially ruled by the astrological planets. This book was written in the cycle ruled by the Sun (1981–2016).

Planetary Hour: Hours of the week, sequentially ruled by the astrological planets.

Plumb Line: String with a lead weight on the end, used to check verticality in building.

Point-de-Jour: Horizon landmark over which the sun rises or stands at a division-point of the day, viewed from a recognized center.

Qiblah: The direction of prayer for Muslims, that is, the direction of Mecca.

Radix (Radical): Generally the natal horoscope, with which an elected horoscope is brought into harmony.

Rig: A straight line on the ground, such as a meridian (q.v.).

Royal Art: Operative Freemasonry.

Solstices: The longest and shortest daylight "days" in the year.

Succedent: The astrological houses that follow the four angles: the second, fifth, eighth, and eleventh houses.

Templum: Area chosen for the observation of omens.

Tesserae: The individual stones that compose a mosaic.

Tide: One of the eight divisions of the day, three hours in length.

Time Capsule: Sealed container of memorabilia buried with the intention that people will dig it up in the future.

Tjösnur (sg. Tjasna): Consecrated posts set up as a boundary fence around a consecrated area in the Norse tradition.

Townyard: An area of forty acres.

Vastu Vidya: A general name for the geomantic traditions of Hindu India.

Vé: Norse sacred enclosure, often V-shaped.

Vébönd: Fence of posts or standing stones delimiting a vé.

Vesica Piscis: Geometrical shape formed by drawing two circles of equal size passing through each other's center. The basis of Ad Triangulum geometry (q.v.).

Vintana: The astrological geomancy of Madagascar, including orientation, numerology, chronomancy, and divinatory geomantic techniques.

Virgate: An area of forty acres (Townyard).

Witch Bottle: Bottle used in foundation rites or as apotropaic magic.

Yattara: Burmese geomancy, including symbolic placement and astrological geomancy.

Bibliography
and Sources for
Further Reading

Ab Ithell, J. Williams. *Barddas; or, A Collection of Original Documents, Illustrative of the Theology, Wisdom, and Usages of the Bardo-Druidic System of the Isle of Britain.* 2 vols. Llandovery and London: Roderio / Longman and Co., 1862–1874.

Addison, William. *English Fairs and Markets.* London: Batsford, 1953.

Addy, Sidney Oldall. *Household Tales.* London: Nutt, 1895.

Alberti, Leon Battista. *The Ten Books of Architecture: The 1755 Leoni Edition* (1452). New York: Dover, 1986.

Alexander, Christopher. *The Timeless Way of Building.* New York: Oxford University Press, 1979.

Allen, Richard Hinckley. *Star Names: Their Lore and Meaning.* New York: Dover, 1973.

Amira, Karl von. *Nordgermanisches Obligationrecht.* 2 vols. Leipzig: Veit, 1882–1895.

Amos, G. S. *The Scratch Dials of Norfolk.* South Walsham, U.K.: n.d. [ca. 1980].

Anderson, B. *Imagined Communities.* London: Verso, 1983.

Andrews, William. *Old Church Lore.* Hull, U.K.: Andrews and Co., 1891.

———. *Ecclesiastical Curiosities.* London: Andrews and Co., 1899.

Arden-Close, Charles. "The Centres of England and Wales." *Geographical Journal* 97, no. 3 (March 1941): 179–81.

Augustine. *City of God.* Abridged version from the translation by Gerald G. Walsh, Demetrius B. Zema, Grace Monahan, and Daniel J. Honan. edited by Vernon J. Bourke. New York: Image, 1958.

Aust, Emil. *De aedibus sacris populi Romani inde a primis liberae rei publicae temporibus usque ad Augusti imperatoris aetatem Romae conditis.* Marburg: Sommering, 1889.

Aveni, A., and G. Romano. "Orientation and Etruscan Ritual." *Antiquity* 68, no. 260 (September 1994): 545–63.

Bächtold-Stäubli, Hanns, ed. *Handwörterbuch des deutschen Aberglaubens.* 10 vols. Berlin: De Gruyter, 1927–1942.

Bader, Karl Siegfried. *Das mittelalterliche Dorf als Friedens- und Rechtsbereich.* Weimar, Germany: Böhlau, 1957.

Baigent, Michael, Nicholas Campion, and Charles Harvey. *Mundane Astrology.* Wellingborough, U.K.: Aquarian, 1984.

Baker, Margaret. *Folklore and Customs of Rural England.* Newton Abbot, U.K.: David and Charles, 1974.

Baker, Steve. *Picturing the Beast.* Manchester: Manchester University Press, 1993.

Bales, Robert F. *Personality and Interpersonal Behavior.* New York: Holt, Rinehart, and Winston, 1970.

Bandmann, Günter. *Mittelalterliche Architektur als Bedeutungsträger.* Berlin: Gebrüder Mann, 1951.

Barnett, Joseph. "On Ideology and the Psychodynamics of the Ideologue." *Journal of the American Academy of Psychoanalysis* 1, no. 4 (1973): 381–95.

Bauchhenss, Gerhard. *Jupitergigantensäulen.* Aalen: Limesmuseum, 1976.

Bauer, Hermann. *Kunst und Utopie: Studien über das Kunst- und Staatsdenken in der Renaissance.* Berlin: De Gruyter, 1965.

Bayet, Charles. *L'Art Byzantin.* Paris: Réunies, 1883.

Bede. *Bedae Opera de temporibus.* edited by Charles W. Jones. Cambridge, Mass.: Medieval Academy, 1943.

Bedos de Celles, Dom François. *La Gnomonique pratique, ou l'Art de tracer avec la plus grande précision Les Cadrans Solaires.* Paris: Didot, 1790.

Behm, Jacob [Jacob Böhme]. *Four Tables of Divine Revelation.* London: Blunden, 1654.

Behmen, Jacob [Jacob Böhme]. *Dialogues on the Supersensual Life.* edited by Bernard Holland. London: Methuen, 1901.

Bell, Walter George. *Unknown London.* London: Lane, 1920.

Bemouilli, Hans. *Die Stadt und ihr Boden.* Erlenbach-Zürich: Verlag für Architektur, 1946.

Bennett, J. A., and Olivia Brown. *The Compleat Surveyor.* Cambridge, U.K.: Whipple Museum, 1982.

Bennett, Jim, and Stephen Johnston. *The Geometry of War, 1500–1750.* Oxford: Museum of the History of Science, 1996.

Benoist, Alain de. *Les Traditions d'Europe.* Paris: Labyrinthe, 1996.

Berlage, Hendrik Petrus. *Grundlagen und Entwicklung der Architektur.* Berlin: Bard, 1908.

Bett, Henry. *English Legends.* London: Batsford, 1950.

Beyerle, Konrad. *Die Gesetze der Langobarden.* Weimar, Germany: Böhlau, 1947.

Bilfinger, Gustav. *Untersuchungen über die Zeitrechnung der Alten Germanen.* Stuttgart: Liebich, 1901.

Bin Gorion, Micha Josef. *Sinai und Gerazim: Über den Ursprung der israelitischen Religion.* Berlin: Morgenland, 1926.

Bion, Nicolas. *De la Construction et des usages des cadrans solaires.* Paris, 1753.

Bischoff, Michael. *Himmels Zeichen.* Nördlingen, Germany: Greno, 1986.

Björnsson, Stefán. *Rymbegla, sive rudimentum computi ecclesiastici et annalis veterum Islandorum.* Copenhagen, 1780.

Blachetta, Walther. *Das Buch der deutschen Sinnzeichen.* Berlin: Widukind, 1941.

Black, William George. *The Scots Mercat "Cross": An Inquiry into Its History and Meaning.* Glasgow and Edinburgh: Hodge, 1928.

Blacker, Carmen, and Michael Loewe, eds. *Ancient Cosmologies.* London: Allen and Unwin, 1975.

Blagrave, John. *A Booke of the Making and Use of a Staffe, Newly Invented by the Author, Called the Familiar Staffe.* London: Jackson, 1590.

Blake, William. *Jerusalem: The Emanation of the Giant Albion.* London: Blake, 1820.

———. *The Marriage of Heaven and Hell.* Lambeth: Blake, 1793.

Blok, Petrus Johannes. *Geschiednis eener Hollandsche Stad.* The Hague, Netherlands: Nihoff, 1910.

Blossfeldt, Karl. *Urformen der Kunst.* Dortmund, Germany: Harenberg, 1994.

Boëthius, Axel. *Etruscan and Early Roman Architecture.* Harmondsworth, U.K.: Penguin, 1978.

Bohn, Richard. *Altertümer von Aegae.* Berlin: Reimer, 1899.

[Böhme, Jacob. *See* Behm/Behmen.]

The Bonesman's Bible. Anonymous East Anglian manuscript, n.d.

Borromeo, Carlo. *Instructions on Ecclesiastical Building.* London: Dolman, 1857.

Borsi, Franco. *Leon Battista Alberti: The Complete Works.* New York: Electa/ Rizzoli, 1989.

Bose, Nirmal Kumar. *Canons of Orissan Architecture.* Calcutta: Chatterjee, 1932.

Botticher, Carl. *Der Baumkultus der Hellenen.* Berlin: Weidmann, 1856.

Botzum, Richard, and Catherine Botzum. *Scratch Dials, Sundials and Unusual Marks on Herefordshire Churches.* Lucton: Botzum, 1988.

Bouche Leclerc, Auguste. *Histoire de la divination dans l'antiquité.* 4 vols. Paris, 1878–1882.

Bradford, J. S. P. *Ancient Landscapes: Studies in Field Archaeology.* London: Bell and Sons, 1957.

Brant, Sebastian. *Das Narrenschiff: Nach der Erstausgabe (Basel 1494) mit den Zusätzen der Ausgaben von 1495 und 1499 sowie den Holzschnitten der deutschen Originalausgaben.* edited by Manfred Lemmer. 2nd edition. Tübingen, Germany: Niemeyer, 1968.

Braunfels, Wolfgang. *Abendländische Stadtbaukunst.* Koln, Germany: DuMont, 1979.

Briggs, Katherine. *A Dictionary of British Folk-tales in the English Language.* London: Routledge and Kegan Paul, 1970.

Brind'Amour, Pierre. *Le Calendrier romain: recherches chronologiques.* Ottawa: Éditions de l'Université, 1983.

Brooke, Charlotte. *Reliques of Irish Poetry.* Dublin: Christie, 1816.

Brown, Ray B., ed. *Rituals and Ceremonies in Popular Culture.* Bowling Green, Ohio: Bowling Green University Popular Press, 1980.

Buck, Adriaan de. "De egyptische voorstellingen betreffende den overheuvel." Dissertation, University of Leiden, 1922.

Bucknell, Peter A. *Entertainment and Ritual, 600–1600.* London: Stainer and Bell, 1979.

Burkert, Walter. *Ancient Mystery Cults.* Cambridge, Mass.: Harvard University Press, 1987.

Burne, C. S., ed. *Shropshire Folk-Lore.* London: Trübner, 1883.

Burt, William Austin. *A Key to the Solar Compass, and Surveyor's Companion; Comprising All the Rules Necessary for Use in the Field.* Philadelphia: Burt, 1858.

Butler, Alfred Joshua. *The Ancient Coptic Churches of Egypt.* 2 vols. Oxford: Clarendon, 1884.

Caldwell, J. L. "Notes on the Ceremonial Procedure for Formally Laying a Foundation Stone." *Journal of the Royal Institute of British Architects* 66 (1961).

Campion, Nicholas. *An Introduction to the History of Astrology*. London: Institute for the Study of Cycles in World Affairs, 1982.

———. *The Great Year: Astrology, Millennarianism, and History in the Western Tradition*. London: Penguin, 1994.

Case, Shirley Jackson. *The Social Origins of Christianity*. Chicago: University of Chicago Press, 1923.

Cashen, William. *Manx Folk-lore*. London: Douglas, 1912.

Castangnoli, F. *Orthogonal Town Planning in Antiquity*. Cambridge, Mass.: MIT Press, 1971.

Cawte, E. G. *Ritual Animal Disguise*. Totowa, N.J.: Brewer / Rowan and Littlefield, 1978.

Cellarius, Andreas. *Harmonia Macrocosmica*. Amsterdam: Janssonius, 1660.

Chambers, William. *A Dissertation on Oriental Gardening*. London: Gregg, 1772.

Chaney, William A. "Aethelbert's Code and the King's Number." *American Journal of Legal History* 6 (1962).

Christian, Roy. *Old English Customs*. Newton Abbot: David and Charles, 1972.

Clemen, Carl. *Die Reste der primitiven Religion im ältesten Christentum*. Giessen: Töpelmann, 1916.

Clouston, W. A. *Popular Tales and Fictions*. Edinburgh: Blackwood and Sons, 1887.

Cobb, Gerald. *The Old Churches of London*. London: Batsford, 1942.

Cockayne, O. *Leechdoms, Wortcunning and Starcraft of Early England*. 2 vols. London: Longman, Green, Longman, Roberts, and Green, 1864–1866.

Codrington, Thomas. *Roman Roads in Britain*. London: Society for Promoting Christian Knowledge, 1919.

Colledge, Eric, ed. *The Mediaeval Mystics of England*. London: Murray, 1962.

Collin, Rodney. *The Theory of Celestial Influences: Man, the Universe, and Cosmic Mystery*. London: Stuart, 1954.

Colonna, Giovanni. *Santuari d'Etruria*. Milan: Electa, 1985.

The Consecration of Liverpool Cathedral. Liverpool, 1924.

Cook, A. B. *Zeus: A Study in Ancient Religion*. London: Cambridge University Press, 1949.

Coomaraswamy, Ananda. "Symbolism of the Dome." *Indian Historical Quarterly* 14 (1938): 1–56.

Cornish, Vaughan. *Historic Thorn Trees in the British Isles.* London: Country Life, 1941.

Cousto, Hans. *Farbton, Tonfarbe und die kosmische Oktave.* Munsing, Germany, 1984.

Cox, J. Charles and R. M. Serjeantson. *A History of the Church of the Holy Sepulchre, Northampton.* Northampton, England: Mark, 1897.

Crane, Walter. *The Bases of Design.* London: Bell and Sons, 1898.

Crawford, Alan. *C. R. Ashbee: Architect, Designer and Romantic Socialist.* New Haven and London: Yale University Press, 1985.

Critchlow, Keith. *Order in Space: A Design Source Book.* London: Thames and Hudson, 1972.

Cross, Lancelot. *The Book of Old Sundials and Their Mottos.* London: Foulis, 1914.

Cubbon, W. *The Treen Divisions of Man.* Douglas, Isle of Man, 1937.

Cumont, Franz. *Astrology and Religion among Greeks and Romans.* New York: Putnam's Sons, 1912.

Curzon, Robert Baron Zouche. *Armenia.* London: Murray, 1854.

Dale-Green, Patricia. *The Cult of the Cat.* London: Heinemann, 1963.

D'Alviella, Eugène Goblet. *La Migration des Symboles.* Paris: Leroux, 1891.

———. "Les Perrons de la Wallonie et les Market-Crosses de l'Ecosse." *Bulletin de la Classe des lettres et des sciences morales et politiques et de la Classe des Beaux-Arts* 11 (1913): 363–407.

Dames, Michael. *Mythic Ireland.* London: Thames and Hudson, 1992.

Daniel, Christopher St. J. H. *Sundials.* Prince's Risborough, U.K.: Aylesbury Shire, 1986.

———. *Sundials on Walls.* London: National Maritime Museum, 1978.

Danielli, M. "Initiation Ceremonial from Norse Literature." *Folklore* 56, no. 2 (June 1945): 229–45.

D'Apremont, Arnaud. *Yggdrasill, l'axe de vie des anciens Nordiques.* Combronde, France: Janvier, 1995.

Darnton, Robert. *The Great Cat Massacre and Other Episodes in French Cultural History.* Harmondsworth, U.K.: Penguin 1985.

Davidson, Hilda Ellis, ed. *Boundaries and Thresholds.* Stroud, U.K.: Thimble, 1993.

de Jong, Karl Hendrik Eduard. *Das antike Mysterienwesen in religionsgeschichtlicher ethnologischer und psychologischer Beleuchtung.* Leiden, Netherlands: Brill, 1919.

Delpech, François. "Rite, legende, mythe et societé: Fondations et fondateurs dans la tradition folklorique de la pénisule Ibérique." *Medieval Folklore* 1 (1991): 1–56.

Deonna, Wademar. *Les croyances religieuses et superstitieuses de la Genève antériure au Christianisme*. Geneva: Imprimerie centrale, 1917.

Descartes, Rene. *Principia Philosophiae*. Amsterdam: Ludovicus and Elzevier, 1656.

Deubner, Ludwig. "Mundus." *Hermes* 68, no. 3 (1933): 276–87.

Dewar, H. Stephen. "Mummified Cats." *Proceedings of the Dorset Natural History and Archaeological Society* 74 (1952).

Digges, Leonard. *Tectonicon*. London: Hodgkinson, 1656.

Digges, Thomas. *A Geometrical Practise, Named Pantometria*. London: Bynneman, 1571.

Dilke, O. A. W. *The Roman Land Surveyors: An Introduction to the Agrimensores*. Newton Abbot, U.K.: David and Charles, 1971.

Ditchfield, P. H. *The Manor Houses of England*. London: Bracken, 1985.

———. *Old English Customs Extant at the Present Time*. London: Redway, 1896.

Dobin, Joel C. *The Astrological Secrets of the Hebrew Sages*. New York: Inner Traditions, 1977.

Dognée, Eugene Marie Octave. *Les Symboles Antiques: L'Oeuf*. Brussels: Muquardt, 1865.

Dornseiff, Franz. "Roma Quadrata." *Rheinisches Museum für Philologie* 88 (1939): 192.

Downes, Kerry. *Hawksmoor*. London: Thames and Hudson, 1969.

Downey, G. *A History of Antioch in Syria from Seleucus to the Arab Conquest*. Princeton, N.J.: Princeton University Press, 1961.

Drake-Carnell, F. J. *Old English Customs and Ceremonies*. London: Batsford, 1938.

Dreier, Franz Adrian. *Winkelmessinstrumente vom 16. bis zum frühen 19. Jahrhundert*. Berlin: Kunstgewerbemuseum, 1979.

Drexel, Friedrich. "Templum." *Germania* 9 (1931): 1–6.

Drinkwater, Peter I. *The Art of Sundial Construction*. Shipston-on-Stour, England: Drinkwater, 1996.

———. *The Sundials of Nicholas Kratzer*. Shipston-on-Stour, U.K.: Drinkwater, 1993.

Duchartre, Pierre Louis. *The Italian Comedy*. Translated by Randolph T. Weaver. London: Harrap, 1929.

Duchesne, Louis. *Christian Worship: Its Origin and Evolution: A Study of the Latin Liturgy up to the Time of Charlemagne*. Translated by M. L. McClure. 2nd revised and expanded edition. London: Society for Promoting Christian Knowledge, 1904.

Dumarçay, Jacques. *The House in South-East Asia.* Oxford: Oxford University Press, 1987.

Dürer, Albrecht. *Underweysung der Messung mit dem Zirckel un richt scheyt.* Nuremberg: [Formschneider], 1525.

Ehrenberg, Kurt. *Baugeschichte von Karlsruhe 1715–1870: Eine Studie zur Geschichte des Städtebaus.* Karlsruhe: Braun, 1909.

Eilmann, Richard. "Labyrinthos: Ein Beitrag zur Geschichte einer Vorstellung und einers Ornamentes." Dissertation. Martin Luther University of Halle-Wittenberg, 1931.

Einarsson, Stefán. "Terms of Direction in Old Icelandic." *Journal of English and Germanic Philology* 43 (July 1944): 265–85.

Eisler, Robert. *The Royal Art of Astrology.* London: Joseph, 1946.

Eliade, Mircea. *Images et symboles: Essais sur le symbolisme magico-religieux.* Paris: Gallimard, 1952.

———. *The Sacred and the Profane: The Nature of Religion.* Translated from the French by Willard R. Trask. New York: Harcourt, Brace and Co., 1959.

Elwin, Verrier. "The Hobby Horse and Ecstatic Dance." *Folklore* 53 (1942): 209–13.

Enking, R. "Zur Orientierung der etruskischen Tempel." *Studi Etruschi* 25 (1957): 541–44.

Evans, E. Estyn. *Irish Folk Ways.* London: Routledge and Paul, 1957.

Evans-Wentz, W. Y. *The Fairy-Faith in Celtic Countries.* Oxford: Oxford University Press, 1911.

Ewing, Peter. "The Saint, the Dragons and the Center of the World." *Practical Geomancy* 3 (1986): 10–13.

Faraone, Christopher A. *Talismans and Trojan Horses: Guardian Statues in Greek Myth and Ritual.* Oxford: Oxford University Press, 1992.

Farrell, Robert T., and Thomas D. Hill, eds. *The Anglo-Saxon Cross.* Hamden, Conn.: Archon, 1977.

Fergusson, James. *The Holy Sepulchre and the Temple at Jerusalem.* London: Murray, 1865.

Fernee, Ben. *Geomantic Survivals in York.* Kingston upon Hull, U.K.: Northern Earth Mysteries Group, 1985.

Fillipetti, Hervé, and Janine Trotereau. *Symboles et pratiques rituelles dans la maison paysanne traditionnelle.* Paris: Architecture et vie traditionnelle, 1978.

Fleischhauer, Werner. *Barock in Herzogtum Württemberg.* Stuttgart, Germany: Kohlhammer, 1958.

Flowers, Stephen. *The Galdrabók: An Icelandic Grimoire.* York Beach, Maine: Weiser, 1989.

Focke, Friedrich. "Szepter und Krummstab: Eine Symbolgeschichtliche Untersuchung." In *Festgabe für Alois Fuchs zum 70. Geburtstage am 19. Juni 1947,* edited by Wilhelm Tack. Paderborn: Schöningh, 1950.

Foster, Richard. *Patterns of Thought: The Hidden Meaning of the Great Pavement at Westminster Abbey.* London: Cape, 1991.

Fougères, Gustave. *Mantinée et l'Arcadie orientale.* Paris: Fontemoing, 1898.

Franz, Marie-Louise von. *Number and Time: Reflections Leading Towards a Unification of Psychology and Physics.* Evanston, Ill.: Northwestern University Press, 1974.

Fraser, George Milne. "The Market Cross of Aberdeen." *Scottish Historical Review* 5 (1908): 175–80.

Fritz, Johannes. *Deutsche Stadtanlagen.* Strassburg: Heitz und Maadel, 1894.

Frothingham, A. L. "Ancient Orientation Unveiled: I–III." *American Journal of Archaeology* 21, no. 1 (January–March 1917): 55–76; 21, no. 2 (Apr.–June 1917): 187–201; 21, no. 3 (July–Sept. 1917): 313–36.

Fulcanelli. *Le Mystère des Cathédrales: Esoteric Interpretation of the Hermetic Symbols of the Great Work.* Translated by Mary Sworder. London: Spearman, 1971.

Gagnière, Sylvain. *L'imagerie populaire en Provence.* Nice, 1946.

Galilei, Galileo. *Operations of the Geometric and Military Compass.* Translated by Stillman Drake. Washington, D.C.: Smithsonian Institution Press, 1978.

Gatty, Mrs. Alfred: *The Book of Sun-Dials.* London: Bell and Sons, 1900.

Geisler, Walter. *Die deutsche Stadt: Ein Beitrag zur Morphologie der Kulturlandschaft.* Stuttgart: Engelhorn, 1924.

Gerbier, Balthazar. *Counsel and Advise to All Builders.* London: Mabb, 1663.

Gerkan, A. von. *Griechische Städteanlagen.* Berlin: De Gruyter, 1934.

Gettings, Fred. *Dictionary of Astrology.* London: Routledge and Kegan Paul, 1985.

Gilchrist, Cherry. *Planetary Symbolism in Astrology.* London: Saros Foundation, 1980.

Giuliano, A. *Urbanistica delle città Greche.* Milan: Il Saggiatore, 1966.

Gobert, Théodore. *Les Rues de Liège, anciennes et modernes.* 4 vols. Liege, Belgium: Demarteau, 1884–1901.

Godwin, Jocelyn. *Robert Fludd: Hermetic Philosopher and Surveyor of Two Worlds.* London: Thames and Hudson, 1979.

Gombrich, E. H. *Symbolic Images: Studies in the Art of the Renaissance.* London: Phaidon, 1972.

Gombrich, E. H. *The Sense of Order: A Study in the Psychology of Decorative Art.* London: Phaidon, 1979.

Gomme, George Laurence. *Folk-lore Relics in Early Village Life.* London: Stock, 1883.

Goudappel, H. M. *Man and Environment in Urbanistic Perspective.* Eindhoven, Netherlands, 1982.

Gradl, Hermann. *Der schöne deutsche Süden.* Stuttgart: Hädecke, 1936.

Grässe, Johann Georg Theodor. *Der Sagenschatz des Königreichs Sachsen.* Dresden: Schönfeld, 1855.

Green, Arthur Robert. *Sundials, Incised Dials or Mass-Clocks.* London: Society for Promoting Christian Knowledge, 1926.

Green, Martin. *Curious Customs: A Guide to Local Customs and Festivals throughout the British Isles.* London: Impact, 1993.

Grimm, Jacob. *Teutonic Mythology.* Translated by James S. Stallybrass. 4 vols. London: Bell and Sons, 1883–1888.

Grimstad, W. N. "René Guénon and the Digital Deception." *Critique* 3, no. 3/4 (1983).

Grinsell, L.V. *Folklore of Prehistoric Sites in Britain.* Newton Abbot, U.K.: David and Charles, 1976.

Groves, Derham. *Feng-Shui and Western Building Ceremonies.* Singapore and Lutterworth: Graham Brash, 1991.

———. "The Hermann Monument." *Transition,* March 1986.

Guénon, René. *La Regne de la Quantité et les Signes des Temps.* Paris: Gallimard, 1945.

Guerber, H. A. *Legends of the Rhine.* New York: Barnes and Co., 1895.

Haff, Karl. *Die dänischen Gemeinderechte.* Leipzig: Deichert, 1909.

Haigh, D. H. "Yorkshire Dials." *Yorkshire Archaeological Journal* 5 (1877): 134–222.

Halden, George Mason. *Setting Out of Tube Railways.* London: Spon, 1906.

Halliday, W. R. *The Pagan Background of Early Christianity.* Liverpool: University Press of Liverpool, 1925.

Hamconius, Martin. *Frisia, seu De Viris Rebusque Frisiae Illustribus.* Antwerp: Franeker, 1620.

Hamkens, Freerk Haye. "Heidnischer Bilder im Dome zu Schleswig." *Germanien* 6 (1938): 177–81.

Hamill, John. *The Craft: A History of English Freemasonry.* London: Crucible, 1986.

Hamm, Ernst. *Die Städtegründungen der Herzöge von Zähringen in Südwestdeutschland.* Freiburg-im-Breisgau: Urban, 1932.

Hancox, Joy. *The Byrom Collection.* London: Cape, 1992.

Harbison, Robert. *Eccentric Spaces.* London: Secker and Warburg, 1989.

Hardt, Mathias. *Luxemburger Weisthümer.* Luxembourg: Bück, 1870.

Hardwick, Charles. *Traditions, Superstitions, and Folk-Lore.* London: Simpkin, Marshall and Co., 1872.

Haring, Hugo. *Schriften, Entwürfe, Bauten.* Stuttgart: Krämer, 1965.

Harland, John. "On Clog Almanacs, or Rune Stocks." *Reliquary* 5 (1865): 121–30.

Harland, John, and T. T. Wilkinson. *Lancashire Folk-Lore: Illustrative of the Beliefs and Practices, Local Customs and Usages of the People of the County Palatine.* London: Warne and Co., 1867.

Harrison, Jane Ellen. *Epilegomena to the Study of Greek Religion.* Cambridge, U.K.: Cambridge University Press, 1903.

Harrison, Stephen. *The Arch's of Triumph.* London: VVindet, 1604.

Harte, Jeremy. "The Power of Lonely Places." *Mercian Mysteries* 23 (1995): 8–13.

———. "Pussycat, Pussycat, Where have you been?" *At the Edge* 6 (1997).

———. "Under the Greenwood Tree." *At the Edge* 1 (1996).

Hartmann, Franz. *The Principles of Astrological Geomancy: The Art of Divining by Punctuation, According to Cornelius Agrippa and Others.* London: Theosophical Publishing Co., 1889.

Harvey, E. Ruth, ed. *The Court of Sapience.* Toronto: University of Toronto Press, 1984.

Haverfield, F. *Ancient Town-Planning.* Oxford: Clarendon, 1913.

Hay, H. H. Dalrymple. "The Tube Railways of London: Their Design and Construction." In *Engineering Wonders of the World,* edited by Archibald Williams. London, n.d. [ca. 1908].

Heggie, Douglas C. *Megalithic Science: Ancient Mathematics and Astronomy in Northwest Europe.* London: Thames and Hudson, 1981.

Heimberg, Ursula. *Römische Landvermessung.* Aalen, Germany: Gesellschaft für Vor- und Frühgeschichte in Württemberg und Hohenzollern, 1977.

Herrmann, Paul. *Nordische Mythologie in gemeinverständlicher Darstellung.* Leipzig: Engelmann, 1903.

Hersey, J. *The Lost Meaning of Classical Architecture: Speculations on Ornament from Vitruvius to Venturi.* Cambridge, Mass.: MIT Press, 1988.

Hesselmeyer, Ellis. "Decumanusstudien Abschließendes zur Dekumatlandsfrage." *Klio* 28 (1935): 133–79.

Hettel, J. N.: "The Cornerstone: Its Significance and Ceremony." *Journal of the American Institute of Architects* (1952): 209–16.

Heydon, John. *Theomagia, or The Temple of Wisdome.* London: Rooks, 1664.

Höfler, Max. *Wald- und Baumkult in Beziehung zur Volksmedizin Oberbayerns.* Munich: Galler, 1894.

Höfler, Otto. *Kultische Geheimbünde der Germanen.* Frankfurt and Main: Diesterweg, 1934.

Hole, Christina. *A Dictionary of British Folk Customs.* London: Hutchinson, 1976.

Holwell, John. *Clavis Horologiæ; or, A Key To the whole Art of Arithmetical Dyalling.* London: Howkins, 1712.

Hopton, Arthur. *Speculum Topographicum, or The Topographicall Glasse.* London: Waterson, 1611.

Hosch, Hans. "Geometria deutsch." *In Die Bauhütte des Mittlealters in Deutschland,* edited by Car Heideloff. Nuremberg: Stein, 1844.

Howlett, England. "Sacrificial Foundations." In *Ecclesiastical Curiosities,* edited by William Andrews. London: Andrews, 1899.

Hutton, Ronald. *The Pagan Religions of the Ancient British Isles.* Oxford: Blackwell, 1991.

Huxley, Francis. *The Way of the Sacred.* London: Aldus, 1974.

Jackson, Nigel, and Nigel Pennick. *The New Celtic Oracle.* Chieveley, U.K.: Capall Bann, 1997.

Jahn, Ulrich. *Hexenwesen und Zauberei in Pommern.* Breslau: Koebner, 1886.

James, E. O. *The Nature and Function of Priesthood: A Comparative and Anthropological Study.* London: Thames and Hudson, 1955.

Jencks, Charles. *Symbolic Architecture.* New York: Rizzoli, 1985.

Johfra. *Astrology.* Amsterdam: V.O.C., 1981.

Johnson, Hildegarde Binder. *Order Upon the Land: The U.S. Rectangular Land Survey and the Upper Mississippi Country.* Oxford: Oxford University Press, 1976.

Johnston, Walter. *Byways in British Archaeology.* Cambridge, U.K.: Cambridge University Press, 1912.

Jones, Bernard. *Freemasons' Guide and Compendium.* London: Harrap, 1950.

Jones, David. *Epoch and Artist.* London: Faber, 1959.

Jones, Inigo. *The Most Notable Antiquity of Great Britain, Vulgarly Called Stone-*

Heng on Salisbvry Plain Restored by Inigo Jones. Oxford, London: Pakeman and Chapman, 1655.

Jones, Prudence. "Broomsticks." *Albion* 4 (1979): 8–10.

———, ed. *Creative Astrology*. London: Aquarian, 1991.

———. *Eight and Nine: Sacred Numbers of Sun and Moon in the Pagan North*. Bar Hill, U.K.: Fenris-Wolf, 1982.

———. *A "House" System from Viking Europe*. Cambridge, U.K.: Fenris-Wolf, 1991.

———. *Northern Myths of the Constellations*. Cambridge, U.K.: Fenris-Wolf, 1991.

———. *Sundial and Compass Rose: Eight-fold Time Division in Northern Europe*. Bar Hill, U.K.: Fenris-Wolf, 1982.

Jones, Prudence, and Nigel Pennick. *A History of Pagan Europe*. London: Routledge, 1995.

Jones, T. Gwynn. *Welsh Folklore and Folk-Custom*. London: Methuen, 1930.

Jonson, Ben. *The Alchemist: A Comedy Acted in the Year 1610*. London: Hills, 1610.

———. *Oberon the Faery Prince*. In *The Workes of Ben Jonson*. London: Stansby, 1616 [first performed 1611].

Khanna, Madhu. *Yantra: The Tantric Symbol of Cosmic Unity*. London: Thames and Hudson, 1979.

Khunrath, Heinrich. *Amphitheatrum sapientiae aeternae*. Hanau: Anton, 1609.

Kidder, Tracy. *House*. Boston: Houghton Mifflin, 1985.

Kinsman, Robert S., ed. *The Darker Vision of the Renaissance: Beyond the Fields of Reason*. Berkeley: University of California Press, 1974.

Kircher, Athanasius. *Arca Noë*. Amsterdam: Jansson, 1675.

———. *Ars Magna Lucis et Umbrae*. Rome: Scheus, 1646.

———. *Musurgia universalis*. Rome: Grignani, 1650.

Kirfel, W. *Die Kosmographie der Inder*. Bonn: Schroeder, 1920.

Knight, Richard Payne. *The Landscape: A Didactic Poem, in Three Books; addressed to Uvedale Price, Esq*. London: Bulmer, 1794.

Knott, Olive. *Witches of Wessex*. Sturminster Newton, U.K. 1963.

Köbel, Jacob. *Geometrey: Von künstlichen Feldmessen, und absehen Allerhandt Höhe, Fleche, Ebne, Weite und Breite*. Frankfurt: Egenolff, 1570.

Kohn, Hans. *The Idea of Nationalism*. New York: Macmillan, 1944.

Kolisko, Lily Noha. *The Moon and the Growth of Plants*. Translated by Marna Pease and Carl Alexander Mirbt. London: Anthroposophical Agricultural Foundation, 1936.

Korth, Leonhard. "Der kölnische Bauer und das Quaternionen-System." *Mitteilungen aus dem Stadtarchiv zu Köln* 14 (1888): 117–24.

Kraeling, Carl H. *Gerasa: City of the Decapolis.* New Haven, Conn.: American Schools of Oriental Research, 1938.

Kruft, Hanno-Walter. *A History of Architectural Theory from Vitruvius to the Present.* London: Foster, 1994.

———. *Städte in Utopia: Die Idealstadt vom 15. bis zum 18. Jahrhundert.* Munich: Beck, 1989.

Kuhn, Adalbert, and Wilhelm Schwartz. *Norddeutsche Sagen, Märchen und Gebräuche.* Leipzig: Brockhaus, 1848.

Laing, Gordon J. *Survivals of Roman Religion.* London: Harrap, 1931.

Lambert, Audrey M. *The Making of the Dutch Landscape.* London: Seminar, 1971.

Lamy, Lucie. *Egyptian Mysteries.* London: Thames and Hudson, 1981.

Langley, Batty. *The Builder's Jewel.* London: Ware, 1741.

Lasswell, Harold D. *Psychopathology and Politics.* New York: Columbia University Press, 1930.

Latte, Kurt. "Augur und Templum in der Varronischen Auguralformel." *Philologus* 97 (1948): 143–59.

Laurie, William Alexander. *History of Free Masonry and the Grand Lodge of Scotland.* Edinburgh: Seton and MacKenzie, 1859.

Lavedan, Pierre. *Qu'est-ce que l'urbanisme? Introduction a l'histoire de l'urbanisme.* Paris: Laurens, 1926.

Laviolette, Jean G. "Iconographie et mesure du temps." *Horlogerie Ancienne* 41 (1984): 7–13.

Lawlor, Robert. *Sacred Geometry: Philosophy and Practice.* London: Thames and Hudson, 1982.

Leadbetter, Charles. *Mechanick Dialling.* London: Caslon, 1773.

Leask, Harold G. *Irish Churches and Monastic Buildings.* 3 vols. Dundalk, U.K.: Dundalgan, 1955–1960.

Le Corbusier. *The Modulor: A Harmonious Measure to the Human Scale Universally applicable to Architecture and Mechanics.* Translated by Peter de Francia and Anna Bostock. London: Faber, 1954.

Legge, F. *Forerunners and Rivals of Christianity.* 2 vols. Cambridge: Cambridge University Press, 1915.

Lehmann-Hartleben, K. "Athena als Geburtsgottin." *Archiv für Religionswissenchaft* 24 (1926): 19–28.

Lethaby, W. R. *Architecture, Mysticism and Myth*. London: Percival, 1891.

Lévi, Éliphas. *Histoire de la magie*. Paris: Baillière, 1860.

Levy, G. R. *The Gate of Horn: A Study of the Religious Conceptions of the Stone Age, and their Influence upon European Thought*. London: Faber and Faber, 1948.

Leybourn, William. *The Art of Dialling Performed Geometrically by Scale and Compasses Arithmetically by the Canons of Sines and Tangents Instrumentally by a Trigonal Instrument Accommodated with Lines for That Purpose*. London: Tooke and Sawbridge, 1660.

Liman, Ingemar. *Traditional Festivities in Sweden*. Stockholm: Swedish Institute, 1993.

Lindow, J. *Swedish Legend and Folktales*. Berkeley: University of California Press, 1978.

Lockyear, Joseph Norman. *Stonehenge and Other British Stone Monuments Astronomically Considered*. London: Macmillan, 1906.

L'Orange, Hans Peter. *Studies on the Iconography of Cosmic Kingship in the Ancient World*. Oslo: Aschehoug, 1953.

Luchner, O. F. *Die Tiroler Stadt*. Munich: Piper, 1914.

Lundquist, John M. *The Temple: Meeting Place of Heaven and Earth*. London: Thames and Hudson, 1993.

Lusher, Geoff. "1300 Applicants for 58 Driver Jobs with the Midland Metro." *Tramways and Urban Transit* 725 (1998): 172–73.

Maass, Michael, and Klaus W. Berger. edited by *Klar und Lichtvoll wie eine Regel: Planstädte der Neuzeit*. Karlsruhe, Germany: Badisches Landesmuseum Kalrsruhe, 1990.

Macarius, Johannes. *Abraxas, seu Apistopistus, quæ est antiquaria de gemmis basilidianis disquisitio*. Antwerp: Moreti, 1657.

MacKenzie, William. M. *The Scottish Burghs*. London: Oliver and Boyd, 1949.

MacLean, Adam. *The Four Fire Festivals*. Edinburgh: Megalithic Research Publications, 1979.

Macleane, Douglas. *The Great Solemnity of the Coronation of a King and Queen*. London: Allen, 1911.

Macleod, Fiona. "Sea-Magic and Running Water." *Contemporary Review* 82 (October 1902): 568–80.

MacManus, Dermot. *The Middle Kingdom: The Faerie World of Ireland*. Gerrard's Cross, U.K.: Smythe, 1973.

MacNulty, W. K. *Freemasonry: A Journey Through Ritual and Symbol*. London: Thames and Hudson, 1991.

Macoy, Robert. *General History, Cyclopedia and Dictionary of Freemasonry*. New York: Masonic Publishing, 1872.

Maier, Michael. *Atalanta fugiens*. Oppenheim: Galler, 1618.

Mann, A. T. *The Round Art: The Astrology of Time and Space*. London: Phin, 1979.

Mann, Ethel. *Old Bungay*. London: Heath Cranton, 1934.

Martin, Alfred J. *Martin's Tables*. London: Fisher Unwin, 1906.

Massey, Gerald: *A Book of Beginnings*. London: Williams and Norgate, 1881.

Matthews, John, and Chesca Potter, eds. *The Aquarian Guide to Legendary London*. London: Thorsons, 1990.

Mayall, Robert Newton, and Margaret L. Mayall. *Sundials: How to Know, Use and Make Them*. Boston: Hale, Cushman and Flint, 1938.

Mazzolani, Lidia Storoni. *The Idea of the City in Roman Thought: From Walled City to Spiritual Commonwealth*. Translated by S. O'Donnell. London: Hollis and Carter, 1970.

McCaffery, Ellen. *Astrology: Its History and Influence in the Western World*. New York: Scribner's, 1942.

McCall, Andrew. *The Medieval Underworld*. London: Hamilton, 1979.

McCrickard, Janet. *Eclipse of the Sun: An Investigation into Sun and Moon Myths*. Glastonbury, U.K.: Gothic Image Publications, 1990.

McFadzean, Patrick. *Astrological Geomancy: An Introduction*. Hull, U.K.: Northern Earth Mysteries, 1985.

———. "Geomancy and Electional Astrology." *Practical Geomancy* 1 (1985): 15–19.

———. "Indian Sacred Geometry, Symbol and Ritual." *Practical Geomancy* 3 (1986): 23–32.

———. "Vastu Shastra: Indian Astrological Geomancy." *Practical Geomancy* 2 (1986): 17–25.

McMahon, E. O. *Christian Missions in Madagascar*. London: Society for the Propagation of the Gospel, 1914.

Menon, C. P. S. *Early Astronomy and Cosmology: A Reconstruction of the Earliest Cosmic System*. London: Allen and Unwin, 1932.

Merten, Klaus. *Schlösser in Baden-Württemberg: Residenzen und Landsitze in Schwaben, Franken und am Oberrhein*. Munich: Beck, 1987.

Meyrac, Albert. *Traditions, coutumes, légendes et contes des Ardennes comparés avec les traditions, légendes et contes de divers pays*. Charleville, France: Petit Ardennais, 1890.

Michell, John. *Ancient Metrology: The Dimensions of Stonehenge and of the Whole World as Therein Symbolised.* Bristol: Pentacle, 1981.

———. *At the Center of the World: Polar Symbolism Discovered in Celtic, Norse, and Other Ritualized Landscapes.* London: Thames and Hudson, 1994.

———. *City of Revelation: On the Proportions and Symbolic Numbers of the Cosmic Temple.* London: Garnstone, 1972.

———. *The Dimensions of Paradise: The Proportions and Symbolic Numbers of Ancient Cosmology.* London: Thames and Hudson, 1988.

———. *A Little History of Astro-Archaeology.* London: Thames and Hudson, 1977.

Michell, John, and Waltraud Wagner. *Masssysteme der Tempel: Die Dimensionen alter Bauwerke als Wiederspiegelung der Dimensionen der ganzen Welt.* Vechelde: Wagner, 1984.

Michels, Agnes Kirsopp. *The Calendar of the Roman Republic.* Princeton, N.J.: Princeton University Press, 1967.

Mistral, Frédéric. *Lou Tresor dou felibrige, ou dictionnaire provençal-français.* 2 vols. Paris: Delagrave, 1932.

Möbius, Hans. *Die Ornamente der griechischen Grabstelen klassischer und nachklassischer Zeit.* Munich: Fink, 1968.

Morper, Johann Joseph. *Bamberg die Mitte Deutschlands: Zur Reichssymbolik der Tattermannsäule.* Bamberg, Germany: Meisenbach, 1957.

Mössinger, Friedrich. "Baumtanz und Trojaburg." *Germanien* (1940): 282–89.

———. "Die Dorflinde als Weltbaum." *Germanien* 10 (1938): 388–96.

———. "Dreischalbrunnen und Dreistufenbaum." *Germanien* 5 (1942).

———. "Maibaum, Dorflinde, Weihnachtsbaum." *Germanien* 10 (1938): 145–55.

Motz, Lotte. "The Winter-Goddesses: Percht, Holda and Related Figures." *Folklore* 95 (1984): 151–66.

Mowl, Tim, and Brian Earnshaw. *John Wood: Architect of Obsession.* Bath: Millstream, 1988.

Muchery, Georges. *The Astrological Tarot.* London: Bracken, 1989.

Mullard, Jonathan. "Turf Sundials." *Ley Hunter* 94 (1982): 32–33.

Müller, Werner. *Die heilige Stadt: Roma Quadrata, himmliches Jerusalem und die Mythe vom Weltnabel.* Stuttgart, Germany: Kohlhammer, 1961.

Mulryne, J. R., and Margaret Shewring, *Shakespeare's Globe Rebuilt.* Cambridge: Cambridge University Press, 1997.

Murtagh, W. J. *Moravian Architecture and Town Planning: Bethlehem,*

Pennsylvania, and other Eighteenth-century American Settlements. Chapel Hill, N.C.: University of North Carolina Press, 1967.

Naredi-Rainer, Paul von. *Architektur und Harmonie.* Cologne: DuMont, 1982.

Naveau, Léon. "Le perron liégeois." *Bulletin de l'institut archéologique Liégeois* 22 (1891): 435–53.

Needham, Rodney, ed. *Right and Left: Essays on Dual Symbolic Classification.* Chicago: University of Chicago Press, 1973.

Newham, C. A. *The Astronomical Significance of Stonehenge.* Leeds: Blackburn, 1972.

Newton, Joseph Fort. *The Builders: A Story and Study of Masonry.* London: Allen and Unwin, 1914.

Nichols, Ross. *The Book of Druidry.* London: Thorsons, 1990.

Nissen, Hemorcj. *Das Templum.* Berlin: Weidmann, 1869.

Oliver, George. *A Cyclopedia of Freemasonry.* edited by Robert Macoy. New York: Masonic Publishing, 1867.

Ortutay, Gyula. *Hungarian Folklore.* Budapest: Akademiai Kiado, 1972.

Ouvrard, René. *Architecture harmonique, ou Application de la doctrine des proportions de la musique à l'architecture.* Paris: De la Caille, 1679.

Owen, Trefor M. *Welsh Folk Customs.* Llandysul, U.K.: Gomer, 1987.

Owen, Will. *Old London Town.* London: Arrowsmith, 1921.

Pagdin, William E. *The Story of the Weathercock.* Stockton-on-Tees, U.K.: Appleby, 1949.

Pálsson, Einar. *Hvolfþak himins.* Reykjavik: Mímir, 1985.

Parker, Derek. *Familiar to All: William Lilly and Astrology in the Seventeenth Century.* London: Cape, 1975.

Pastor, Eilert. *Deutsche Volksweisheit in Wetterregeln und Bauernsprüchen.* Berlin: Deutsche Landbuchhandlung, 1934.

Patai, Raphael. *Man and Temple in Ancient Jewish Myth and Ritual.* 2nd edition. New York: Ktav, 1976.

Pattenden, Philip. *Sundials on an Oxford College.* Oxford: Roman, 1979.

Pearce, Alfred John. *The Text-Book of Astrology.* 2 vols. London: Cousins, 1879–1889.

Pearson, David. *The Natural House Book.* London: Octopus, 1989.

Pennick, Nigel. *The Ancient Science of Geomancy: Man in Harmony with the Earth.* London: Thames and Hudson, 1979.

———. *Anima Loci.* Bar Hill, U.K.: Nideck, 1993.

———. *The Celtic Cross: An Illustrated History and Celebration*. London: Blandford, 1997.

———. *Celtic Sacred Landscapes*. London: Thames and Hudson, 1996.

———. *The Celtic Saints: An Illustrated and Authoritative Guide to These Extraordinary Men and Women*. London: Godsfield, 1997.

———. *The Cosmic Axis*. Bar Hill, U.K.: Fenris-Wolf, 1985.

———. *Crossing the Borderlines: Guising, Masking and Ritual Animal Disguises in the European Tradition*. Chieveley, U.K.: Capall Bann, 1998.

———. *Dragons of the West*. Chieveley, U.K.: Capall Bann, 1997.

———. *Earth Harmony: Siting and Protecting Your Home—A Practical and Spiritual Guide*. Chieveley, U.K.: Capall Bann, 1997.

———. *Einst war uns die Erde heilig*. Waldeck: Huebner, 1987.

———. "Geomancy." *Cambridge Voice* 1969.

———. *Geomancy*. Cambridge: Cokaygne, 1973.

———, ed. *The Geomancy of Cambridge*. Bar Hill, U.K.: Institute of Geomantic Research, 1977.

———. *Haindl Rune Oracle*. New York: U.S. Games Systems, 1998.

———. *The Inner Mysteries of the Goths: Rune-lore and Secret Wisdom of the Northern Tradition*. Chieveley, U.K.: Capall Bann, 1995.

———. "Karlsruhe: The Omphalos of Baden." *Mercian Mysteries* 24 (1995): 10–16.

———. *Das kleine Handbuch der angewandten Geomantie: Wie wir heute Landschaft und Siedlung wieder in Einklang bringen können*. Amrichshausen, Germany: Neue Erde, 1985.

———. *Labyrinths—Their Geomancy and Symbolism*. Bar Hill, U.K.: Fenris-Wolf, 1984.

———. *London's Early Tube Railways*. Bar Hill, U.K.: Runestaff, 1988.

———. *Mazes and Labyrinths*. London: Hale, 1990.

———. *The Mysteries of King's College Chapel*. Cambridge: Cokaygne, 1974.

———. *Natural Measure*. Bar Hill, U.K.: Runestaff, 1985.

———. "The New Geomancy, Canary Wharf: Devilsend?" *Practical Geomancy* 3 (1986): 14–16.

———. *The Oracle of Geomancy: The Divinatory Arts of Raml, Geomantia, Sikidy and I Ching*. Chieveley, U.K.: Capall Bann, 1995.

———. *Runic Astrology: Starcraft and Timekeeping in the Northern Tradition*. Chieveley, U.K.: Capall Bann, 1995.

———. *Sacred Geometry: Symbolism and Purpose in Religious Structures*. San Francisco: Harper and Row, 1982.

————. *The Sacred World of the Celts: An Illustrated Guide to Celtic Spirituality and Mythology*. London: Thorsons, 1997.

————. *Secret Signs, Symbols and Sigils*. Chieveley, U.K.: Capall Bann, 1996.

————. *Secrets of East Anglian Magic*. London: Hale, 1995.

————. *Skulls, Cats and Witch Bottles: The Ancient Practice of House Protection*. Bar Hill, U.K.: Pennick, 1986.

————. *The Subterranean Kingdom: A Survey of Man-made Structures beneath the Earth*. Wellingborough, U.K.: Turnstone, 1981.

————. *Wayland's House*. Bar Hill, U.K.: Nideck, 1993.

Pennick, Nigel, and Paul Devereux. *Lines on the Landscape: Ley Lines and Other Linear Enigmas*. London: Hale, 1989.

Pennick, Nigel, and Helen Field. *The Goddess Year*. Chieveley, U.K.: Capall Bann, 1996.

Pennick, Rupert. "The Secret Vehm." *Symbol* 3 (1984): 20–23.

Petrie, Flinders. *Measures and Weights*. London: Methuen, 1934.

Pirenne, Maurice. *Les Perrons de l'arrondissement de Verviers*. Verviers: Fèguenne, 1930.

Plassmann, Joseph Otto. "Die Stufenpyramide." *Germanien* 12 (1940): 91–102.

Plunket, Emmeline M. *Ancient Calendars and Constellations*. London: Murray, 1903.

Porter, Enid. *Cambridgeshire Customs and Folklore*. London: Routledge and Kegan Paul, 1969.

Prætorius, Johann. *Blockes-Berges Verrichtung*. Leipzig: Scheiben, 1669.

Prayon, F. "'Deorum Sedes': Sull'orientamento dei templi Etrusco-Italici." *Archeologia Classica* 43 (1991): 1285–95.

Prise, M. de la. *Méthode nouvelle et générale pour tracer facilement les cadrans solaires*. Caen: Le Baron, 1781.

Ram, Raz. *Essay on the Architecture of the Hindus*. London: Parker, 1834.

Raman, Bangalore Venkata. *Sri Muhurtha or Electional Astrology*. Bangalore: Raman, 1976.

Ratcliff, Edward C. *The English Coronation Service: Being the Coronation Service of King George V and Queen Mary, with Historical Introduction and Notes, together with Extracts from Liber Regalis, Accounts of Coronations, etc.* London: Society for Promoting Christian Knowledge, 1936.

Rees, Alwyn, and Brinley Rees. *Celtic Heritage*. London: Thames and Hudson, 1967.

Reitzenstein, R. *Die hellenistischen Mysterien-religionen nach ihren*

Grundgedanken und Wirkungen. Leipzig: Teubner, 1927.

Reuter, Otto Sigfrid. *Germanische Himmelskunde*. Munich: Lehmann, 1934.

———. *Sky Lore of the North*. Translated by Michael Behrend. Bar Hill, U.K.: Runestaff, 1985.

Ries, Nicolas. "La Croix de Justice." *Les Cahiers Luxembourgeois* 1 (1938): 45–51.

Ringbom, Lars-Ivar. *Graltempel und Paradies: Beziehungen Zwischen Iran und Europa im Mittelalter*. Stockholm: Wahlström and Widstrand, 1951.

Roberts, W. J. *Some Old London Memorials*. n.d. [ca. 1900].

Robson, Vivian E. *Electional Astrology*. New York: Weiser, 1972.

———. *The Fixed Stars and Constellations in Astrology*. London: Aquarian, 1969.

Rochholz, Ernst Ludwig. *Deutscher Glaube und Brauch im Speigel der heidnischen Vorzeit*. 2 vols. Berlin: Dümmler, 1867.

Roder, Christian. *Villingen*. Heidelberg: Winter, 1905.

Roe, Anthony. "Every Which Way." *Mercian Mysteries* 16 (1993).

Roger of Wendover. *The Flowers of History: Comprising the History of England from the Descent of the Saxons to A.D. 1235*. London: Bohn, 1849.

Rohr, Rene R. J. *Sundials—History, Theory and Practice*. Translated by Gabriel Godin. Toronto: University of Toronto Press, 1970.

Rokeach, Milton. *The Nature of Human Values*. New York: Free Press, 1973.

Romano, G. *Archeoastronomia Italiana*. Padua: CLEUP, 1992.

Roscher, Willhelm Heinrich. *Omphalos: Eine philologisch-archäologisch-volkskundliche Abhandlung über die Vorstellungen der Griechen und anderer Völker vom "Nabel der Erde."* Leipzig: Teubner, 1913.

Rossi, A. *The Architecture of the City*. Cambridge, Mass.: MIT Press, 1982.

Röttingen—Stadt der Sonnenunhren. Röttingen, 1995.

Rousseau, Felix. *Namur, ville mosane*. Brussels: Renaissance du Livre, 1948.

Roux, Georges. *Ancient Iraq*. London: Penguin, 1992.

Rushen, Joyce. "Folklore and Witchcraft in Tudor and Stuart England." *Popular Archaeology,* April 1984, 33–36.

Ruskin, John. *The Seven Lamps of Architecture*. London: Smith, Elder and Co., 1849.

Rybczynski, Witold. *The Most Beautiful House in the World*. New York: Viking, 1989.

Rykwert, Joseph. *The Idea of a Town: The Anthropology of Urban Form in Rome, Italy and the Ancient World*. Cambridge, Mass.: MIT Press, 1988.

———. "On the Palmette." *Res* 26 (1994): 10–21.

Saintyves, Pierre. *Corpus de folklore préhistorique en France et dans les colonies françaises.* 3 vols. Paris: Nourry, 1934–1936.

Salmon, William. *Palladio Londinensis, Or the London Art of Building.* London: Ward and Wickstead, 1734.

Salzman, Leon. "The Psychology of Religious and Ideological Conversion." *Psychiatry* 16 (1953): 177–87.

Santillana, Giorgio de, and Hertha von Dechend. *Hamlet's Mill: An Essay on Myth and the Frame of Time.* Boston: Gambit, 1969.

Sartori, Paul. "Ueber das Bauopfer." *Zeitschrift für Ethnologie* 30 (1898): 1–54.

Saward, Jeff, and Deb Saward. "Let Sleeping Dogs Lie." *Symbol* 4 (1984): 10–11.

Scarry, Elaine. *The Body in Pain: The Making and Unmaking of the World.* Oxford: Oxford University Press, 1985.

Scheingraber, Wernher, and Wilfried Bahnmüller. *Volkskunst im Bayerischen Oberland.* Freilassing, Germany: Pannonia, 1978.

Schiaparelli, G. V. *Astronomy in the Old Testament.* Oxford: Clarendon, 1905.

Schmid, Peter. *Structural Completion for an Integral, Biological Architecture.* Eindhoven, 1975.

Schumacher, Fritz. *Der Geist der Baukunst.* Stuttgart: Deutsche Verlags-Anstalt, 1938.

Schwabe, K-H, and G. Rother. *Angewandte Baubiologie: Beispiele aus der Praxis.* Waldeck: Hübner, 1985.

Schwenk, Theodor. *Das Sensible Chaos.* Stuttgart: Freies Geistesleben, 1976.

Schwilgue, C. *Description abrégée de l'horloge de la Cathédrale de Strasbourg.* Strasbourg: Dannbach, 1843.

Scullard, H. H. *The Etruscan Cities and Rome.* London, 1967.

Services for Use in the Diocese of Chelmsford. London: Society for Promoting Christian Knowledge, n.d. [ca. 1936].

Shute, John. *The First and Chief Groundes of Architecture.* London: Thames and Hudson, 1563.

Siebs, Benno Eide. *Grundlagen und Aufbau der altfriesischen Verfassung.* Breslau: Marcus, 1933.

Simpson, Jacqueline. *European Mythology.* London: Hamlyn, 1987.

Sircello, Guy. "Beauty in Shards and Fragments." *Journal of Aesthetics and Art Criticism* 48 (1990): 21–35.

Skinner, F. G. *Weights and Measures: Their Ancient Origins and Their Development in Great Britain up to A.D. 1855.* London: HMSO, 1967.

Small, John William. *Scottish Market Crosses.* Stirling, U.K.: Mackay, 1900.

Smith, E. Baldwin. *The Dome: A Study in the History of Ideas.* Princeton, N.J.: Princeton University Press, 1950.

Smith, Worthington G. *Dunstable: The Downs and District.* Dunstable, U.K.: Homeland Association, 1904.

Snyder, Gary. *Good Wild Sacred.* Madley, U.K.: Five Seasons, 1984.

Somerville, Boyle. "Orientation." *Antiquity* 1 (1927): 31–41.

Sperling, Otto. "On the Mechanisms of Spacing and Crowding Emotions." *International Journal of Psychoanalysis* 29 (1948): 232–35.

Speth, G. W. *Builders' Rites and Ceremonies: Two Lectures on the Folk-lore of Masonry.* Margate, U.K.: Keble's Gazette, 1894.

Spieß, Karl von. *Bauernkunst, ihre Art und ihre Sinn.* Vienna: Österreichischer Bundesverlag, 1925.

Steiner, Rudolf. *Wege zu einem neuen Baustil: "Und der Bau wird Mensch."* Dornach: Rudolf-Steiner-Verlag, 1992.

Stephenson, Rob. "The Old Sun-Dial: Key to Trellech's Past." *London Earth Mysteries Circle Journal* 2 (1990).

Sternberg, Thomas. *The Dialect and Folk-Lore of Northamptonshire.* London: Smith, 1851.

Stilgoe, John R. *Common Landscape of America, 1580 to 1845.* New Haven, Conn.: Yale University Press, 1982.

Stirling, William. *The Canon: An Exposition of the Pagan Mystery Perpetuated in the Cabala as the Rule of all the Arts.* London: Elkin Mathews, 1897.

Stone, Alby. "The Cosmic Mill." *Mercian Mysteries* 24 (1995).

———. "Goddess of the Black Stone." *Mercian Mysteries* 15 (1993): 19–21.

———. "The Nine Sisters and the Axis Mundi." *Mercian Mysteries* 16 (1993): 1–4.

———. *Straight Track—Crooked Road.* Wymeswold, U.K.: Heart of Albion, 1998.

———. *Ymir's Flesh: North European Creation Mythologies.* Wymeswold, U.K.: Heart of Albion, 1997.

Stoob, Heinz. "Dithmarschens Kirchspiele im Mittlealter." *Zeitschrift der Gesellschaft für Schleswig-Holsteinische Geschichte* 77 (1953): 97–140.

Storr, Anthony. *Human Destructiveness.* London: Chatto and Heinemann, 1972.

Stratmaim-Dohler, Rosemarie. "Zur Baugeschichte des Karlsruhers Schlosses." In *Planstädte der Neuzeit,* edited by Michael Maass and Klaus W. Berger,

276–96. Karlsruhe: Badisches Landesmuseum Kalrsruhe, 1990.

Stroebel, Hermann. *Ludwigsburg: Die Stadt Eberhard Ludwigs—Ein Beitrag zur Geschichte der Landesfürstlichen Stadtbaukunst um 1700.* Ludwigsburg: Ungeheuer & Ulmer, 1918.

Stuart, Alec. *The Septiform System of the Cosmos.* London: Clowes and Sons, 1924.

Sturmy, Samuel. *The Art of Dialling by a New, Easie and Most Speedy Way.* London: Eglesfield, 1683.

Svendsen, Peter Juhl. *Rundetarn Opklaret: Katedralens Mysterium.* Copenhagen: Sphinx, 1987.

Szanto, Arpad. "Roma Quadrata." *Rheinisches Museum* 88 (1939): 160–69.

Szanto, Gregory. *Perfect Timing: The Art of Electional Astrology.* Wellingborough, U.K.: Aquarian, 1989.

Tafuri, Manfredo. *The Sphere and the Labyrinth: Avant-Gardes and Architecture from Piranesi to the 1970s.* Cambridge, Mass.: MIT Press, 1990.

Temple, Robert K. G. *Conversations with Eternity.* London: Rider, 1984.

Thibault, Gérard. *L'Academie de l'Espée.* Leiden: Elzevir, 1628.

Thom, Alexander. *Megalithic Sites in Britain.* Oxford: Clarendon, 1967.

Thonger, Richard. *A Calendar of German Customs.* London: Wolff, 1966.

Thorn, Thorskegga. "Spinning Myths and Folktales." *At the Edge* 6 (1997): 25–29.

Thorndike, Lynn. *The History of Magic and Experimental Science.* 8 vols. New York: Columbia University Press, 1941.

Thorsson, Edred. *Futhark: A Handbook of Rune Magic.* York Beach, Maine: Weiser, 1984.

Thulin, Carl. *Die Götter des Matrianus Capella und der Bonzeleber von Piacenza.* Gießen: Töpelmann, 1906.

Tihon, Ferdinand. "Notes sur les Perons." *Bulletin de l'Institut archéologique liégeois* 40 (1910): 19–34.

Tille, Alexander. *Yule and Christmas.* London, 1899.

Tilley, Christopher. *A Phenomenology of Landscape: Places, Paths and Monuments.* Oxford: Berg, 1994.

Tournaire, Albert. *Le sanctuaire d'Apollon.* Paris: Fontemoing, 1902.

Trier, Jost. "Irminsul." *Westfälische Forschungen, Mitteilungen des Provinzial-Institut für westfälische Landes- und Volkskunde* 4 (1941): 99–133.

Tristram, H. B. *The Land of Moab.* London: Murray, 1873.

Trubshaw, Bob. "From Mountain to Temple to House." *Mercian Mysteries* 23 (1995).

————. "The Metaphors and Rituals of Place and Time: An Introduction to Liminality, or Why Christopher Robin Wouldn't Walk on the Cracks." *Mercian Mysteries* 22 (1995).

————. *The Quest for the Omphalos*. Loughborough, U.K.: Heart of Albion, 1991.

————. "Weaving the World." *At the Edge* 6 (1997): 20–24.

Tuan, Yi-Fu. *Space and Place*. Minneapolis: University of Minnesota Press, 1977.

————. *Topophilia: A Study of Environmental Perception, Attitudes, and Values*. Englewood Cliffs, N.J.: Prentice-Hall, 1974.

Udal, John Symonds. *Dorsetshire Folk-Lore*. Guernsey: Toucan, 1970.

Urton, Gary. *At the Crossroads of the Earth and Sky: An Andean Cosmology*. Austin: University of Texas Press, 1980.

Valdenaire, Arthur. *Das Karlsruhe Schloss*. Karlsruhe: Müller, 1931.

Valeton, I. M. J. "De modis auspicandi Romanorum." *Mnemosyne* 17 (1889): 275–325; 18 (1890): 418–52.

————. "De templis romanis." *Mnemosyne* 20 (1892): 338–90.

Vallance, Aymer. *Old Crosses and Lychgates*. London: Batsford, 1920.

Van Der Meer, L. B. "Iecur Placentinum and the Orientation of the Etruscan Haruspex." *Bulletin van de Vereeniging tot Bevordering der Kennis van der Antike Bescaving* 54 (1979): 49–64.

Van Doesburg, Theo. *Principles of Neo-Plastic Art*. London: Lund, Humphries and Co., 1969.

Van Gennep, Arnold. *Le Folklore de la Flandre et du Hainaut français (Nord)*. 2 vols. Paris: Maisonneuve, 1935–1936.

Vaux, Roland de. *Ancient Israel: Its Life and Traditions*. London: Darton, Longman and Todd, 1961.

Vėlius, Norbertas. *The World Outlook of the Ancient Balts*. Vilnius, Lithuania: Mintis, 1989.

Vernaleken, Theodor. *Volksüberlieferungen aus der Schweiz,* aus Vorarlberg, Kärnten, Steiermark, Salzburg, Ober- und Niederösterreich. Vienna: Seidel, 1858.

Vitruvius. *Vitruvius on Architecture*. Translated by Frank S. Granger. 2 vols. London: Heinemann, 1931–1934.

Voysey, Charles F. Annesley. *Reason as a Basis of Art*. London: Elkin Mathews, 1906.

Wagner, Waltraud. *Zeit, Das Fortschreitende oder die Ordnung*. Vechelde: Wagner, 1981.

Waite, Arthur Edward. *The Book of Ceremonial Magic.* London: Rider and Son, 1911.

Warburg, Aby Moritz. *Heidnisch-antike Weissagung in Wort und Bild zu Luthers Zeiten.* Heidelberg, Germany: Winter, 1920.

Ward-Perkins, J. B. *Cities of Ancient Greece and Italy: Planning in Classical Antiquity.* London: Sidgwick and Jackson, 1974.

Warren, Charles. *The Temple or Tomb.* London: Bentley, 1880.

Waschnitius, Victor. *Perht, Holda und verwandte Gestalten.* Vienna: Hölder, 1913.

Watkins, Alfred. *Must We Trade in Tenths? Being a Plea against Decimal and for Octaval Coinage, etc.* Hereford, U.K.: Watkins Meter Co., 1919.

Waugh, Albert E. *Sundials: Their Theory and Construction.* New York: Dover, 1973.

Weinstock, Stefan. "Martianus Capella and the Cosmic System of the Etruscans." *Journal of Roman Studies* 36, nos. 1–2 (1946): 101–29.

———. "Mundus patet." *Mitteilungen des Deutschen Archäologischen Instituts, Römische Abteilung* 45 (1930): 111–23.

———. "Templum." *Mitteilungen des Deutschen Archäologischen Instituts, Römische Abteilung* 47 (1932): 95–121.

Wensinck, Arent Jan. *The Ideas of Western Semites Concerning the Navel of the Earth.* Amsterdam: Müller, 1916.

Werner, Paul. *Schmuck am Haus.* Freilassing, Germany: Pannonia, 1978.

Wheatley, Paul. *The Pivot of the Four Quarters: A Preliminary Enquiry into the Origins and Character of the Ancient Chinese City.* Edinburgh: University of Edinburgh Press, 1971.

Willoughby, H. R. *Pagan Regeneration: A Study of Mystery Initiations in the Graeco-Roman World.* Chicago: University of Chicago Press, 1929.

Wither, George. *A Collection of Emblemes, Ancient and Moderne.* London, 1635.

Withington, R. *English Pageants: A Historical Outline.* Cambridge, Mass.: Harvard University Press, 1918.

Wood-Martin, W. G. *Pagan Ireland: A Handbook of Irish Pre-Christian Antiquities.* London: Longmans, Green and Co., 1895.

———. *Traces of the Elder Faiths of Ireland.* 2 vols. London: Longmans, Green and Co., 1902.

Wren, Christopher. *Parentalia.* 20 vols. Oxford: Oxford University Press, 1924–43.

Wright, Arthur Robinson. *British Calendar Customs: England.* edited by Thomas East Lones. 3 vols. London: Glaisher, 1936–1940.

Yates, Frances A. *The Rosicrucian Enlightenment.* London: Routledge and Kegan Paul, 1972.

Yeats, William Butler. *A Vision.* London: Laurie, 1925.

York, Michael O. *The Roman Festival Calendar of Numa Pompilius.* New York: Lang, 1986.

Young, Arthur M. *The Geometry of Meaning.* New York: Delacorte, 1976.

Zaborsky-Wahlstätten, Oskar von. *Urväter-Erbe in deutscher Volkskunst.* Leipzig: Koehler & Amelang, 1936.

Zaehner, R. C. *Mysticism, Sacred and Profane: An Inquiry into some Varieties of Praeternatural Experience.* Oxford: Clarendon, 1957.

Zinner, Ernst. *Deutsche und niederlandische astronomische Instrumente des 11. bis 18. Jahrhunderts.* Munich: Beck, 1967.

Index

Page numbers in *italics* indicate illustrations.